THE ANARCHIST BASTARD

SUNY series in Italian/American Culture
Fred L. Gardaphe, editor

The Anarchist Bastard

Growing Up Italian in America

JOANNA CLAPPS HERMAN

excelsior editions

State University of New York Press
Albany, New York

Photo on previous page: Grandpa Becce sitting on a cow.

Published by State University of New York Press, Albany

For information, contact State University of New York Press, Albany, NY
www.sunypress.edu

Excelsior Editions is an imprint of State University of New York Press

Production by Ryan Morris
Marketing by Fran Keneston

Library of Congress Cataloging-in-Publication Data

Herman, Joanna Clapps.
   The anarchist bastard : growing up Italian in America /
Joanna Clapps.
      p. cm.
   Includes bibliographical references.
   ISBN 978-1-4384-3631-9 (hardcover : alk. paper) 1. Herman, Joanna
Clapps—Childhood and youth. 2. Herman, Joanna Clapps—Family.
3. Italian Americans—Connecticut—Waterbury—Biography. 4 Italian
Americans—Connecticut—Waterbury—Social life and customs.
5. Waterbury (Conn.)—Biography. I. Title.
   F104.W3H47 2011
   973'.0451—dc22

                                                            2010031915

10   9   8   7   6   5   4   3   2   1

To every single Claps, Clapps, Becce, Scarpa, Padula, Semprini, and all those who have joined us. Especially to my beloved sister Lucia, my wonderful Billy, to delicious James and Heather and to my Donna

Contents

III.
BEFORE AND AFTER TINFOIL:
THE BECCE FAMILY

IV.
E' POI? AND THEN?

Acknowledgments

Can anyone write a book without their people? *Non posso*. There have been so many people who have been with me in this, who always read what I write, who care about what I've written, who want me to write.

My husband has been at my side every word, sentence and paragraph, who insisted for years—"You have to write about Waterbury."

My sister, Lucia Mudd, has been with me every single step of my life and my writing and thinking. Her family, John Mudd, Peter Mudd, William Mudd, and Anna Mudd, all of whom have supported my work.

Myra Goldberg, has read and reread, who was there when we were girls living in the Village and together we decided that since we were readers we would be writers. We were young and certain and young and uncertain, but we grew up together and now we're ladies and grandmothers together of the spectacular Ariella. I thank my beautiful goddaughter, Anna Resnikoff, for her inimitable self and for Ariella.

Edi Giunta, Annie Lanzillotto, Maria Laurino, Nancy Carnevale, without whom there wouldn't be an Italian American world of women writers for me.

My wonderful friends and fellow artists Judy Solomon, Linda Sherwin, Theresa Ellerbrock , Karen Wunsch, and Jane Olian.

Toby Miroff who gave me the courage to write what I wanted to write despite how terrified it made me to do it. And who has helped me finally to be myself.

Others who are part of the world of writing and ideas as writers, brothers, friends.

Joseph Sciorra, George Guida, and Peter Covino.

Then there are those for whom it simply wouldn't matter if I wrote or didn't. All of my Waterbury cousins who keep the flame.

My mother and father both of whom were wonderful storytellers, all of my aunts, uncles, and cousins who helped me remember and told me things I didn't know, who helped me bring these stories to life. Paul Claps who was especially helpful with the Claps material.

James Peltz who is the very best editor I know, who says things like, Sure you can do that. I think we can get that in too. Why don't you try it and we'll see how it goes. Does anyone else have an editor that good? No.

His kind and helpful assistant, Amanda Lanne. Amelia Krales who prepared all the photographs for this book.

Finally, James and Heather and Donna Ann without whom life just wouldn't be fun.

The following pieces are reprinted by permission of the publishers:

"*U Bizza di Creanza:* A Piece of Politeness," *Alimentum.* Fall 2010.

"My Aboriginal Women," *Lavanderia: Wash, Women and Word.* Fall 2009.

"My Homer," *Speaking Memo,* edited by Luisa Del Giudice, Palgrave. October 2009.

"Words and Rags," edited by Joanna Clapps Herman and Lee Gutkind. New York: Other Press. Fall 2006.

"*Papone,*" *Don't Tell Mama: The Penguin Book of Italian American Writing,* edited by Regina Barreca. Penguin. 2002.

"Coffee And," *The Milk of Almonds: Italian American Women Writers on Food and Culture*, edited by Edvige Guinta and Louise DeSalvo. New York: Feminist Press. 2002.

"Notes from an Unredeemed Catholic," *The Critic* 48:2. (Chicago). Winter 1993–1994.

"Two," *New England Sampler.* December 1980.

With and Without Words

An Introduction

Once at a party I met a really crazy woman—who happened to be Italian—and who loved to read books and talk about them. I found myself gripped in conversation with her, talking to her about reading and about being Italian even while I recognized that there was something very crazy about her. My hostess came by and said, with ill-hidden irony, "I see you two are enjoying yourselves." She came close to rolling her eyes at me as if to say, What are you doing with this one?

As I drove home from the party I gazed out into the dark night wondering: why *had* I spent the whole night talking to a crazy woman? In my sad reflection in the car window I saw the answer. I was that *desperate*, that *lonely*, and that filled with longing to talk to someone who knew intimately both of my spheres, my Italian world and the life of the mind, that I didn't care that she had been a lunatic.

That ride home was the beginning of a long search for a world that joined both my lives together.

For many years I had lived with a divided consciousness without realizing it. My "Italian" world was in Waterbury, Connecticut, with my family, where I grew up and where my large clan still sprawls. My adult life, husband, son, work life, intellectual and cultural life has been made in Manhattan where I moved when I was twenty-one. It wasn't something I thought much about. I simply lived this divided life. I went home to Waterbury and I came home to New York. Neither place knew much about the other.

I have always loved my family inordinately—my grandparents, my parents, my sister, *all* my aunts and uncles *and* cousins and their wives and husbands and children and grandchildren too. They made me and make me still. They are the waters I swam in first and swim often in my imagination, in my heart, and in my writing. When I sit at their tables drinking and eating and talk, talk, talking I could sit there forever—leave never.

Yet I did. Physically in 1963 and emotionally—fully—really only in the last few years. It's only recently that my life has come to belong to me before it belongs to anyone else. Where I come from loyalties belong first to your tribe, then your parents and siblings, then your husband or wife and children, then to your neighborhood, church, and maybe eventually to yourself last and only a little bit. Any more than that and you are the kind of person who doesn't put others before yourself—self-centered—the worst you can be. It's hard to overturn what were really good values for another time and place. It was a good way of life: full of vitality, fun, passion, joy and profound connections with an intense sense of the past and the immediate present as central and important. It wasn't about always moving toward somewhere else in the future. Still, because of my deep connections and loyalty to my Italian family it is only recently that I have come to feel I can write what I want about them despite what I know will be their grave confusion and disappointment, even disapproval. I am violating a basic rule—all loyalty to the family: keep all of the difficult stuff—all that was painful or sad or angry or rude—within the family. I'm still in the pull of that loyalty but no longer enough to stop me from doing the work.

While it took me more than forty years to sort out what coming from my immigrant family in Waterbury into modern life in America has meant, it didn't feel like that at first. I was an Italian kid, born in America who grew up first in the '40s and '50s with my family. Then it was the '60s: I was a college student involved in the civil rights movement, then a young hippy. After that I came into the consciousness of feminism and psychotherapy, and traveled in Europe while I was working and living in New York. All these cultural changes shifted the ground under my feet so radically that it took the next forty years to sort out all the implications and consequences. Even though I was living in New York, working, dating, marrying, divorcing, going to wild parties, *and* still very attached to and visiting my family, at a certain point the gap between where I came from and where I lived grew disorientingly wider. When I married a second time and had my son James—the toll grew even heavier.

All that I knew about family, being a wife and mother, came from Waterbury and what I had learned as a young New York woman simply didn't hold against the original forces of motherhood and family. I didn't know how to negotiate where I had come from to where I was. The penalties were great. I had no idea how to reconcile work and family, religious difference and cultural values. Family and the self.

Along the way, my reading, which has accompanied the whole of my life, led almost inevitably into writing. My husband would urge me to turn my attention to writing about my Italian family and I would look at him in confusion. What would I write about? There was only a dark silence in the place he was asking me to call up into language.

I was married, I was a mother. I hadn't lived in Waterbury for twenty years, I was teaching writing at City College, but I was still so utterly *of them*, a part of them, that I had no words to bring to my pages about them. You can't write about that which is so much a part of yourself that you can't step back from it, consider it, think *about* it. "But it's such great material," my husband would say. I'd stare at him wanting to understand what he was suggesting.

I knew he was right yet I didn't have a single word to say on the subject. All that was still immersed in the languageless me.

I grew up speaking English. I listened to Rock and Roll from its very beginnings. and yet my deepest Italian *at-one-ness* with my family remained utterly intact.

I was so muted by this *at-one-ness* because there was no air inside me between me and them. At the heart of my Italian family's life and ways is that you live in it, you are it. Self-consciousness is embarrassing—everything is wrong about it. Waterbury is about work, obligation, and responsibility, then spontaneous being. Being and doing are at our center. Not about self-consciously taking stock of experience. We sang songs and told stories, but we didn't talk about singing songs and telling stories. That would be silly. You went to the movies to be there. Not to be separate from it. You don't talk about it afterward, except perhaps to say things like—"I cried. It's so great. You should go see it."

Just as important, the absolute loyalty to my family assumes that you don't talk about the stuff that doesn't make us look good—to anyone outside the family and only in whispers in the family. If you talk about the bad stuff you're breaking a dead center rule. Everything about my place in this good world—a place that has deep virtues that my life in New York doesn't have—held me mute. So it was both against the rules *and* impossible to do.

The ride home from that party where I only wanted to talk to the craziest person in the room because she was Italian and because she had the sensibility of a serious reader made me aware of what it was that was so completely missing from my life: It took a long time, but eventually I began to find people like me: Italians who care about both kinds of life equally. Meeting and getting to know Edi Giunta, Maria Laurino, Annie Lanzilotto, George Guida, Joseph Sciorra, Adele LaBarre all helped me to find new waters to swim in. In these seas people care very much about family, the immediacy of life: about children, dogs, gardens, cooking and eating, about coffee, wine, and especially about garlic. *And* we care about reading, writing, and ideas that engage the questions of what our culture is made of—the willingness to look at and think about, write about who we are. A world where you can be, do, *and* reflect upon. A world where you can have family and the self. These people comprise my second great tribe, who know me, who are me.

The more I have examined my Italian world, come to understand it and to write about it, the clearer it has become to me how mute I had been made by the utter discontinuity between the world I was born into and my life in New York. It took the larger part of twenty years to be able to fully unloosen my word hoard against this wordlessness. But here, at long last, it is.

JOANNA CLAPPS* HERMAN
THE UPPER WEST SIDE, NYC

---

*Claps is a southern Italian name. There is a very long list of people with this name in the phone book of Basilicata, our province: Francesco Claps, Leonardo Claps are typical names. (My grandfather inexplicably added the second "p" at some point long after he had come to America.). I've always been sad not to have a vowel to announce me to the world. But it's my father's name and I am my father's daughter, so Clapps it is, Italian, whether it sounds Italian or not.

I

HOMER IN WATERBURY: THE BACKDROP

My Homer

I often say that I was born in 1944 but raised in the 15th century because although I was born in Waterbury, Connecticut, in a New England factory town, in post–World War II, I grew up in a large southern Italian family where the rules were absolute, and customs antiquated. My sister and I were doing the jitterbug to Chuck Berry's "Maybelline" coming from the radio on the kitchen counter, my father was singing Nat King Cole songs in the shower and my grandfather was singing *"Vicin' 'u mare,"* and *"Non sona più la sveglia"* under the grape arbor.

My grandparents were all born and raised in two tiny paesi, Tolve and Avigliano, in Basilicata, the backwater of a backwater. Naples is "the North" to us. Roughly old Lucania, Basilicata is composed of steep parallel mountains precluding easy communications, making it one of the least known parts of Italy. Even Calabria, to our south, the famously backward toe of our famous boot, is better known. Sicilians have the wild pride of their stunning and infamous island. But if you are *Lucanə* [‹ *Lucano*, It.] you are from a place that even other Italians barely know. *"Abash,"* my grandmother said when I asked her what she thought of the Tolvesi, her people. Real low, said this southern Italian woman who was filled with pride of blood, pride of self, pride of her American prosperity. It is still one of the poorest regions in Italy. There is little tourism, less industry, a place more deeply connected to the past than the present.

Is this why layers of the great ancient cultures that swept through Sicily and Southern Italy have been preserved? The Greeks were powerfully present in this part of the world beginning in the seventh century BCE. Though all the ancient Mediterranean cultures left their imprint in the region, the deposits of Greek colonization are among the most richly apparent. Just to point out two strikingly obvious remnants: throughout the south of Italy and Sicily, there are the stunningly beautiful Greek temples, as well as the countless regional museums crammed with statues of Greek deities, so voluminous that they are literally stuffed into cabinets, in room after room, museum after museum, without note or comment. There are simply too many of them to catalog. The Greek colonial world seems more richly inscribed than any of the other ancient empires. What I am exploring here is perhaps a subtler layer, remnant of that Greek "new world," one inscribed in cultural mores and oral traditions. Though subtle, they were, and are, so strongly a part of my people as to have successfully survived up to, and right alongside, the intense transforming forces of post–World War II America. My grandparents carried with them an ancient world preserved as if in simple, breathing amber, and passed it onto us, not as a relic but as our everyday lived reality.

The archaic ways with which I was raised were so natural as to be effortless. Absolute tribal cultures keep you busy. There are a lot of rules to keep. We were so preoccupied with making sure we lived according to the absolute customs of our family, that we never questioned them.

But once I left my sealed Italian existence, and went out into the modern urban world, I found myself at the doorway to the 1960s. Even though I was of the second generation, born in America, I had so little ability to reconcile the southern Italian immigrant life I had come from with the one I moved to, that I found myself mute. But the word mute isn't quite accurate. I was so literally stunned, "out of it," "out of tune," *stunnada*, that I had ability neither to form thought nor to find a language with which to describe this switch. So, for many years, I lived in two irreconcilable loci.

Only long after I left Waterbury, did I begin to understand the distance between these cultures and only fairly recently, some forty-five years later, have I discovered a perspective to help me understand why these two places are so irreconcilable. There is a single author who acts as a useful guide to the land and tribe whence I came. Homer and his epics, *The Iliad* and *The Odyssey* are my guidebooks. At first, I thought it humorous that there were so many particulars I recognized at once in his epics, but gradually I began to appreciate that Homer wasn't telling us about a mythical, distant people, but rather stories about a tribe like mine.

One of the major functions of myth is to embody and teach the values of a culture. In its stories are embedded the culture's codes of behavior. In Homer I found a means of understanding why the eighty-nine-mile journey from New York to Waterbury actually represented a span of millennia. Homer's archaic terrain is as familiar to me as the Formica table in my mother's kitchen.

So in reality, it makes more sense to say I was born in 1944 but raised in Homer's time. It was the 15th century, but 15th century BCE! Although during my childhood, life in America would soon be closing in on the posthistorical, second half of the 20th century, much of what formed the paradigms of our family life had to do with pre-Christian, prehistorical ideas of pride and honor, shame and hospitality, of singing and storytelling, the palpable reality of dreams, and a strict code of what it meant to be a man and a woman. What was emphasized was shame not anxiety, honor not accomplishment, hospitality rather than individual ambition, song and storytelling, not writing.

This psychogeography will be familiar to other Sicilian and southern Italian Americans. Even the basic Homeric concepts were at the heart of the ethos in which we were raised. We watched our parents, grandparents, even those of us not born in Italy, experience a lifelong preoccupation with *nostos*, or the longing for home or return, which lies at the heart of *The Odyssey* and the immigrant experience. There is the idea of *nekyia*, the calling up of ghosts or the dead, as well as all the stuff of daily life in a southern Italian family. There are the linked concepts of *moira* or fate, and time or reputation. *Moira* is someone's share or portion of what life gives, but really implies fate or that which is inevitable. Aunt Mena, who had more than her share of misery, always said, "What are you going to do?" with a cosmic shrug. There is the companion concept of time, the share of gifts or prizes accorded someone, depending on their heroic deeds and commensurate with their set of obligations and risks taken. We can think here of the heroic stature of Achilles but also the idea of the *primo figlio* [< *primogenito*, It.]. There is of course, the idea of *kleos*, glory or fame, but more literally "reputation," what people will say about you. Etymologically, *kleos* comes from the word for *call*, so inherent is what is said about one out loud. One of my grandmother's favorite rhetorical questions was, "Ma whadda the people gonna tink?" making it clear people thinking badly of us was not a risk we could take. Perhaps most important however, is the idea of *xenia*, in both Homer's world and in mine, which defines the absolute obligations on either side of the guest-host relationship. More specifically, the term defines coded responses to a stranger or a foreigner's arrival. Finally, in my family, there are the distinctly Homeric practices: the singing of songs and the telling of tales.

There were the stories about "the other side," (again, *nostos*), but there were also repeated oral cycles about set characters told with the same refrains and phrasing. Their oral storytelling practices could easily have been studied by Milman Parry and Albert Lord, who would have found in Waterbury the same extemporaneous composing, using age-old narrative strategies of repetitious epithets and oral formulae. These stories reflected the values by which we lived, the values that were transmitted to my generation as they had been for centuries, explaining who was foolish or corrupt, and what constituted virtuous behavior. There were stories about the outsized behavior of men who contended with terrible and startling events. There were stories about scandalous and virtuous women.

Indeed, one of the main characteristics of a good woman in my family, almost as important as being a good cook and being utterly faithful, was her skills with thread and needle, a key measure by which the women in Homer are judged. Penelope could have sat at her loom on my grandmother's farm with ease, just as my grandmother had when she was a girl in her mother's home.

I mention in passing that one grandfather ran a large pig farm—remember that upon his return to Ithaca, Odysseus finds his first *xenia* with Eumaios, his loyal swineherd who sits "Odysseus down on brush and twigs he piled up for the visitor, flinging over these the skin of a baggy wild goat warm and soft, the swineherds own good bedding" (Book 14, lines 50–60), before "the stranger ate his meat and drank his wine ravenous, bolting it all down." Eumaios says to Odysseus, "It's wrong my friend to send a stranger packing even one who arrives in worse shape than you. . . . Here I sit my heart aching for him, my master, my great king, fattening up his own hogs for other men to eat." Fattening pigs, butchering and roasting them, were all a part of our everyday life. My other grandfather, indeed all the men on my father's side, including my uncles and my father, were blacksmiths, later iron-workers. In Book 10 of *The Iliad* we hear: "And the bellows . . . blew on the crucibles, breathing with all degrees of shooting, fiery heat, a blast for heavy work, a quick breath for the light, the pace of the work in hand all precisely gauged." This same "fiery heat . . . the pace of work in hand, all precisely gauged," along with the forge, the bellows, the anvil and hammers, were as much a part of our landscape as they were for Hephaestos, the smith who makes Achilles' new suit of armor before he finally enters battle with Hector.

So, to begin, let us drift into dreams. In Homer, dreams, augurs, omens, and prediction are part of the landscape. What they mean, who interprets them, and what they predict, are essential pieces of Homeric reality. So too were they for us. When we wandered into the kitchen of the ranch house my father had built for us in 1950 (from plans he had cut from our newspaper, the *Waterbury Republican*), and we were still stupid from sleep, we plopped ourselves down on the green vinyl chairs at the white Formica and chrome-legged kitchen table, we typically started our day the same way: "I had this dream last night," or, "You'll never guess what I dreamed last night," or, "It was the darnedest thing last night."

And every day these introductions were interrupted by my mother turning away from her preparations, her face strung with the same worry, "Was it a good dream or a bad dream? If it was a bad dream have something to eat before you tell it. If you don't eat something your dream will come true." She stopped us before we could continue to speak. She said this every day and every day it had the same annoying, disruptive effect of breaking the mood of our still loose-limbed trances, that paranormal state between sleep and waking, between the unconscious and the conscious. Dreamscapes in my home were ones that were clearly between the lands of the spirit and the flesh. It was that site where you followed neither the rules of sleep nor wakefulness, the one you traveled from one place to the other. We reveled in the telling, but we wouldn't know what the dreams meant until we told our grandmother who had her own code of signs, augurs, and predictions.

My superficially Americanized mother's worries about our dreams were intense and real. Only food had the power to stave off the forces of the dream life. Dreams had the power to follow us into consciousness. By the time you ate a piece of bread or took a swig from the glass bottle of milk, the somnolent trance had been disturbed, and thus my mother's goal achieved. An interruption of the corporeal dampened these forces from the other cosmos. My mother lived, and so we lived in turn, in a universe where spirits walked at our side, where dying loved ones appeared at bedsides to say good-bye or to tell us good news, where dead baby brothers walked up the stairs calling out for Mama.

Then we always proceeded to tell our dreams. While the coffee was being poured from the percolator, the Sunshine 'Merican bread or Spinelli's Italian was being toasted, we took turns telling what had happened in our dreams. The wilderness of our dreams was brought into the kitchen: lions roared, we walked naked down streets, people chased us, or large dogs lunged for our jugular. We pleaded before authorities that didn't see we hadn't committed an offense. We were innocent and powerless. Or we flew, our arms were wings, we pumped ourselves up toward a sky as real and as meaningful to us as Penelope's eagle swooping down on her geese. Dreams were deeply embedded in our ordinary daily life. Although we had no official oracles or diviners for interpretation, my illiterate grandmother served as the diviner and interpreter, having brought with her an ancient code of interpretation from Italy's deep South. Strong spirits, signs, and oracles, were all part of my grandmother's sphere, and so in turn, a part of ours.

Underlying all the unspoken assumptions in our kitchen was the idea that dreams portend and then reveal the truth, just as they do throughout Homer. To take a single important example from *The Odyssey*, there is the crucial moment between Penelope and Odysseus, after he has returned to his home disguised as a beggar and they finally sit together on either side of their hearth, the symbolic center of the household. Penelope tells him her recent dream in which an eagle swoops down and kills her geese. The geese represent her suitors. In the dream the eagle settles, then speaks to her in Odysseus's own voice. Odysseus, whose chair is drawn up near to hers, his identity still hidden beneath rags, responds like this: "Twist it however you like your dream can only mean one thing. Odysseus has told you himself—he'll make it come to pass. Destruction is clear for each and every suitor, not a soul escapes his death and doom" (Book 19). Although Penelope makes the disclaimer, "Ah my friend, dreams are hard to unravel, wayward and drifting things, not all we glimpse in them will come to pass . . ." (Book 19, lines 625–650), within a few lines she is essentially colluding with this beggar about the contest she's going to hold over the stringing of Homer's bow, which we all know only Odysseus can possibly string. It's in this crucial scene that Homer, the master storyteller, leaves us with the "does she or doesn't she know" question. This moment is one of the critical turning points of the story and the meaning of the dream is at its center. Dreams bring knowledge from beyond. My grandmother typically sat in an old worn upholstered chair next to the wood-burning stove telling us family dreams and interpreting what extraordinary messages they carried to us.

My grandmother's interpretations of all our dreams had the same mythic importance to us. Long after her own four daughters were married—my generation was already in college—my grandmother dreamed that a man had come and abducted one of her daughters. Sick with worry, she kept saying to herself, "No, no it's not true. I have all my daughters, all my children are safe." Still the dream haunted her. After a few days one of her daughters came to her profoundly upset. Her own daughter was pregnant and was going to be married immediately. This was in the very early 1960s when such news was still a horrifying breech of our sexual code. My grandmother's response was to start laughing with relief and pleasure. "Oh thank god. That's what my dream meant. I was so worried. *Figlia mia*, it's okay. No one took her. It's just that she's going to be married." And she told her daughter her dream. We have here another embedded Greek myth: the Persephone and Demeter story where sex and marriage are seen as the abduction of a daughter.

In Waterbury we told our dreams, we sat under grape arbors in the warm weather eating and drinking, singing and telling stories. Both grandfathers made cellars filled with innumerable barrels of wine each Fall so that the long tables so frequently filled with guests could be served abundantly throughout the entire year. In Homer too, a home without plenty of good wine and food to offer guests, either familiar or strange, was a home in shame.

My father loved to tell this story about the importance of wine to his family. His grandmother, his father, and his father's closest friend Canio stood solemnly in the cellar passing around the first taste of Canio's wine. They were the arbiters. The glass was passed in turn to each. No one said a word for a moment. Then Mamanonna, my father's grandmother, broke the silence grimly: "Canio's season is shot to hell." Poor Canio's wine wasn't any good and so now he had no way to welcome guests to his home.

In the south of Italy, a place of poverty, it was deemed essential that you conceal that meagerness and share abundantly what you had so little of. The poorer members of my family had to find a way to fulfill this duty even if it was a hardship because hospitality marked the essence of seeing ourselves as a civilized people.

Because after the fall of Troy Odysseus travels for ten years to return home, always in a perpetual state of *nostos*, one of the great concerns of this epic is *xenia* or hospitality. His journey is often defined by those who help or hinder his way home, those who violate the code of *xenia* and those who uphold it. *Xenia* is at the very heart of this epic. One could say it is the central value. Kalypso and Circe break this code by not helping Odysseus to get on with his journey.

The true horror of *xenia* being violated is made clear when we meet the Cyclops who not only does not extend proper hospitality but threatens instead to make his guests into dinner. This is to say, if you are so inhospitable as to not observe *xenia* properly, you turn into a creature who instead of feeding his guests, eats them. In *The Odyssey* good *xenia* is good character.

For us in our closed communities, these were the absolute rules: we were not sure if that which lay beyond our neighborhoods would welcome us, so the rules of hospitality required rigid certainty. If you were a stranger in the land (an immigrant), away from your own people, would you be welcomed or harmed? In fact, you could say *xenia* marked for us the essence of our morality. It is based more than anything on obligation, rather than love or friendship. The host must more than welcome the guest or even the stranger. Family and friends herded strangers to our tables and our beds. If members of the family had to sleep on two chairs pushed together instead of a bed, and if children had to sleep on tables, then so be it. Hospitality determined our reputation as *custumade* ("with custom or courtesy"). To be *scustumade*, or without custom or courtesy, was shameful. If we took a walk to a neighbor's house to ask about some incidental piece of information and they left us standing at the door and did not invite us in, the full force of my mother's scorn rose in her, "They didn't even invite us in. They didn't even make us a cup of coffee." Nothing could be more ill-mannered.

My grandmother was loath to leave her pig farm, especially on the very rare occasion when no one else was going to be home; she'd protest, "*Ma* [But] what if the people come and nobody *è ca* [is here]?" In my own household, there were many occasions when, although we had plans go out, when a Pontiac or Terraplane appeared with friends, relatives or *paesani*—they might only have driven from across town— our plans immediately changed. We might be, and often were, already in our car. Dad could be backing the car down our driveway, but guests had arrived at our door. Lucia and I would look at each other and sigh. We knew the car would be pulled back up the driveway. "Put the coffee on, Lucia. Jo, get the cold cuts and a jar of pickled eggplant from the cellar." Later we'd bring the cookies in from the roasting pan where they were kept in the garage cupboards. We were going to be sitting on the porch, or at our kitchen table for the rest of the night, visiting and telling stories.

Lucia and I would roll our eyes at each other, but so embedded were these values in my family that we never dared to question this practice. My father and mother reassured our guests, "Come in, come in. No, no we weren't really going anywhere. How nice to see you Uncle Dominic and Aunt Carmela," even if we had just seen them the night before. "We weren't going anywhere." It was essential that you deny reality because, "You don't want them to think we don't want them in our house." Lucia and I would never have dared display our sullen responses to our company. We would never have wanted to be seen as *scustumade*.

Telemachus, as Odysseus and Penelope's son, like us, was the inheritor, and therefore the upholder of this code. In fact, in the first four books of *The Odyssey*, Telemachus, as both host and guest, displays the primacy of place that *xenia* holds in the Greek homeland. We are shown here a terrible violation of *xenia* by the suitors who have stayed too long, who are eating and drinking Penelope and Telemachus out of house and home. This behavior is considered so terrible that if it is not at one with the suitors' plan to kill Telemachus, it does nonetheless signal a grievous violation of the Homeric ethic.

We first see Telemachus's moral fiber when Athena arrives at his door disguised as a guest, "Mortified that a guest might still be standing at the doors . . . he clasped her right hand and relieved her at once of her long bronze spear. . . . Greetings dear stranger. Here in our house you'll find a royal welcome. Have supper first then tell us what you need" (Book 1, lines 140–144). He escorts her to a high chair of honor, taking only a low chair for himself. Water is brought so that the disguised Athena might wash her hands before she is lavishly served. Only after all this has been attended to—and this is the key to *xenia*—does Telemachus ask his guest for a name and identity. The code of *xenia* rests on the fact that the host must be willing to take a guest into his household and take care of him before he has any idea of who he is.

Here is a parallel story that is part of my family's myth cycle. My mother often tells of the hordes who would visit her home when she was a child:

And I do mean hordes, these people would come up from New York and bring their friends and their friends' friends to stay with us or even sometimes live with us for the summer. It was their summer vacation and we were happy to have them. We'd wait on them hand and foot. This was our fun. To have company. People would come and live with us, with their children and everything. They'd take over our bedrooms and we'd sleep on the sun porch. We set out platters of my mother's home made *prosciutto* and sausage. We'd cook and clean for them.

Up the farm—whoever came there was always welcome. There were people who came to the door and asked for sandwiches. They were drifters. Once a big man came to the farm and he was Russian and he said, "Mama, can I have something to eat?" So my mother made him a sandwich and gave him something to drink, she looked down at his legs and they were a mess, full of sores and pus. So she had him take his shoes and socks off. Then she got down on her hands and knees and bathed his leg with disinfectant. This is a perfect stranger: she never asked his name! He never asked her for this and she got a basin and took off the old bandages and washed and cleaned his feet and legs and cleaned them and put ointment (a substance made up largely of oil) on them and wrapped them up

again. He was a big Russian guy, Big John. He had burned his
feet with gasoline. I don't know how that happened, but my
mother felt so sorry for him. When my father came home he
said, "What are you doing?" She said, "He doesn't have any
place to live. You have any work for him?" So my father asked
the guy, "You want to work for me?" Big John called my
mother "Mama" and us girls "Little Mama." He worked on the
farm for a long, long time.

There are a couple of Homeric values encoded here. First, one wel-
comes a stranger, especially a stranger in need. One offers him food,
drink, even the ancient value of bathing the stranger when the stranger
enters your house, particularly his feet, since presumably he has been
traveling and his feet are dirty and tired. Most importantly, one does
not ask his name until these other needs have been attended to. This
task is not beneath the woman of the house—in fact it enhances her
status—to attend to these welcoming duties. She is the one who knows
the value of welcoming the stranger. And although Big John was not
given the comfort of a lustrous rug and mattress and settled under the
eaves of the porch, as Odysseus is with Nausicaa's family, he is given a
job and a bed and a place in my grandparents' household. He worked
and lived in the little house for the men who worked on my grandfather's pig farm for a long time, ate all his meals at my grandmother's
ample kitchen table, and there was certainly always wine with dinner.

If this narrative echoes, as it surely does, the Nausicca chapter filled
with details of bathing and welcome, food and drink, the two details
that especially caught my attention are the way my mother says casually,
and only in passing, "She didn't even ask his name." This was so much a
part of the fabric of the culture that she barely notices its importance.
But Homer would have noticed.

My mother's tale parallels yet another Homeric story—and I assure
you no one in my family ever read Homer until I did—the story of
Odysseus's encounter with Euryclea, his childhood nurse and the family
retainer. In Book 19, after Penelope and the beggar (Odysseus) have
concluded their talk at the hearth, Penelope says, in line 364: " But
come women, wash the stranger and make his bed, with bedding, blankets and lustrous spreads to keep him warm . . . then tomorrow at day-
break bathe him well and rub him down with oil." Penelope is showing
her superior virtue by offering even a beggar the finest *xenia* (notice the
lustrous spread, beyond the bathing and bedding).

Because Penelope's maids are not virtuous—they have been con-
sorting with the violating suitors—they now actually mock Odysseus

Grandma Becce and Uncle Rocky roasting a pig

instead, so Euryclea steps in to perform this righteous task. "The work is mine   wise Penelope bids me now and I am all too glad. I will wash your feet for both my own dear queen and for yourself." At that point there is a foreshadowing of recognition. "You're like Odysseus, to the life! Then she took up a burnished basin she used for washing feet and poured in bowls of fresh cold water before she stirred in hot." And it is at that moment that in bathing his feet, just as my grandmother bathed and oiled the drifter Big John's feet, before *she* knew his name, that Euryclea recognizes the beggar as her master. She started to bathe her master . . . then in a flash, she knew the scar. This beggar, this hero, is finally among his own people. This is the beginning of his stunning homecoming.

I often say jokingly about Homer: I know these people. When my grandmother washed and dressed the legs and feet of the drifter Big John in so similar a posture as Euryclea washing Odysseus's feet, I would like to suggest that Homer would have recognized my grandmother and that is why I recognize in him the people whence I came.

II

THE UNSAYABLE:
THE CLAPPS FAMILY

Peter and His Brothers

Who wants to dig up all the stuff that hurts or makes us feel stained, all that flutters up just before we justly press it back? My father's family's tragedies all lived in that place for him and so too in turn for our family. He was wracked with pain and shame and he wanted to stay as far away from all of those memories as he could. But sometimes they would fight their way to his surface and Lucia and I would hear fragments of what he had lived through.

The rules were clear during these times. Listen and be quiet. We were at a ritual purification. He'd become very sober. He'd say what he had to say, then push it back down. "Let's talk about something else," he'd declare as soon as he could. We were to bear witness and stay silent with him until he was ready to say something again. Often years would pass between such cleansings.

We were left with the uncertainty of whether we were actually supposed to know what happened to him in his early life.

This is terra under my feet, the terrain my family stood on. We've lost my father and lost the way to what happened behind those silences. Complicating our loss is a freedom. Now that he and my mother are both gone, Lucia and I can explore as much as we are able what did happen, especially to Michael.

My grandfather Clapps's house for Sunday dinner: There would have been a huge meal of soup, macaroni with sausages, meatballs, roasted meat with roasted potatoes, vegetables, salad. The women and the girls worked together to wash and dry the dishes, soaking and saving the roasting pans for last. We're all under each other's feet but it goes quickly. "Here put this away. What did I do with my wedding band and watch? Oh my God, I thought I lost it."

We're so stupefied with food that the grownups all go to take naps.

Our generation has been outside under the grape arbor at the table. We did tricks on the iron railings, somersaults, cartwheels in the grass. We searched for four-leaf clover for a long time. We walked down the long steep hill to Sacred Heart. We lit candles there and came back up.

Now we're back in the kitchen. The grownups slowly get up from their naps. The women set the table again for desserts, coffee, fruits, nuts, anisette. After a while, the table is littered with nutshells, crumbs, flakes of crusts, and nougat candy boxes. I picked the one with the lady with the lace headdress. Grandpa Clapps is drinking more wine.

Everyone else is sipping anisette and drinking coffee.

The kids are still restless and we're not paying attention. My cousin Paulie has his parakeet with him. The parakeet is flying around the kitchen landing on curtain rods, on Paulie's shoulder. Pastries, fruit, nuts, and the talk lengthen and loosen into silky strands of the other.

Grandpa is sitting in his seat at the head of the table. Uncle Paul is sitting to one side of him. We're all crowded together. My father is there next to Uncle Paul. They're happy, laughing, the talk is drifting around the things they always talk about, the old country, the other side, how good the water tastes there, how the air is so much better, cleaner, the sky is clearer. I wanted to go home and play with my Becce cousins, ride my bike.

". . . brilliant, he was really so brilliant, you couldn't believe it," Uncle Paul is saying. "He could make anything, build anything. That's just the way he was."

Are they bragging again about some relative? They often do. I look at my father. He has a vague smile on his face. As if he's looking deep into somewhere else.

I'm bored. I don't want to stay here all afternoon. Maybe we can go swimming if we leave soon enough. The lake is probably warm enough by now. I imagine the winter's traces of this June day against my skin.

"Yes, it's true," Uncle Paul is saying, "and so good too. You know once he built a whole radio all by himself, No one helped him. That's just the way he was." He's smiling. There is a brightness in the room, a sweetness about the mood. What a wonder, this lovely relative.

There were so many vague stories in this part of my family. Things would come up at Sunday dinner, who knew whom they were talking about. Maybe someone from the other side. But that day it came into focus very slowly, then sharply, that we were talking about the most forbidden subject—my father's brother Michael. The one subject no one was ever, ever to mention. But it was Uncle Paul talking. My father's favorite uncle. He wouldn't interrupt him. I wanted to ask a question, but I knew not to do it.

Just as it began to come into focus that we were really hearing about Michael—my father's second oldest brother, my uncle Michael, who had killed himself—I could see my father's face set and freeze. This is too difficult for him. "Okay everyone. Let's change the subject. That's enough of that now. End of discussion." And everyone would sink into a leaden silence. We left to go home soon after that.

My father lost all his brothers, one by one, and was the only male child left to his despotic father.

He had a sister too, Mena (Filomena), named after Mammanonna, Aunt Mena, to us. In the end, they were the two surviving children of five births. Neither of them was much favored by their father. Both suffered terrible violence at his hands. Once my aunt was bitten by a dog when she was a little girl and she was so dirty and neglected, they couldn't find the bite on her skin until they bathed her. Later, when she was a teenager, her brother Frank would take her out with him so that she could meet her friends. Otherwise, Grandpa Clapps would beat her. That was the only way she got out of the house. Another time, she was under a street light talking to a neighborhood kid and someone told her father she was talking to a boy. He came and got her and beat her so badly on the way home that he broke her nose. That was when she went to live with Uncle Paul.

When Frank died, my grandfather said, "Now, I have no one left." Two of his children were standing with him by the grave, my father and his daughter Mena. The first male child born to Giuseppe and Beatrice died in infancy. So he was barely a brother to any of the children.

But this is about Peter and his brothers, Frank and Mike, and how he lost them.

Lucia and I knew very early that we weren't allowed to talk about my father's brother Frank. My mother told us our father had an older brother who had died very early in their courtship days. We knew that even mentioning his name was forbidden. "It upsets him too much. So let's just not talk about it," my mother explains to us. But my mother liked to talk and to tell us what she knew. My sister remembers the day my mother told us this family history. Lucia remembers just exactly where we were on the cracked sidewalk, coming up that slight incline toward North Main Street, the first time my mother told us about our father's family story. Maybe he had been yelling the day before and she wanted us to know why he got like that sometimes. We might have been walking back from Aunt Toni and Uncle Al's house on Shelly Street where we went to play with Diane. Lucia remembers exactly because my mother telling us was inscribed in her soft skin so deeply, so excruciatingly, that her life was changed forever by that story, by that day. "It was too sad," Lucia says now, "too painful. I couldn't believe that

Dad had so much pain to live with. I knew that I had to protect him, to take care of him after that. To make sure I never caused him any pain. And that we could never talk to him about any of this." That small child, too tender herself, took on the job of protecting her large, strong, pain-laced father.

"Dad's mother was down in Middletown in the hospital."

"When Frank died, you can't imagine what that did to your father. It was horrible. Oh, how he cried and cried. I thought he'd never get over it. He loved his brother so much. Frank was such a nice, nice man. And handsome, too. But he just had a way about him that was so lovely, that even though I was madly in love with your father, I could see how attractive he was. And I didn't really have eyes for anyone but your father. Frank was the one who taught Dad how to be an ironworker. They were really close. We were keeping company at the time his brother got sick, but after Frank died we didn't go out for a year. We kept the mourning for a full year. It was fine. We were in love and we were happy just to be with each other. But for your father it was really terrible.

"Then, once after we were married and living on Ward Street, one day I said to your father, 'It's time for us to go to the cemetery to visit Frank's grave.' Your father walked out of the house and slammed the door without even talking to me. I didn't know what I had done wrong. Aunt Vicki and Uncle Joe lived right down the street from us and he went down there. Aunt Vicki told me he went down and he cried his heart out. 'You'd better not talk to Peter about this, Rose,' she said. 'He can't take it.' After that I never said anything. I just went by myself to the grave. I didn't realize it was going to do that to him. I just thought we should visit the grave. I never brought it up again after that.

"This is how much your father loved his brother. When we were first keeping company and we were falling madly in love, I can't tell you how handsome your father was. One day he sat me down and he said, 'I have to tell you something. I love you but I love my brother Frank more than I love you.'

"'That's fine,' I said, 'I'm glad you love your brother. I'm very glad you love him.' And then he had to lose him too. He had to lose him, too."

It was in the "too" that so much of the pain is lodged.

Joe Clapps, his father, was a violent drinker, a womanizer, and Dad's mother was institutionalized when he was a very small child.

Was it that day that my mother told us about Michael, too? "Your father had another brother too, Michael. And he died too. He killed himself. That was a long time ago when the boys were young.

"Michael was a very bright boy," my mother tells us, "a very intelligent young boy. Aunt Dora told me. He was so bright. He would go in the basement and he would create the darndest things. You wouldn't believe it. He was always tinkering with things. Aunt Dora told me," my mother confides in us as we walk through the spring afternoon, "that Michael built a short wave radio completely on his own in the cellar and that his father got mad about something and went down to the basement and smashed it to smithereens.

"Then he got involved with some bad kids and they robbed a store and that's how all the trouble happened," my mother continued the story. "How he got roped into that I'll never know. It makes you want to bawl your eyes out.

"He got involved with these young men and what happened was this. There was a furniture store on South Main Street and they broke into it to rob it. They went in the back window and they were caught.

"So he got put in jail that night. It wasn't that big, nothing big. But Peter's father let him sleep there at the jail all night.

"So then Mecca, Grandpa Clapps' drinking buddy, heard about it. Mr. Mecca said, 'Come on now. We've got to take him out.' But Grandpa Clapps was just furious. So they went and they got him out. I could imagine, never talked to him probably, never said a word, just walked ahead of him. And they went home. Aunt Dora told me all of this," my mother says. "So Mikey went in his bedroom, changed his clothes, climbed out the window and he was going down Bank Street and he had a gun. Now this bad kid that he got involved with must have given him the gun. So Mikey sees two policemen coming toward him. He wasn't doing anything. He was just standing there, but goodness knows he thought they were after him. He shot himself. Not to go through what he went through again. And the policemen were not after him. He was out. He was free. But it was too late.

"Later they found a bank book with his name and a balance of $400.00. But no one knew anything about it."

Years later, long after my father died, my mother added another chapter to Michael's story.

"Peter's father had a *paesan* who had a son who was not a very nice son. And the father wanted him to have a good job and work. The family was Aviglianese. My father-in-law never turned down a *paesan*. And he gave the kid a job. This son didn't want to work so he was going to fix it so that my father-in-law would have to fire him. Then he wouldn't have to show up anymore at the shop. After a while, Peter's father had to fire him because he wouldn't do the work

"So then his father, the *paesan*, probably bawled him out pretty good, you know all the trouble he had caused his father. The kid got mad that my father-in-law fired him. I don't know what he wanted for the shop to just pay him. So this young man got a hold of Mikey and made a pal out of Mikey to get back at my father-in-law and turned him *malandrine*, a bad person, bad like him.

"Why Peter thinks this kid did this because the *paesan*, the father, kept going to visit Peter's father and he kept saying, "Oh Joe, I'm so sorry. I'm so sorry." So that's what they deduced. The father put my father-in-law in jeopardy by insisting he give his son a job.

"So that's how Mikey, who was such a good kid, got involved with these bad kids.

"Dad never talked about this. He told me about this just a little while ago. I never asked him any questions. Dad was a couple of years younger than Michael. If Michael was nineteen, Dad must have been sixteen. He worshiped his brilliant brother Michael.

"Uncle Paul and Aunt Dora took Dad to New York to get his mind off his brother.

"Maybe he told me this because we were riding around. Maybe we went by a place where they used to play, Hamilton Park or somewhere, and he told me this. It was just recently, late in his life."

After my mother died and we emptied her apartment and boxed up all her notebooks and files and costume jewelry and fifty-four photograph albums, I was casually going through her things and picked up a small vinyl photograph book. There sat one photograph of my father and his two brothers.

Neither Lucia nor I knew this photograph existed. When I called her to say, "Lucia, I found a picture of Dad with his two brothers," she said, "Are you sure?"

Actually I wasn't. We had only seen two tiny photographs of Michael that my mother kept. My father didn't want reminders of his brothers around. We had seen just a couple of Uncle Frank. And when she said that I thought, of course, this can't be of them.

"Where did you find it?" By then we had decided together to try to find out as much as we could about our father's family. Lucia sent for the admissions card to the Middletown Hospital for our grandmother, Beatrice Coviello. We called cousins to ask them to tell us what they knew. We found Michael's gravesite—where he was buried far away from the rest of the family—in the children's section of the cemetery. I had been there only once before with my mother. That day she had told me that the site didn't even have a grave marker so she had put one there for him. Lucia sent for Michael's death certificate.

"I found it in that small blue photograph book Mom kept on her coffee table."

"Are you sure? We both looked through that book a million times."

"I know. Maybe it isn't. Maybe it's just some friends. Dad looks like he's maybe fifteen in it. He's taller than both of the guys in the picture. But I'm pretty sure it's Uncle Frank."

But it was Peter and his brothers. It was. The only photograph of the three of them together in existence. We have no idea where it came from. How it was that we had never seen it before? How it came in our mother's possession? How come she never mentioned it to us? But there it was.

Mike is in the middle. My father is to one side, Frank is to the other. It's just before Michael shot himself. There are three young men. Handsome, skinny, full of life, smiles, simple, direct, no fuss, full of "young guy here we are" stuff. Mike has his arm around my father's waist. Frank has his arm around Mike's shoulders. My father's long arm dangles around Mike. They are linked. Completely intact. As they would very soon never be again.

There's no hint of trouble or anguish. Frank hasn't worked at the Naugatuck Rubber for one solid year, on his father's orders, in a closed shop breathing in the toxic fumes that would lead to his leukemia. Mike hasn't gotten into trouble with the *malendrin'* yet. He hasn't taken a .32 Colt Automatic and shot himself in the right temple in a public place.

"But that's enough. Let's not talk about this anymore. End of discussion."

Paulie *e 'u Gagaron'*

My cousin Paulie knew things that Lucia and I didn't. He's always known them. We had a few fragments and lived sometimes in the sad caresses of our family's history, but he knew the facts. He knew every byway of the ruins of our family, every cracked stone, heard every desolate wind that blew over our ruins, because he was born and raised at the center of the eroded pile that is our Clapps family. In the middle of it. Subjected to it. Haunted by it. Made by it. Unmade by it. He doesn't like to talk about it. He pushes it away. But every bone of his was constructed and grown on that terrain.

Chiu o men' (more or less) Paulie is our age, chronologically our peer, but he has never been of our generation. He was the solitary member of his own generation. Being the member of a generation means that you are clearly marked as at one with the next round, with others of your family. But, by the time he was born, his first cousins, those who should have been his generation, were married and starting their own families. How does anyone occupy a generation by themselves? It's a lonely station. So he didn't belong to a group of brothers, sisters, or cousins, who would have played with him every day, told him he was being a baby, embarrassed him into being braver than he actually was, argued with him, pinched him, sanctioned his bad behavior. Reminded him that all grown-ups were stupid and crazy. So although he sat only slightly to one side of us, he wasn't of our generation either. He occupied a solitary outpost.

Paulie stood slightly to one side of all the action. His days and nights were mostly spent with the people who should have been his grands and greats, grandparents, great aunts and uncles. And he was left alone with the terrifying secrets of our family. Like what had happened between his father, my Uncle Paul, and his Uncle Joe, my grandfather. What was that all about? Why didn't they speak for twenty years?

His father, Paolo Clapps, my beloved great Uncle Paul, was the precise opposite of his brother, Giuseppe Clapps, my grandfather. Whereas his brother Joe was despotic, a bully, violent, an alcoholic, a philanderer, father of at least one illegitimate child, Uncle Paul was *un proprio gallanthomo*, deeply gallant, full of dignity, grace, sobriety, generosity, and deep loyalty. One of the kindest men I have ever known. A real gentleman.

Dora LaGuardia, Paulie's mother, my Great Aunt Dora, was Uncle Paul's profoundly shy, hardworking, loving companion. She was so shy and reticent that as a girl she spoke with hesitations and hems and haws often ending her sentences with sounds rather than words. She was comfortable with working, always working. That they came upon one another and married was itself a bit of fate's sleight of hand.

Uncle Paul and my grandfather were driving up to New Jersey so that Uncle Paul could visit the daughter of an *Aviglianese* family whom he was courting. On the long drive, they stopped to have Sunday dinner in Stamford, Connecticut, with a different *Aviglianese* family. No *Aviglianese* would think of driving near another without stopping to visit. There they had a sumptuous Sunday dinner. The *minestra* was a rich broth made from chicken and a pork bone, filled with greens, tiny meatballs, pieces of chicken, pepperoni, an *Aviglianese* soup that sets a soul straight when the world is all wrong. After that there was a pasta, light and silky, handmade by a young woman who lived with this family. The roast was succulent, the potatoes crisp and brown with olive oil and butter, the *torta* was sweet, the coffee strong. All of this food had been prepared by the agile hands of the younger sister of this family, who was so excruciatingly shy she rarely said anything throughout the meal. When their bellies were filled and it was time to leave this table and be on the road, my grandfather turned to his younger brother and said, "Why should we drive all the way up there? Ask this young woman to marry you instead. Just look at the way she cooks." Then he turned to their *Aviglianese* hosts, "Make her come out of the kitchen." She was young and strong, slender and pretty but *quieta, quieta*.

My Aunt Dora never knew her own mother, who died soon after she was born. Instead she was raised by a stern father and a stepmother who beat her daily. She was allowed to leave Avigliano only because her sisters were coming to America. That day she mostly stayed in the kitchen, listening to her relatives propose this shocking, thrilling idea.

As reticent as she was capable, Aunt Dora was as unable with language as her hands were fluid and quick. A sleight of hand of the gods had revealed their fortune in the luster of golden broth and floating pieces of rich green *cicoria* and *scarole* of Dora LaGuardia's *minestra*. My Uncle Paul proposed marriage to my Aunt Dora that afternoon and their lives were joined. Ah that *minestra*. What a golden soup it was.

Many of the girls of Avigliano were trained early to be fine seamstresses, famous for their embroidery, their perfect seams, their fine, tiny hand-stitching for hems, buttonholes. That was true of Dora LaGuardia and the Clapps sisters, too. While the soft flawless turn and binding of fabric was for our girls, heating, shaping, and tempering the hard, tough materials of steel and iron was the destiny of all the young Clapps men. There are records as far back as the 1700s of our people as blacksmiths and farriers in Avigliano, but it's clear this trade goes back many more centuries. The records in Avigliano are deep with this name recorded there; blacksmithing was part of their presence in Avigliano. As soon as the male children became old enough, they were trained by their fathers, grandfathers, and uncles to work with anything made of iron and steel. They could make the delicate twists of the decorative ornamental work that graced fences, gates, grilles, and *balconie* as well as the varied range of sturdy agricultural tools, hoes, hatchets, sickles, knives, and horseshoes. They lived by the flowing fires of orange and red, where they heated, hammered, bent, and shaped these metals into beauty and tools for work. When my tall, strapping young grandfather, Giuseppe Clapps, arrived at the Battery in New York City in 1903, his uncle met him with an extra large pair of overalls so that he could start work that afternoon as a blacksmith's helper. Each of the brothers took up their family trade as soon as they arrived in America. They were blacksmith helpers, second finishers, finishers in ornamental iron.

Once the whole Clapps family was reassembled here in America, an inevitable immigrant family opera of wild love, marriage against family wishes, multitudes of babies, great success, horrible failure, illness, and, of course, death and madness occupied their stage. Family members died in the flu epidemic. Businesses were begun, struggled for, thrived; great wealth was accumulated. Then those same businesses failed.

In 1921, Uncle Paul and his equally gentle brother, Uncle Willie, decided to start a scrap iron business together: Clapps Brothers Scrap and Steel Co. Over the course of the next twenty-two years, they succeeded and failed, and succeeded and failed with the hindrance of a corrupt partner once, a good brother-in-law's advice another time, then the depression of the '30s. They worked, struggled, thrived, and prospered. Then there was great success, real wealth, ease, the joy and satisfaction of hard work paying off. They had seventeen men working for them. They had their own barges to send the scrap metal directly to Pittsburgh. They bought brand new cars every year. They had bank accounts all over New Jersey. They went out to nightclubs, took everyone out to dinner.

Uncle Paul and Aunt Dora took great pleasure in sharing their prosperity. My father talked often about Uncle Paul: "I can't tell you what it meant. Uncle Paul would hand me a shiny ten-dollar gold coin. But Uncle Paul was like that, so generous, so kind. I can see him looking down at me when he hands me that piece. You have no idea what that meant to a raggedy kid like me. It was all the money in the world."

Uncle Paul and Aunt Dora were devoted to each other. But they were also those two devoted people who took care of anyone in their larger family in need—creating in their very beings a place of refuge and sanctuary. If problems came to any part of our family, they were the most devoted people who stepped in and took care. If there was worry or need, they lent a helping hand, bought the groceries, and left money in the sugar bowl. Uncle Paul picked up those with troubles, drove them places; whatever the need, he provided. Aunt Dora nursed and succored them back to health, her kitchen alchemy cooking them back from family illness and tragedy. She scrubbed, sewed, and crocheted them back to rightness. Aunt Dora would move into someone's home to nurse them and ease their misery. Many of the children born to the extended family were taken in by Uncle Paul and Aunt Dora when their own families were unable to care for them. Their home was the haven in the storms that blew all across those rough times. He was the uncle and she was the aunt who stood by their nephews and nieces as the tragedies multiplied and took over my father's family.

While Aunt Dora and Uncle Paul took care of everyone in the family, they were the Anna and Joachim of our family. Plain and right, devoted and kind, generous and inclusive. But like Joachim and Anna, for all of their rightness, the fates and fortunes withheld from them the greatest bounty. The final and most essential blessing eluded them.

They were without a child.

This must have been a cause of lamentation. There may have been miscarriages, heights of hope and depths of disappointment. Perhaps out of this terrible absence their devotion to their nieces and nephews was increased. I know with certainty that my own father's kindness and generosity was directly a result of Aunt Dora and Uncle Paul's love and care. I'm sure his life wouldn't have been as full of love and happiness without them. If the rage in my father came from his father Joe Clapps, his capacity for love came from Uncle Paul.

While my two great uncles, Uncle Paul and Uncle Willie, struggled and strived, failed and then pushed their way to the heights of success, my grandparents, Giuseppe Clapps and Beatrice Coviello's family was descending into tragedy and chaos. They were having one child after another. She lost her first baby, Francesco, at eight months, to pneumonia in 1910. Within a few months, she was pregnant with her second son—so her first surviving child was conceived, carried, and born into her grief. He was also named Francesco. She had three more babies within five years. After each birth she had severe postpartum depressions. With which baby did this start? Did the death of her first-born, followed by an immediate pregnancy, start this descent? There were a lot of babies and a lot of postpartum depression. Along the way, my grandparents had moved to Waterbury and my great-grandparents moved in with them to help raise the family.

There are many versions of how and why my grandmother Beatrice descended into madness. One is that my grandfather was so mean to her, so violent and so crushingly cruel that one day she just snapped. Another is that her mother-in-law joined in the violence against her. Another is that her own mother was never right in the head. just ran in her family. Which begets which? My father always said very simply, "My mother had a weak mind."

My Uncle Paul thought the world of his sister-in-law, Bessie. He loved her. To him, she was the dearest, dearest person. What she put up with from her husband was as horrible as it gets, and it finally drove her mad. She, like so many in the family, dreaded when her husband went down the stairs to fill his wine jug too often because he wasn't just going to drink, he was going to turn into the mean drunk he inevitably became. A number of times Bessie called my Aunt Dora and Uncle Paul to come and take one or another of her children to save them from their father's violence. If she couldn't protect herself, she'd protect them. Uncle Paul drove up after work in the dark to pick them up, bring them home and raise them as if they were his own. Perhaps his brother or his mother, *Mammanonna*, called too. Maybe Uncle Paul also came when my grandmother Beatrice tried to boil Mikey in the water on top of the stove. Was that one of those times?

Of course, my cousin, Paulie, knew all of this. He understood the *Aviglianese* dialect, knew all the family secrets, where the skeletons in every closet resided, his own family's hard times and miseries, including those that took place before he was born. Even if his parents didn't tell him all of this directly, he'd be in the next room and they'd be talking this over in the *Aviglianese* dialect. But when they talked to each other, "it was as if they'd forget I was there. Or forget I heard every word they were saying. So I learned things I was never supposed to know. Yet I never spoke to anyone about it. It didn't seem right. It wasn't my place. And, besides, it was too painful for everyone. I could never, never, for instance, talk to your father about his brother Mikey and what happened to him. Often we'd go for long, long bike rides at four-thirty in the morning after you girls had left Waterbury and he would unburden himself to me; he'd talk to me about everything he was worried about, but he never once spoke about his brother Mike and the suicide. Never once. What I know about that I know from overhearing my parents talking about it in the kitchen while I was sitting in the living room watching television. I've often wondered: Didn't they know I could understand every dialect word they were saying?"

Then long after Aunt Dora and Uncle Paul had given up the hope of having a child, long after they had provided solid ground for their nieces, long after Bessie was permanently placed in an institution, after Michael killed himself, and Frank had died of leukemia, and long after their brothers' and sisters' children had grown and married and were having their own children, Aunt Dora got pregnant and had my cousin Paulie. Finally all their great dreams were fulfilled.

At that point, Uncle Paul's and Uncle Willie's business was at its strongest and most prosperous. They were dismantling transportation buses for the Third Avenue Railway Company in New York City, doing it quickly and very profitably. Was that the reason that Uncle Paul and Uncle Willie decided to empty all of the bank accounts all over New Jersey and pour every single penny they had accumulated back into their now thriving business? They bought all new trucks and invested in new machinery; they were roaring along the road of well-earned success. When America became fully involved in World War II, it stopped the dismantling of anything that had wheels. The U.S. government froze the price of scrap metal for the war. Their bank books had been emptied at exactly the wrong moment and their business went under.

Uncle Willie went to work for his wife's family and Uncle Paul took a job at Waterbury Iron Works where his brother Joe was one of the bosses. It was an absolute loss for him, a real comedown from the life he had been living. Now he had his final dream, a male child, but he was left with the emptied bank books and lost dreams. And he was left living with his cruel older brother, my grandfather, whom Uncle Paul had watched mistreat Bessie and his children. He went to work as a laborer in the shop where my grandfather was part owner and shop foreman. He was back under his older brother's thumb.

So my cousin Paulie's life began late in his parents' lives and, while it began at the crest of their joy and success, too soon after his arrival the three of them fell into Waterbury and landed in the midst of the wild terrain of my grandfather's meanness and misery. They lived above my grandfather on the second floor of the house my grandfather owned. From that perch, Paulie was privy to every whisper and scream of my family's mostly hidden saga. His childhood was fevered with the heat of these secrets.

My father was Paulie's first cousin, but by the time they moved to Waterbury, my father and mother had married and Lucia and I were born within a couple of years. My sister's life and mine centered much more around my mother's large sprawling family. We were born into and brought up with all of our cousins on the Becce side of the family. Just as in Middle Eastern families, first cousins in my family are like siblings. We were all raised in each other's hair. We were each other's best friends, each other's rivals, each other's best and worse. My first wild crushes were on my older male cousins. They were so handsome, classically Italian handsome. Large dark eyes, thick dark hair, strong chins, strong athletic bodies. So cute. We practiced our flirting on them. They were charmed and amused. They teased us, bragged about the scooters they built out of fruit boxes and old roller skates and about the dangerous hills they raced down with their friends in the middle of traffic. They won, natch. They laughed with us, at us, swaggered off into their larger worlds of newspaper routes, seriously souped-up bicycles. With all that and girlfriends, they picked us up and threw us over one shoulder, put us in our place. When we were with them, we'd pull our white ruffled blouses off one shoulder to practice our four- and five-year-old girly wiles on them. Later they taught us how to dance the Lindy, allowed us to be with them until the sun set when they went downtown to meet and neck with their girlfriends.

Paulie was robbed of all that. Although he'd spend time with us and the Becce children, there was always something that set him apart from us. He didn't belong fully in either world of either generation. He was singular and isolated, living in the house that was a memorial to all the pain that had befallen all of these older people. The larger part of their lives was over by the time he was toddling around.

In addition to being the only member of this halfway-between generation, and living in a house full of much older people, he was the last precious gift in his parents' lives and they hovered protectively over him as if the gods would arrive at any second and take from them this last treasure too, the most important treasure of all—their only child. *E` figlio masculine.*

They hovered over his every precious step. When he ran, they were afraid he'd fall. "Paulie, Paulie," they called after him, "be careful." When he rode a bike, they hovered as if it would be their own aging bones that might hit the pavement if the bike wobbled and tipped over.

He came over to our house all the time. He played with my sister and me and all our other cousins from my mother's side of the family, but he was always a little apart, a little different. Most of it was because he was being raised by his older, hovering parents who had had to wait too long, who had had to bear too many losses—of pregnancies, perhaps, of Michael, of Bessie, of Uncle Paul's business—and who, once they finally had Paulie, were always warding off their own fear, "Be careful, Paulie. Oh, Paulie, don't do that. Oh, Paulie, you'd better not." Not. Not. Not. All of our stock and status rested with who was willing to go the fastest, the longest, take the greatest risk. Hesitation was simply not anything we had any tolerance for. We had contempt for all our New York cousins because they had hay fever, they didn't know how to run fast, they couldn't race to the top of the hill on their bikes.

Another thing that set Paulie apart was that he was raised with the knowledge that he would be responsible for his parents too soon in his own life. That his fate was tied to theirs in an even more profound way than most children feel. When he became a teenager, my Aunt Dora was afraid that every young girl was going to do something bad to him. "*Beh*, be careful, Paulie, those girls, Paulie. Be careful. They want your money. Hmpf."

As he came into adulthood, he felt his own life had to be put on hold because, "I knew where my duties were. I had to be responsible for my parents. I discussed this many times with your mother. And she tried to tell me that I had to have my own life. Who else was going to do it? I had to put my own life on hold."

Even getting his license, which in our world was a cause of tremendous joy and freedom had a terrible extra cost for him. While my sister and I were never allowed to see our grandmother because my father insisted on protecting us from this misery, as soon as Paulie got his license, he went with my mother every single week because by then Beatrice was failing. Sometimes he drove my mother and his mother there twice a week.

He tells me now that my mother would say he didn't have to come in with them if he didn't want to. But "I wouldn't let the women go in alone. I just could not do that to them.

"That place was terrifying. She was in a locked institution. And they didn't just unlock the doors to let us in. We go through a series of locked doors and they'd lock those same doors behind us. You can't image the clang of those doors behind us. There were inmates screaming constantly. It was terrifying. People going wild, I mean climbing the walls.

"But, I have to tell you something that you might not believe, but it's true. It's really true. In the midst of this, of all these locked doors and screaming, your grandmother Bessie had the calmest smile, the most serene smile. There was peacefulness about her. I was in awe of her. Every time I visited her, I was amazed at her serene disposition, that beautiful consistent smile. She didn't seem fazed by the persistent loud screams coming from the various wards. She had made peace with her surroundings and her fate. It didn't seem to get to her. Even I could see she was a lovely lady just like my father always said about her. And your parents had been so kind to me. I just had to do this for them."

So while we were protected, he was expected to drive, to do, to give up being a teenager hanging around the Dairy Queen and drive to the locked mental institution.

Raised in these dusty shadows, he alone grew up knowing too much. The Clapps family was filled with silences, secrets, torn yellowed fragments of stories. "I lived in dread of hearing your grandfather call me to come and do something for him. He terrified me. He was so imposing and tall, so frightening. 'Come here, Paulie. I want you to . . .' and then whatever he wanted me to do I simply had to do it. No matter what, I had to obey. And how I dreaded when I'd hear his footsteps going down to the cellar to get more wine. Now he was going to be vicious. He always did. We'd hear him from upstairs yelling at Aunt Elisa, screaming really horrible stuff at her. You can't imagine what it was like in that house. He was such a bully, such a mean bully."

Those were our ways. If a family elder called, you had to obey. "Even after the big fight between my father and him, still, I had to go. Of course a big part of that fight was what he had done to Mike. My father never forgave him for what happened with Mike.

"Michael was so talented, so very, very talented. The things he could build. He could make anything. He was mechanically inclined. Well, you could say a mechanical genius. You can't imagine how much my father loved Michael. Your father and Michael were his sons, as far as my father was concerned.

"Mikey had one of those minds. Once he built a shortwave radio out of nothing, out of parts he found around. It was perfect. He did it all by himself. I don't know how he did it. One day for no reason whatsoever your grandfather went downstairs and smashed it to smithereens. To smithereens. Oh he made my father so mad. I'd heard my father talking this over with my mother many, many times in dialect—about how bad he was to Mike, to Bessie, to all his children.

And that's why Uncle Paul had to take Mike home to live with him sometimes. That's one of the things he always held against his brother. He was sure that his brother was the cause of Mike's suicide. That's what my father thought. Well, that excruciating pain never went away for my father. He never recovered from that.

"But the weird thing is that really, underneath, my father knew that his older brother had no backbone. He was a scardy-cat. You know we'd go up to Vita and Paul Salvatore's house in Townplot quite often on Sundays to play cards, maybe twice a month. They would play cards and I'd go into the other room to watch television. It was a big house and the living room was far away from the kitchen. I'd sit there by myself and watch their TV, cowboy shows and so forth.

"That's how it always was. They'd be singing, talking loud, even shouting in Italian as they slapped down the cards. But I wouldn't really be paying attention to them.

"So that night," Paulie continues, "there was the usual shouting coming from the kitchen, but I didn't pay any attention. That was normal. I was engrossed in my cowboy show, naturally. But then gradually I realized that this was a different kind of shouting.

"I walked out toward the kitchen and I stood in the doorway. My father's face was beet, beet red. His face was right in Uncle Joe's face. I had never seen my father like this. You know, my father was the mildest mannered guy. My father wasn't as tall as Uncle Joe, but he had huge arms and huge hands. He was very strong. Very strong.

"'You? You, you're going to do what?' my father yelled at Uncle Joe. I could see that Uncle Joe was scared. Actually scared. I had never seen him like this. Frankly so was I. I was actually trembling. But Uncle Joe was shaking like a leaf. I don't know what set that particular argument off. I could see the terror in his face. I thought he was going to well, how can I put this nicely, well, relieve himself right there sitting in the chair.

"Then Paul Salvatore's son came in. You know he was a police detective and he knew how to deal with situations like this. He got in between them. Now Uncle Joe was protected, he was so relieved. I could see it in his face.

"So now, all of a sudden, from being terrified he was full of bravado, 'I'm going to kick you out of my house,' he screamed at my father.

"Now my father called his bluff! 'Oh yeah,' he said. He was still furious. 'You? *Che gagarone,* * *tu*? You think you're going to kick me out

---

*Gagarone, cacarone, as in *caca*—one who is so frightened as to shit his pants.

of that house?' He knew who his brother really was, a bully who was all talk but no backbone. So my father said to him, 'Don't ever dare show your face at my door! If you do, I'll come down in the middle of the night and strangle you in your sleep! You'll never know what happened to you. In your sleep!' And he actually made a circle with his hands. 'The only way I'll leave that house is feet first. You just try to get me out. You *gagarone*!' Even though Uncle Joe owned the house.

"My father had finally called his bluff. At the shop, your grandfather was very imposing. You know how tall and imposing he was, domineering, a dictator at the shop. But he couldn't fool his brother. He knew his brother better than anyone did. So after that fight, my father wouldn't speak to Uncle Joe. Even though technically he worked for Uncle Joe at the shop, my father simply would not take orders from him. Would not talk to him. Would not listen to him. All of Uncle Joe's orders had to go through Chippy to my father. He could never forgive his brother for what he had done to his wife or his children. He knew how his brother had terrorized his family and he couldn't forgive him for that.

"My father had loved your father, and Mikey, and all his nieces and nephews like his own children. They were his children, so to speak, before I was born. When Mikey killed himself because of your grandfather, you can't imagine how my father felt about that. He never got over it. Never. Never. And the way he had treated Bessie too. And your father too. And that night it all came out in that fight.

"Uncle Joe and Aunt Elisa got up, put on their coats and left right away. We stayed for quite a while and my father tried to calm down. We were there for hours. Eventually, we went home and that was that. Aunt Elisa came up a few days later to say that Joe felt terrible about what had happened, but it was too late. My father wouldn't speak to him.

"Later on, of course, when Uncle Joe started to get Alzheimer's many years later, one day we heard him climbing up the stairs. Now he never came up the stairs—even when they had been speaking. But that day we heard him coming up the stairs. We all recognized his footstep and we were all waiting to see what would happen. Finally he got to the top of the stairs and knocked on the door. 'I've got to see your father,' he said to me. My father said immediately, '*En beh*, Joe, what is it?' After all those years. There he was. Uncle Joe started crying. Even my father started crying. They hugged. 'I'm so sorry for what I did. For everything,' Uncle Joe said, 'Bessie had too many children too fast. That's what did it. I'm so sorry.' And they both cried together. But that was much much later on."

My Father Telling Stories

My father grew up very much in the oral traditions of singing and storytelling around the table. Both were a part of his daily life.

By the time he died, he had told all his stories hundreds of times to all of us who knew him. He was a fine storyteller—regularly pulling an old favorite out of his story hoard. Often we'd be sitting at one of our tables, having coffee after our afternoon naps and we'd be talking about whatever, and my father's attention would drift off into a fixed gaze—above and away from the table, maybe to the freezer door, somewhere between remembering, daydreaming, and being in a trance. His eyes might close slightly. He'd have a half-smile playing around his mouth, but he had definitely left the kitchen for another plane. At some point, he'd shift the heft of his body in his chair and take stock of his audience. He'd choose one of us sitting at the table to bring the whole audience to attention. "Billy Boy," he might say to my husband, "you have to listen to this. You will not, you can not; there is simply no way to believe what just happened down at the North End Social Club. You know there's Silly Mo, Crazy Mo, and Dirty Mo." He had gone off to compose his most recent tale or he had returned with it burnished new. He had returned with his story to tell.

He considered his point of view, his audience, weighed language and figures of speech, in short, he composed them. Each time a story was told, it had the classical dimensions of the oral tradition, certain repeated phrasings, a repetition of image, theme and form and, no matter how many times he repeated the story, with almost no variation. I had always thought it was strange the way he would leave and return while sitting with us—breaking into whatever conversation was going on while he had, it seemed to me, so rudely, gone off into his own

39

world. His departure and return with the story was so much a part of the life we led that it was only after he died that I realized he left us at those moments to compose his stories, to re-prepare them, an actor about to take the stage That is, he was in the artist's ecstatic state in the original sense of the Greek word—*ecstasis*—meaning out of the body; *sta* is to stand or be in a place, *eco* is out of or away from, which is of course at the heart of every artistic creation. He would have been annoyed and embarrassed if I had explained this to him. He'd have looked down and away from my face. Being self-conscious about anything was not as things should be. Unless he was reflecting on something. At times he'd be quite philosophical and articulate in his reflections. But he told stories as naturally as any bard does.

His voice was his instrument. It was a deep resonant voice that projected into whatever room or space he occupied. He sang all day long to accompany his life; he whistled long elaborate songs and he told stories at the kitchen table. He didn't have to push his voice out—it went out large and booming and filled air around him. Like any good storyteller, he used it with modulation, nuance, and pleasure. He told us stories about his youth, his work life, the political life of Waterbury, his family, and his oddball friends.

Oak Street

My father talking about moving into the house on Oak Street in 1924 when he was eight years old:

> I think it was either two thousand four hundred dollars or three thousand four hundred dollars for that house, but you should have seen it, what a mess it was. I wondered why my father bought it, child as I was, but he never was one with money. He was a good earner, but he never was a money manager. He'd been kicking around, block to block, rent to rent and I guess he finally decided, maybe my brother had gotten old enough to influence him, to convince him to settle down.
>
> There was this adjoining property next door, there was no wall, just a dirt bank, there was no driveway, no cement walks, no fences. The back half of the house wasn't even there, it didn't exist. There was an outhouse, no plumbing, no inside plumbing. And I can remember the stark first night we spent there. We went into the house, I think it was 1924. That would make me seven years old, I'm pretty sure that it was—I

can remember sitting on this threadbare floor, that's what it was, threadbare, no linoleum, and I can remember Mammanonna saying, "*L'auita da Di'*," with the help of God, "*L'auita da Di'*."

Scialababola

My father talking about his father and making wine:

My father was like a bachelor, because my mother was in the hospital. Mammanonna was the housekeeper and he was free to bring the guys in. He had to be king, had to be the *scialababola*, meaning spendthrift or wasteful, but also with the connotation of carefree or generous. As a matter of fact, it was kind of a joke on Oak Street. If someone asked for a glass of wine, the answer would be "What do you think this is, Joe Clapps' house?" That's all these men lived for . . . uh, well was to guzzle wine in unbelievable amounts. One year, one of my father's gang, Mr. Passarento's wine had spoiled. It was a great tragedy. I can remember my father saying with all the melancholy he could muster, "Passarento's shot to hell." He meant his social career was dead for that year.

The winemaking went on every October. How many hundreds, I could almost say thousands, of boxes of grapes we lugged up and down those cellar stairs (the wine press and barrels were in the cellar). Then we would have to cart the *vinazzio* (the grape skins after the grapes have been pressed) back up the stairs. What a mess that was. My father used to make as much as eleven barrels for home consumption. Can you imagine that? Eleven barrels for him and his buddies? He had to be the *scialababola*, the king host.

But everybody had to make the wine; he just made the most. Even Canio on his four dollars a week, somewhere, somehow he managed to save up money for the grapes for the wine. Don't ask me how. There ware all kinds of schemes to get the most out of the grapes, like add sugar or water, take the press apart and re-squeeze the grapes and the casings.

My father, Mammanonna, and Canio were experts in wine judging. When it came time to test the new wine, the moment of truth, it was a very solemn occasion. I remember them drawing a glass of wine and the three of them standing

in a circle passing the wine, silent. Reserving judgment. It
went from my father to Mammanonna to Canio. Canio was
the last in line. That year it was a particularly good wine.
Canio tasted it and then he said, "*Stu vine . . . ca u solo remain-
ishe bia emboad.*" ("This wine is SO powerful, if the sun goes
down while you are drinking it, you won't be able to find your
way home.")

Canio Becomes a Citizen

My father talking about his father and Canio:

There is this person, Canio: he was a nice man, he was a beautiful man. He was a cuckold, you know. My father was having
relations with his wife. They lived upstairs from us. He was
like a clownish figure in a way, but in another way he would
come out with these things. He was beautiful. My father and
he were good buddies. Canio, he was terrific. He would
become speechless, but I mean mute, totally mute, when he
was drunk. He would go to speak, his cheeks would puff out
and not a sound would emerge.

Now, in 1940, there was general hysteria going on
throughout the country because of the impending war or
because the war had started in Europe. Now, Canio was in a
rush to get his citizenship papers. He didn't want to be
deported back to Italy to go into the Italian army. So he's
going to high school for a couple of weeks to learn the basic
questions—Lincoln's birthday, George Washington's birthday.
Comes the big day and he's going to become a citizen. He's
going down to appear before the court and they are going to
ask him these questions, and he's going to give the answers.
My father is going to sponsor Canio for his citizenship. You
know he was going to say to the judge, 'I know this man' and
so forth and so on. Canio comes over to get my father.

Now the ritual at home was that my father would come
home for lunch everyday. Grandma would make him lunch
and fill Grandpa up with these *L'ambionze* (their word meaning a huge glass of wine), that's what they were *L'ambionze*
(literally it means a greedy fill) of wine.

But now Mammanonna's eyes were failing at the time; she
was very, very old. And this particular day, she got a hold of a

bottle of Mt. Vernon whiskey. It was half-full. She goes down-stairs, she takes this bottle and finishes filling it with wine, and puts it on the table.

Now can you imagine what a dynamite concoction this was? So Canio comes in. My father was having his dinner. Canio knew that. He was all excited. Of course, right away, the first thing Canio has got to have a glass of wine. Grandma fills up this glass of dynamite. And Canio picks it up and down it goes. The glass is empty, there's no such thing as an empty glass in the Clapps' household. Grandma fills it up again. Now up to this minute my father hadn't finished his *minastre* (soup) so he hadn't tasted it yet. And Canio has put the second one down the hatch. Now my father finishes his dish of *minastre*, he picks up his glass and tastes it and he catches on right away that this is not straight wine. 'What the hell did you do here?' And then they realized what had happened. But it's too late now, Canio is paralyzed. They try to rehearse the questions: "What's George Washington's birthday?" Canio's cheeks are puffing out, his face is red as a beet and nothing, but I mean nothing is coming out. If the joint was on fire, he couldn't holler help, that's how speechless . . . honestly, that's how para-lyzed he was.

"*Ca' fa mo?*" [Actually, what the———are we going to do now? but which my father nicely translates as, what are we going to do?] We're going to go down there anyway.

Well, as circumstances would have it, Canio wasn't the only person that was frightened. The whole Italian community was frightened, and there was a whole big gang down there, so much so that they swore them in, en masse. So he escaped. No individual was asked any questions. That's the happy ending to that one.

The Aviglianese Society

My father talking about the Aviglianese Society:

At the time, I'm like nineteen or twenty years old. To me this is a greenhorn society. I want no part of this. I was a wise guy. I see myself as a young American. But not to say no, I said yes. Well, at the time World War Two is starting and Italy had invaded Ethiopia, this was Italian Empire dreams again. But this is ridiculous. This little country in Africa whose whole army probably consisted of two men and two goats and uh . . . It was embarrassing, but in these Italians' minds, the Italian army is going to go marching forth and invade Ethiopia. The whole Italian community's patriot fervor burst out. All the Italian women were sending their wedding rings to Italy to raise money for Mussolini. Well, at this time, I went down to be sworn in to the Aviglianese Society. They were having a heated debate. There was a member of the society who had gotten sick and he needed help with his doctor bills. There was a serious hour-long debate over whether they should pay his doctor bills.

When that debate was over, someone makes a new motion. "Let's send Mussolini five hundred dollars." Bing, bang, the motion is first, seconded, and passed. All the women donated their wedding rings for the gold value. It was comical, but it was tragic, but comical. That was the only meeting I ever attended.

Mammanonna

Peter Clapps talking about his grandmother who raised him after his mother was hospitalized:

Mammanonna was the envy of the Oak Street women because my father had a salary every week. She used to get the then-fabulous unheard of sum of twenty dollars a week to run the house. And I remember one of the fights they had (they used to fight real bad, my father was a son of a bitch), and I remember him throwing it up to her, "Who gets twenty dollars a week?" She was no patsy to him, though. She was no *"povere figlio mio"* (she wasn't the typical Italian mother who is always saying *"povere figlio mio,"* my poor son). She would fight back. My God, what ferocious fights they used to have. But I mean Mammanonna and my father, neither one of them were housekeepers, by any means. Mammanonna was a worker, a good solid person. She was a good cook and she was an excellent hostess. The whole crowd from New York used to love to come down and taste her fabulous cacciatore. She was terrific like all the old Italians; all the Italian girls were terrific in making homemade sausage and they didn't leave anything out. They weren't dusters or furniture polishers, you know.

Rocco Lauro and the Sausage

My father talking about Rocco Lauro, his father's friend:

This Rocco Lauro, ah, was a compulsive thief. I could tell you a thousand conniving stories about this man. But anyway, he was good friends with my father. So this one day, he comes walking in our house and our house was *scialababola*, open, no locks, open windows, open doors. And there hanging in the kitchen was a string of sausage and peppers drying out. Well this man being the compulsive thief that he was, he couldn't help it. He had to have one of those strings of sausages. And he takes one and puts it around his neck under his shirt collar, just like a tie, and puts his coat on top and he's all set and he's walking out. Who comes walking in but my father and his whole gang. There is no escape. He has to come back in. He's got to sit down; he's got to play cards. He used to love to play cards and they were saying take off your coat. "No, *I tengo poco raffreddore* [I have a little cold]." And he couldn't take off his coat. And one more game, one more game. "I have to go."

"But you can't go, you've got to stay." To make a long story short, he wound up staying the entire night. The sausage melted, it ruined his shirt, the collar, the jacket. What a mess it made out of everything.

He went home. He told his daughter Fannie what had happened. He was happy, proud. Now he said to Fannie, "You get on the phone and call Joe Clapps and ask him to supper tomorrow night." So my father goes down there the next night to have supper and they have sausage for supper. Fannie keeps laughing and laughing and asking my father, "Joe, how do you like the sausage? Is it good? Do you want some more?" Finally, she tells him the story and they have a good laugh together.

Local Politics

My father talking about local politics:

Hayes was Mayor of Waterbury from 1930 to 1939. He was simultaneously lieutenant governor as of 1938. He was probably going to be the next governor of Connecticut. He was the son of an Irish immigrant who had made a great deal of money by owning and running liquor stores. Hayes was well educated, very much respected and revered in Waterbury. He was very good looking; his prematurely grey hair gave him an air of distinction. He was a dramatic figure and campaigned on a white horse. He owned many businesses including the vaudeville theater in Waterbury—*Jake's*. He was indicted by a grand jury in 1939. Although it was never proven that he directly gained from the corruption that was taking place both in Waterbury and throughout the state at that time since he was both mayor and lieutenant governor, he went to jail.

It is a popular myth in Waterbury that it was his friend Dan Leary, the city comptroller, who was corrupt and did make a great deal of money corruptly on city and state government levels. Hayes was given a Cadillac by a large group of admirers from Waterbury when he returned from serving his jail sentence. Hayes was the mayor. He was the son of a respectable Irish woman who had money. He was a flamboyant kind of a boy. He was a very handsome bachelor all of his life. He had all kinds of girlfriends hanging on his arms. A real movie guy. His partner, Dan Leary, was a very clever Irishman, but these politicians had these leanings that they had to stick their hands in the till. Now Hayes didn't need the money and still today it remains a question about whether he took any. They emptied the city treasury. They really did a job, but it was fun to see them flashing around town. In the city parades., they'd be riding these beautiful white horses and they would wear these wide Texas, huge ten-gallon hats and white suits with beautiful boots with spurs. They were such heroes.

They were politically powerful. Now times had changed and so from total prohibition, a weak beer was allowed—three-point-two alcoholic content. It was weak beer, but everyone closed their eyes. Leary owned the Red Fox Brewery; it was lousy beer, but every tavern owner had to take this Red Fox beer. They were riding high, wide and handsome. I remember as a little boy one time at the Sacred Heart Church Bazaar, this Hayes and Leary came waltzing in. It was very important for them to make these tours to show their faces. They had to leave a dollar at each stand. The Irish people had to see them do those things. They came to this stand where there's a gambling wheel. Now this is a church, but they need money so they have this wheel. You pick a number and you had to lose; the general public had to lose. This Leary puts a dollar down on this number and it comes out. Now he has seven dollars. He bets the seven dollars, he wants desperately to lose. Don't you think the number comes out again. Now he's got forty-nine dollars. Oh my God, this is what the stand took in for the night! He looks at Hayes, and Hayes looks at him. Now he didn't dare put the whole forty-nine dollars down because he knew the table didn't have that much money. So he puts the money down on the table and leaves it there. The whole crowd is watching; they ooh'ed and aah'ed.

One night my gang went to a political rally. We were kids, we had no use for politicians. We were too young to vote anyway, but we would go for the free cider and donuts. This particular night he was drunk. They used to drink pretty good. The entire entourage is sitting up on some kind of a makeshift stage and Hayes is making a speech. But this is his gang, he doesn't have to sell himself to them. They love him. They are feasting their eyes on him. He comes up with that old chestnut, "You can fool half of the people half of the time, and some of the people some of the time," and it goes, "you can't fool all of the people all of the time." He gets two-thirds of the way through it and he's laughing so hard he can't finish it. That's how hard he's laughing. The rest of the entourage on stage is twittering nervously, but they don't know how far he's going to go. There is Pat Cantillion looking up at Hayes with actual adulation in his eyes. Now here is this poor working stiff, and I'm only a kid and I'm thinking to myself this guy's zinging the people and they don't even know it.

There was some suspicion about him, because they were flashing around town. There was all kinds of talk about deals, kickbacks, etcetera. Sure as heck, in the next election, it came out so close that he won by only two or three votes and Leary, who was the comptroller, lost by two or three votes. That meant that the new comptroller was a Republican. He started examining records and some were missing and it came to a grand jury investigation. It was just like someone being caught with their hand in the cookie jar. Hayes actually went to jail. Here's the son of a wealthy man and mayor of the town for nine years and he went to jail. They got ten to fifteen years.

Leary skipped town and went to Chicago rather than serve a jail sentence. Son of a gun, didn't he start another business selling religious articles. I don't know how many years later, something like ten, twelve, fifteen years later, somebody spotted him in Chicago and reported him. They picked him up and he had to come back and served his jail sentence. Leary said, for publication mind you, "Well if you're in politics and you can't help your friends, then what the hell are you doing in politics?" That was his answer. But the heartbreaking part was Hayes' mother. She was a respectable woman. He didn't need the money, he didn't have to do that to her.

The Boys

My father talking about hanging around on the street with his friends.

Oh what memories! You hung out with the boys every minute you could in front of the store. That was the social center of Oak Street, of the hill. It was a big, big gang. We had a lot of good times. A million games of kick the can. There was this man, Garbatini, he, he wasn't all there like. And he had the audacity to think he was a singer. So right away our swift evil Oak Street minds start working, see. "Garbatini, you go outside and sing for us; let your voice blend with the night air." All the while we are steering him like, go over by the stairs. Meanwhile I've got two baskets of tomatoes up on the porch. The tomatoes are there to be dried out. Georgie Graham, Harold Graham and I are up on the porch. He starts singing, "Tell me that you love me . . ." Swoosh, swoosh. Ah, those were the days.

One night we were hungry. I mean we were always hungry. We had young boys' appetites. None of us had two dimes to rub together. So in the store we go; who bumps into the lights, the lights go out, the store is dark. I reach into the ice cream cooler and dig into the vanilla with my hands, see, and dig up this huge mass of dripping vanilla ice cream and out the door we go and over the hill to share the spoils. We are passing this messiest of messes from one pair of filthy hands to the next. We couldn't care less. When it's finished, back to the store we go. I quietly pick up the cover to the ice cream cooler and there in the ice cream tub are five black streaks across the vanilla.

The Shop

My father talking about working at the Waterbury Iron Works:

Now we talk about the shop. It was so slow that my father and Andy and Chippy would alternate three days a week. The industrial world was just coming out of the dark ages, so to speak. A lot of people had been hurt by machinery in the factories. The insurance companies clamped down on the factories to have guards around the machinery. They must have made literally thousands of guards for different companies. They had become mandatory. My brother used to go down to the rubber company on a Friday night and he wouldn't come back until Monday morning. He would have to work during shut-down times, Friday nights, Saturday, and Sunday. And that's what kept the iron works going during the Depression.

I started working in 1935. At the time, unions were pretty weak, but they were emerging. We'd get out on these jobs and pretty soon these desperate men that needed jobs would come on the jobs. They were actually ready to do physical combat over the work. There were union men and union guards. There were several incidents so the shop knew they had to do something about the union business. So they called in the union and explained that the shop didn't have enough work to keep two outside men going all the time. So they come up with this illegal setup, where we could work in the shop and outside, too. It was illegal but, at that time they banded their views in desperation to get dues paying members. This meant that my wages went from forty cents an hour to ninety cents an hour. Sometimes with the rubber shop, I would work seven days a week. I'd make seven-twenty a day. That makes forty-nine dollars a week. That was a fortune. That's when I met your mother. She looked at me and said where did this guy come from? But this was also the time when my brother got sick. Well, I was not ready to but I was forced into running jobs. There I was, a kid running jobs. All the men from the union would look at me suspicious-like and say, "Where the hell did this kid come from?" They'd start needling me and take advantage of me. There I was a kid telling grown men what to do. There was no kid supposed to run a job. A punk, is what they called me. It was conflict, conflict all the time. Bad times, at that time, but on the other hand, they were so desperate to get a day's work that they overlooked the rule.

Walter

Working in the shop at this time was a man named Walter. He was quite a character. He was a necessary nuisance. We had to have him around because none of the old-timers, like Chippy and Andy, could drive. He would make the deliveries. The shop was so quiet because of the lack of work. Not like today at all, with the machines whirling and the hammering and banging. My father would make endless trips back and forth between the shop and the office all day long. When he entered the shop, the latch on the door gave a loud click. Walter would be hovering next to the stove. The shop was cold. It only had two stoves. We'd save wood for the stove and chisel coke from the foundry. When Walter heard the latch click, he knew the door was opening, my father was coming into the shop now, so he would pick up a file and head vigorously somewhere as if he was putting this file where it belonged. When my father would leave the shop to go back to the office, back he would go to the stove. He'd hear the click again and he'd pick up the same exact file and head off again.

On Friday night we got paid. We would go over to a local tavern, all of us, the whole shop. There were seven of us. The highest pay was eighteen dollars, the rest of us got sixteen dollars for forty hours. Take out sixteen cents for Social Security and you had fifteen eighty-four. The idea was we used to go over there to play cards. We'd play pinochle. We'd buy a round of beer, seven beers. The losers would buy the beer. The beer was ten cents a glass. After three rounds, the man would bring us a huge platter of sandwiches. They were wild. They were made from dark rye bread with ham and cheese and tomatoes. We would demolish them. We had worked all afternoon, and we were young and lusty in those days, and I mean we would demolish them. But the arithmetic didn't add up. We had only spent two dollars and ten cents and out would come that platter of sandwiches like clockwork. But you know that's the sad part of my life. We used to enjoy each other so much and we were fresh. How stale life has become.

On these Friday nights, he would drink all his pay. He'd go in a joint and buy the whole bar a drink. This was a dream world to him. He would like to have been a big spender, but he didn't have the money. But in his drunken state, he'd do these things and in the morning he'd have the fearful prospect of facing his mother and no board money. He lived with her and she was very strict with him. She knew she couldn't trust him and she'd insist that he pay his board. Now he'd wake up and he'd have to get the money somehow. So he would turn to chicken stealing, and sell them for half a buck apiece.

One day he was trying to give me lessons on how to steal chickens "properly," if you will. You have to sneak up on them and you can't make any noise because they start squawking. Then it's all over with, you might as well take off. But if you grab them, and you twist the heads quick, and shut the sons of bitches up, then you're okay. That's how he'd make his board money.

The Unsayable

My father had all the confidence that intelligence, great good looks, a strong body, a passionate Italian nature and a remarkable sense of humor can and does bring. If, before he grew into the hot-tempered, passionate young man he became, he hadn't had a childhood marked by a series of tragedies, this confidence might have slipped over into arrogance. But his early years were embedded in events so excruciating only the dimensions of melodrama can frame them. Those events were the simple facts of his life. His outsized gifts were tempered by outsized miseries. And rage. A rage against the fates, a rage against his raging father, and all the rest. He tried to balance his good fortune of finding a woman he loved deeply, having two children against all of this roiling pain all of his adult life. Sometimes he lost that battle and the fights in our home were epic. Quite often, he was the uncle who rounded up all his nieces and nephews to go swimming and get ice cream.

My father told stories as often as he sang, but about his mother and his brother Frank, whom he lost so early in life, he rarely spoke at all. About Michael, never. Whenever he did talk about Frank or his mother, he said the same few minimal things. Uncomfortably and without pleasure. As if these stories had to be occasionally, ritually expelled to give him a brief respite. Here are a couple of the fragments that would come out about his mother: "I was about three. I remember she put me in a dirty bath. The water was cold. It had the hair from my father shaving in the bath the night before. I knew she wasn't right, even then. One time, I was so little, around that same time, when they were going to take her away, I was standing down at that big apartment building on Oak Street—that's where her parents lived—and I didn't want to go home. I was afraid to go home. I was standing there on the corner with my mother's mother. I can still see her looking down at me, sad-like, saying, '*Poverell*, what are they going to do with him?' She had a weak mind," he added matter of factly about his mother. "What are you going to do?" He shrugged.

Once he had shrugged, he turned away to make it clear that he didn't want to talk about this anymore. If anyone asked him another question, he'd shift in his chair. Often that anyone was me—I was filled with curiosity about these strange stories, this crazy mother who would make her son take a dirty bath, a cold bath, behaving in a way that was the very opposite of mothering. "Dad, what did you think when she was doing this?" "Nothing, I knew even then that she wasn't right." Then he'd say, "Okay, that's enough of that topic. Let's get onto a cheerier subject." And then the subject was closed until, and only if, he brought it up again. His face at those moments was quiet, his eyes slightly closed, gazing off into his weird beginnings.

"Your father doesn't like to talk about it," my mother would explain to my sister and me when my father wasn't around. "He really didn't know her. He never really had a mother. She went to Middletown when he was only six, just a baby. And she was a raving beauty, they say." My mother was in charge of this material from my father's life. She would package it for us, hand it over contained, as if to tell us what this information meant in our lives. Sometimes she told him too.

It was all *manca, magra, meno.* I don't know when I first knew that there was a grandmother whom I did not know.

Maybe people are visiting from New York. My mother is serving coffee an' in the kitchen, "We went to see Peter's mother last week. She doesn't recognize us when we go. She doesn't know us. It's so sad. But we go." This is her way, I will discover, of her opening and closing this package quickly, neatly. "My husband had a hard time of it. All those troubles."

Eventually: "They say she was so beautiful. They say that men used to turn to watch her walk down the street. They followed her home and asked her to marry them without even knowing her name. She was that beautiful. Just an angel.

"And in those days you had to know the family. She was walking with her sister, her sister told me this story," cups are poised or surreptiously sipped.

"Well, I think this fella was a German or an Irish fella. But he followed her home. And he followed her up the stairs. The girls didn't turn around or look at him or anything. They didn't say a word to him. They went inside. You just didn't talk to strange men back then.

"Then he knocks at the door. Her brother, Uncle Pete, opens the door. 'Who are you? 'What do you want?'

"'That woman who just walked in. She's not your wife is she?'

"'I said, 'Who are you and what do you want?' Uncle Pete was a small man, but he was her older brother.

"'I saw her on the street and I want to marry her,' the guy said. Uncle Pete just slammed the door in his face. First of all you had to be Italian and second of all you had to be Aviglianese. I don't know if this fella was German or Irish. But can you imagine how he felt?"

Poor fella. "What a waste. She was that beautiful." The guests murmur their assenting sense of waste.

Once a year my mother would decide it was time to go to Middletown to visit the raving beauty. Although Middletown is the name of a quiet little New England town in Connecticut, when I was growing up if someone said, "They're down at Middletown," about a member of their family, it was a sentence filled with discomfort and shame. One of your own was down "there," at the place whose euphemistic name conjured up abhorrence. Our discomfort was so great that we couldn't bring ourselves to use the name of the institution for the place where our damaged and broken went. Instead we used the name of the town, Middletown.

When my mother announced that it was time for the visit, she would insist, "It isn't right just to leave her there like that." A Saturday would come when a mysterious deadliness would descend over our kitchen. I can see my parents coming out of their bedroom all dressed up as if they were going out, but each wearing a strained expression that concealed something important. My mother wearing a hat with a veil, gloves, matching shoes and pocketbook. My father wearing a suit. My mother carried a gift, wrapped with a ribbon. She looked solemn, dutiful. My father looked miserable. "You have to spend the day at Aunt Vicki's today. We'll be home late," my mother said with great seriousness.

"Where are you going?" we'd ask. "Why can't we come?" That was how we became aware that she was in Middletown. You belong in Middletown the kids said to each other when they wanted to say that you were nuts.

"The nurses always steal her stuff. Whatever we bring her is never there the next time," my mother would say of these visits, huffing with fury at her good work undone, the unfairness of her husband's mother being treated like this.

If my father went reluctantly, looking unusually strained, sad, unable to look us in the face, he returned drained of all his high handsome color, drained of hope. He had visited the undead. His unmother.

It must have been after days like that one that I would get down on my knees by my bed and clasp my hands together to pray. Please, dear God, let her be all right. Please, dear God, let her know who my father is. Please, dear God, let her have a clear mind. In my intensity, I was sure I could bring her back to us, that Lucia and I would go and visit her and she'd be so happy to meet her granddaughters. My father would be so happy. I was convinced this could and would happen.

My father's grandmother, his father's mother, raised my father and his brothers and sister. But my father apparently was her favorite. He was the baby and she saved him from the bleakness of his motherlessness. Mammanonna was a tall, large-boned woman who ruled her family like the peasant matriarch she was.

A family story tells of another young man who followed her home. Giuseppe, a young blacksmith and ironworker, noticed Beatrice, a young seamstress, on the streets of lower Manhattan; she was exquisitely dressed completely in white. He followed her onto the subway up to 118th Street, another Italian community. "He fell madly in love with her and was determined to marry her. When it turned out that they were both Aviglianese, her older brother, Pietro, insisted that she marry him. All that is left of their courtship is that my grandfather is reported to have written his mother back home in Avigliano, "I want you to give me your blessing to marry this girl. But if you don't, I'm going to marry her anyway." But why would his mother object?

My grandfather Giuseppe Clapps was the privileged oldest surviving Italian son. Although he hadn't been raised as the *primo figlio*, first-born son, but rather as the *secundo*, he was the first member of his family sent to America. His brilliant, talented older brother, Michele was set to follow him to America when he died suddenly at the age of nineteen. The reign of succession had changed. I have no idea how this may have impacted what became a reign of terror for his wife and children. Was it because it wasn't the role he had been raised to? Did it never sit deeply inside of him? Or did ascending late to this feudal position bring him power he didn't know what to do with? He and his mother, Philomena, were two fierce spirits. Once she came to America, he—as her oldest surviving son and, therefore, a figure of complete importance—reigned with her, prince and regent, then king and queen mother. His father apparently was a sweet, playful man, who loved jokes and tricks, music and wine. It was Francesco whom everyone loved, but it was Philomena, Giuseppe's mother, who was obeyed by the rest of the family.

"Oh they fought all the time. All, all the time. Terrible fights. They were wild," my father would say about his father and grandmother, "They were two strong people. And, as such, they both wanted their way. But that's the way it was. Nobody made much of it. That was just the way it was. Oh, but I remember they were terrible to each other. But, for me, my grandmother was my champion. She really loved me."

I'm not sure when *Mammanonna* came to live with her oldest son and his wife. Probably after my grandmother Beatrice's troubles began—after she began to have too many children too close together and suffered from severe postpartum depressions. Can it be that no one knew there was something wrong before she married? Did this only become apparent when she began to have children? Misunderstood postpartum depressions, alcoholic, violent husbands, too many births too fast: none of this can have been terribly unusual for women in that time. Not all of those women wound up in institutions.

My grandparents had moved from New York to Connecticut after my grandmother had her first babies. The few shreds of information I have about this grandmother take place in Waterbury.

The first house my grandmother (always called Bessie in America by those who loved her) lived in with my grandfather was a three-family wood frame house, standard housing in Waterbury in the early part of the century. Although each apartment was separate, there was great intimacy among the families who lived under the same roof. A neighbor who lived upstairs from my grandparents told my mother many years later that my grandmother was a lovely young mother. "A raving beauty and always well dressed. What a fine seamstress. She made all the children's clothes, too. She kept them dressed so beautifully. I remember Peter when he was a little boy, he had a sailor suit she made him. What fine work she did. But her mother-in-law, Mammanonna, was mean to her," the neighbor said.

"I used to find your husband's mother out on the stairs crying, 'My mother-in-law is driving me crazy. I don't know what I'm going to do. She gave me a terrible beating today. She's always hitting me.'"

This is what the woman who lived upstairs from my grandmother told my mother. Is it true? Is it *the* truth? Each one of the scraps is only suggestive of all that isn't there. It's the what's not there that tells so much. So far, we can say with some certainty that she was pretty and a seamstress. That her mother-in-law was a strong woman and probably beat her. Was this so unusual back then?

When did Mammanonna come to live with her? Why did she come to live with her? Was it to help her with her babies when she went into postpartum depression? Why didn't Beatrice's own mother or sister come to help her? They lived nearby, but I know almost nothing about those great-grandparents.

Certainly after she became institutionalized, my grandfather was a ladies man, his tall handsome looks drawing many women to him. But really I assume, as was common in that culture, he always had women. Did this contribute to her depression? Before my mother married my father, Grandpa Clapps asked to speak to my mother. "People will tell you we're a bad family. Not to marry my son. But it's not my fault. The women always came to me. I don't go after them." Later, when he had Alzheimer's Disease, he'd get very *agita* and say to my mother, "The police are going to come and get me."

"No, Pa, the police aren't coming. It's okay." Once or twice he climbed up on the roof of the garage to escape them. My mother, my father, my cousin Paulie would all have to talk him down.

"You don't know how bad I was. I was bad. They have to come and take me away," he'd whisper to my mother.

"I don't think you were that bad, Pa," my mother would try to reassure him.

"No, you don't know. All you should say is, 'I'm sorry you're that way.'"

Beatrice's younger sister, Margaret, whom I met only a few times, once said to me, "It was his fault—your grandfather's—what happened to my sister. She came to stay with us once after she had one of the children. And he came down to see her only one time the whole while she was with us. And when he was leaving, she started to cry. He didn't leave her any money. She felt so bad." This was her sister's explanation for the fact that my grandmother wound up institutionalized from when she was twenty-five until she died at the age of eighty-three.

If he was so terrible to her and didn't care for her, why didn't her family rescue her from him? Why didn't they give her money? If he beat her, if his mother beat her, why did she have to stay with him and his fierce mother? Why did she only come and stay with her sister once after she had a baby? To me, there's culpability on both sides. Or maybe none. Maybe, just as my father put it, "she had a weak mind."

I have only a couple more scraps to add to this upmap, this not a story, this untelling.

My sister and I went to see an old friend of my father's after he died. It had only been in the previous year that he had begun to take each of us separately to visit Angie: "Come on, there's an old friend of mine I want you to meet." Previously, I hadn't really been aware of her. She lived in a sweet dilapidated old house. When you entered, it had a kind of stale smell. On each of these two visits when I entered, once with my Dad, once with Lucia, the house was dark except for the television.

When we went to visit her recently, she was sitting in the front room right near the television, in the same chair she had been sitting in when I had visited her with my father. Both her chair and the television are just inside the front door. She can't move easily and so doesn't get up. She calls to you from her chair when she hears you at her front door, "Come on in." She had been hit by a car as a girl, although later in our visit she got up with the help of a walker and awkwardly went over to a sideboard to show us some photographs.

Angie's family and ours were from Avigliano, the same small village in Basilicata, so they were paesans as well as neighbors who lived across the hall from my father's family when he was a baby. That must have been the second house they lived in in Waterbury. Angie's family had witnessed on a daily level the disintegration of my father's mother.

Angie says at one point in our visit, "Bessie, that's what they called her, was always worse after she had a baby—what do they call that postpart—" she hesitated. Lucia finished the phrase for her.

"She used to throw dishes out of the window. She was always doing things wrong. My own mother was a saint. She would help the family out, make dinner for the kids. A lot of times, she was the one who made dinner for them. Or they would of had nothing to eat. And we didn't have much ourselves.

"Yeah, my mother was a saint and she took care of both families. Made all their clothes too, for all the children. Or they wouldn't have had any clothes to wear. My mother was a fine seamstress. She did really fine work."

"But where was Mammanonna?" we asked.

"Oh sometimes she had to go to church, she went every day, or to the store. So my mother would watch the kids. I had to help. I changed your father's diapers. He was just a baby.

"Mammanonna would see me and she'd grab me and give me a smack, 'Sweep the floor.' I was just a kid. But that's how it was in those days. You had to listen. My mother would send me over. I was a big girl so they acted like I was older. Mena, your father's sister, was my friend.

"Yeah we kids had to help out. And my mother she worked so hard. Your father was just a tiny baby.

"The men, my father too, they were all drunks—drinking every night. Then they'd get up and go to work the next day like it was nothing. But they drank every night. That's what they were. Now they call them alcoholics. We didn't call them that, but they were drunks. That's what they were. And mean, too. My father, your grandfather, all those men.

"Your grandmother would do strange things—like once she was going to put Mike in boiling water on the stove. I went and called my mother, 'Mama, come quick. Bessie's cooking Mikey.' She was never right, she wasn't right in the head." Here it is—the most unsayable thing of all. My grandmother, in some version of trying to bathe her son, almost succeeded in *cooking* him. "*Mama, come quick. Bessie's cooking Mikey.*" I'm sure my father had been told this story. I know he remembered that his mother bathed him in cold dirty water. Bathing, a mother cleaning her children—in the hands of his mother meant something really bad or worse. Your mother might cook you. It must have been water heating on the stove. It can't have been boiling or Mikey would have been badly burned and or died. But she put him in heated water on the stove.

I'm not sure how to fit Angie's scrap into this mapping. In this version, Mammanonna is barely a presence. So religious she goes to church instead of cooking dinner for her family. Angie's mother is the seamstress, not my grandmother, though still a very fine seamstress. But it's true, Aviglianese women are well known for their needlework. So none of this makes any sense to me as delivered by Angie, who is one of the few people still alive who knew my grandmother.

Mammanonna was a renowned cook, a great hostess, a fierce worker. I know it wasn't that Mammanonna was too old or incapable of taking care of this family since this is precisely what she did until she died. When my own parents met and fell in love, she was still taking care of my grandfather's house, helping to arrange his assignations, cooking for his wine-drinking cronies. She taught my mother how to make an Aviglianese tomato sauce so that my father could have the sauce he grew up with and loved made by his new bride. The idea that she would go off to church and let a neighbor cook and sew for her family just doesn't add up.

Her piece of this story must sit off to one side now. Unless I create a scrap of my own, invent a piece of narrative to hold these shreds together. Can Mammanonna and Pappanonno have gone back to live in New York for some time between the first beatings—"She's driving me crazy"—and the time when Angie called to her mother, "Mama, come quick. Bessie's cooking Mikey"? During that time did Angie's kind and accomplished mother cook and sew for Bessie's vulnerable family until Mammanonna returned? Conflation of these events is the only explanation that I can come up with to make sense of these snippets of Angie's.

My Aunt Mena would take her daughter to see her mother. I didn't know that. I didn't know that our generation was ever allowed to meet her.

"You did?" I was shocked. To me, my grandmother was in an unen-
terable place, a home so strange, so forbidden it was off the map. It had
never occurred to me that an ordinary person could go there. "What
did she say?"

"Well, she's not all there, you know. It's kind of strange. But I
talked to her. She didn't understand much. But she could understand
some of what I said."

"What did you say to her?"

"Well, I told her that I am Mena's daughter, that Mena is my
mother."

"'Oh no,' she said to me. 'That can't be. She's just a little baby.'"

Did she remember her other children? Her mother-in-law? The
beatings? Did she remember that she looked like an angel? That my
grandfather was going to marry her, whatever his fierce mother
thought? Was her life frozen when she still made beautiful tiny sailor
suits? Did she remember giving baths to her children?

There is one other scrap I can add. After a long life of wine,
women, and song, my grandfather Giuseppe came down with
Alzheimer's. Eventually, after years of home care, my mother changing
diapers, cleaning up after him, he wound up at the same hospital as my
grandmother. My parents went down to visit and brought him some
Hershey Bars. "Do you want to go and see your wife?" my mother asked
him.

"I'm going to bring this to Bessie," he said, taking one of the candy
bars my parents had brought to him.

"'Did you bring that for me?'" Bessie asked my grandfather, my
mother tells us, "When he went up to her on the porch where she was
sitting. She was looking at him so sweetly and smiling.

"He peeled back the wrapper and broke off a piece to give her.
Then he held it up to her lips. He fed it to her piece by piece.

"When she was looking up at him, she seemed to remember something. Like she still knew who he was," my mother always said when
she told this story.

"'Will you come and see me again?' she asked him as she ate the
Hershey Bar. He nodded, feeding her the last piece."

It was at this point in the story that my father, who would have
been looking off out the window over the kitchen sink acting as if he
was thinking about other things and not really paying attention to what
my mother was saying, would turn his head back, rejoining us at our
kitchen table, coming back from the land of the other.

At this point, he'd take over the story to tell the same final detail
about his mother and father. "You know," he'd said, "the porch we were

on had an iron railing." He always had the same half a smile on his face, would shake in wonder and admiration as he said, "When the candy bar was finished, he went over to the iron railing and gave it a professional shake as if to see if it had been properly installed. Then we left."

Peter and his brothers

Beatrice Coviello (Bessie) and Giuseppe Clapps:
my father's parents on their wedding day

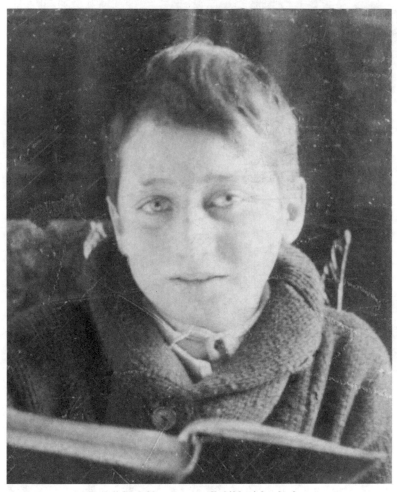

Michael Claps as a small child with a book

From left: cousin Johnny Maneri, Lucia Mudd, Grandpa Claps, me,
Mammanonna and a Stolfi cousin

The men as Waterbury Iron Works at the shop during the Calder Era

Comune di *Avigliano*

ESTRATTO DEGLI ATTI DELLO STATO CIVILE

Atto di Nascita dal 1875 in poi *1887*

Num. *213* d'ordine *Claps Giuseppe*

L'anno mille *ottocentottantasette*, addì *Ventuno* di *Marzo* a ore *anti*meridiano *nove* e minuti *quarantacinque* nella Casa Comunale.

Avanti di me *Angelo Cavaliere Dottore Telesca Sindaco*

Ufficiale dello Stato Civile del Comune di *Avigliano*, è comparso *Francescantonio Claps*, di anni *trentadue*, *ferraio* domiciliato in *Avigliano*, *il* quale mi ha dichiarato che alle ore *anti*meridiane *nove* e minuti —— del dì *Venti* del *suddetto* mese, nella casa posta in *Via Annità* al numero *trentadue*, da *Domenica Maria Filomena Salvatore sua moglie filatrice seco lui convivente*

è nato un bambino di sesso *maschile* che *egli* mi presenta e a cui dà il nome di *Giuseppe*

A quanto sopra e a quest'atto sono stati presenti quali testimoni *Giuseppe Romano*, di anni *trentotto*, *contadino* e *Vito Larossa*, di anni *trentotto, Conta-dino*, entrambi residenti in questo Comune. *Letto il presente atto agl'intervenuti si è solo da me sot*

TIP. CAV. L. CRESBATI-UGGI

Giuseppe Claps's birth certificate

Il presente passaporto consta di venti pagine

N. del Passaporto

1613

N. del Registro corrispondente

1

IN NOME DI SUA MAESTÀ

VITTORIO EMANUELE III

PER GRAZIA DI DIO E PER VOLONTÀ DELLA NAZIONE

RE D'ITALIA

Passaporto

rilasciato a *Claps Giuseppe*

figlio di *Francesco*

e di *Salvatore Filomena*

nato a *Avigliano*

il *20 Marzo 1887*

residente a *Avigliano*

in provincia di *Potenza*

di condizione *fabbro*

accompagnato da fratello
Raffaele di Pietrantonio

Guiseppe Claps' passaporto (cover)

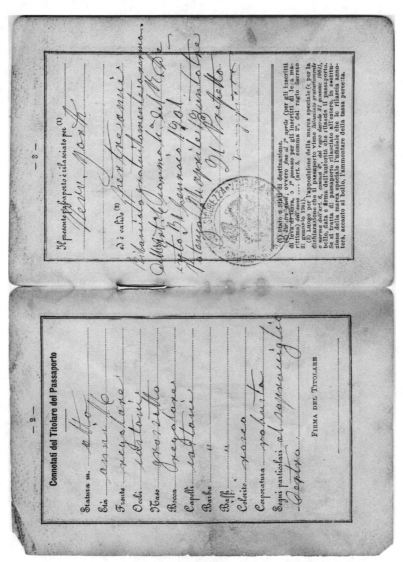

Passoport (inside pages)

Beatrice Coviello and Giuseppe Claps' marriage certificate (page one)

Stato di New York – Città e Contea di New York – Io James Smith assessore della Città di New York – Col presente certifico che, addì 26 del mese di luglio a. 1909, al municipio della Città di New York ho legalmente celebrato il matrimonio fra il Sig. Giuseppe Claps del N.º 208 Ovest, 27ª Strada, Manhattan New York e la Signorina Beatrice Coviello del N.º 315 Est 118ª Strada Manhattan New York, i quali ambedue sono in età legale a contrarre matrimonio e che da richiesta da me eseguita, non risultò veruno impedimento al detto matrimonio. Inoltre certifico che le seguenti persone, cioè: Clemente Gagliardi e Pietro Coviello furono presenti e diventarono, sottoscrivendosi, testimonii al suddetto matrimonio. —
Firmato: James J. Smith, Assessore della Città di New York. 9º James Weldon, Commissionario degli atti pubblici della Città di New York.

Traduzione conforme all'originale allegato

NUOVA YORK 27-8 '09

FIRME N.º 20063
DIRITTI LIRE 6
ART.
77

Church of Our Lady of Lourdes
Waterbury, Conn.

BIRTH CERTIFICATE

Name of Child _Pietro Claps_

Date of Child Birth _September 17, 1916_

Name of Father _Peppino (Joseph)_

Maiden name of Mother _Beatrice Coriello_

Baptized _May 14, 1917_

Attest _Felix Saoglio –_

Waterbury, Conn., _May 28_ 192_5_

Church of Our Lady of Lourdes
Waterbury, Conn.

BIRTH CERTIFICATE

Name of Child _Michele Claps._

Date of Child Birth _January 16, 1915._

Name of Father _Joseph_

Maiden name of Mother _Beatrice Coriello_

Baptized _April 18, 1915._

Attest _Felix Scoglio_

Waterbury, Conn., _May 28_ 192_5_

Michael Claps and Pietro Claps' (my father) two birth certificates.

COMUNE DI AVIGLIANO
PROVINCIA DI POTENZA

UFFICIO DI STATO CIVILE

CERTIFICATO DI NASCITA

L' UFFICIALE DELLO STATO CIVILE

Visto il registro degli atti di nascita dell' anno 1888

Parte I Serie = N. 450

CERTIFICA

Che COVIELLO Beatrice

E' NATO in questo Comune

il giorno Sedici del mese di Giugno

dell' anno Milleottocentoottantotto

Si rilascia per uso consentito.

Avigliano, lì 7-4-1966

L' UFFICIALE DELLO STATO CIVILE
(Giuseppe Viggiano)

Naturalization papers for Giuseppe Claps

III

BEFORE AND AFTER TINFOIL:
THE BECCE FAMILY

The Anarchist Bastard

Vito Becce, *un' anarchista,* my grandfather, a *primo figlio,* a first-born male child, imbued with and accorded a potentate's sense of privilege, had the exacting certainty that such a figure knows. Among the subjects under his rule, along with his wife and children, were the usual s*trisciliat',* mess of animals: rabbits, chickens, goats, sheep, cows, horses, asses kept on a farm. One scorching hot summer day when the smell of the manure floated across the rocky hills like a limp rotting flag, a particularly unruly *ciucio,* an ass, pulled against the relentless toil my grandfather insisted he'd have from the *ciucio.* The *ciucio* decided to be just like my grandfather and he became an *anarchista,* too. He dug his hooves in and refused to be ruled. The mule wouldn't move. "*Faccia tosta!*" my grandfather screamed at the beast and beat it but the creature brayed back just as loudly, pulling its head to one side, then the other. Grampa beat the *ciucio* harder. Two furious animals, nose to nose. *Tutt'e due, tutt' insiem', che faccia brute, faccia tosta, capo tosta.*

Which was more stubborn, on that sticky summer day, as Grampa tried to get the ass to haul a load of stones to the barn behind the house? Grampa, enraged that the creature would defy him, beat the ass even more than usual that day. Just as *capo tost',* the ass kicked until he landed one on Grampa. Grampa was so mad he grabbed the ass by his ears and bit him so hard he tore a hole in his ear.

Ciucio commanda ciucio: the adults found it hilarious when one of us kids tried to tell another what to do. One ass commands the other, they'd say. Their faces floated above us laughing as they made clear the absurdity of any insignificant trying out its authority on another insignificant. Aunt Rose, Grampa's teenage sister, a lively, nervy girl, only recently brought over from "the other side," happened to walk up through the garden as he pulled out the ass hairs caught in his teeth.

"Vitucci'!" she bent over laughing. He didn't think it was funny and screamed in a rage, "*Manag' a diavol'! Ammazati!* Damn the devil! I'll kill you!"

After that, the *ciucio* kicked the anarchist more savagely every time he went near him, so Grampa had to sell *ma sonna ma beech*. "Hey, my father had to have it done yesterday, not today," my mother says, "And here this *ciucio* not doing his work. Can you imagine?" Her voice pitched in disbelief when she told this story.

"So when the buyer came to look at the *ciucio*, my father said—oh he was a tricky devil, my father was—,'I'm going to tell you something. This *ciucio* is so calm and I'm going to prove to you just how calm he is. *La figliola viena ca'*, show the man how calm *le bestia* is.'" My mother always laughed at her father's outrageous trick when she told her version of this story eighty years later, "So when Mama went to the barn to bring the *ciucio* my father told her to make sure she led the ass directly away from him.

"Don't bring him anywhere near where I'm standing," my tricky grandfather told his wife.

"That way the man," my mother continued, "would see how calm the *ciucio* was, so calm that his young wife could easily manage this beast." The ass, as wily as grampa, left the farm with its new owner.

Once Grampa had sold the *ciucio*, it was turned into a family story. Eventually he even allowed his sister to tell her part, laughing with her when it was safely in the past and someone who wasn't him had clearly been bested.

Grampa's eyes always gleamed as he pounded the edge of the chipped white enamel table whenever he filled the kitchen with this story. We threw back our heads and roared our approval, heehaw laughing at our wild outrageous patriarch. Being *facciadosta, capodoste*, was who we were: We never gave in.

Vito Becce ruled his fiefdom with all the tyranny of the minor feudal lord he was—the *anarchista* despot. He believed that every form of regulation or government is immoral and that the restraint of one person (particularly himself) by another (anyone else on earth), is a form of evil that must be destroyed. *Anarchism* comes from the Greek, meaning without government. Like so many first-born males in Italy, what he most deeply believed was that he should be the only form of governance: he answered to no rule but his own. All his subjects, however, answered to him.

Vito was given to bouts of fury at the all and sundry "*sonna ma beech* bastards"; this included the priests, the government, even the traffic lights on the streets, anyone or anything that thwarted his wild propulsion forward into America. A pig farmer, he befriended the mayor of Waterbury, all the local politicians, brought them home to eat at his table, played poker with them down at City Hall, by virtue of his very gregarious nature and by way of making his way in America as a decent capitalist. I wonder how he explained this to himself. I have no idea. It was never discussed.

When she was four or five years old one of my cousins stayed at the farm during the day while her mother was working. She told me later, "Everybody was running around to get everything just right, everything ready for lunch. Then the trucks would come thundering up in front of the house and you'd just wait in terror. You never knew what might start him off. He'd come in looking to find fault: if something had been left in the dish rack, *that* might set him off. Or he'd come in jolly, singing and laughing, and have a story to tell and the whole atmosphere on the farm would change. It was so confusing. Do you remember that Grandma would never answer the phone? I was there one day when Grandma took an order from New York on the phone and she got it wrong. They fought so bad. Everything was in Italian. Everyone would be screaming by then. I didn't know what they were saying. She'd come back at him. He started hitting her. I used to run and hide under the dining room table."

My mother, his second child and favorite daughter, claimed: "Before my baby brother drowned in the lake he wasn't like that. I remember him singing all the time. But after Pasquale died, I remember the first time he came down from the pigs like that, mad, and I thought, this isn't like my father. I was only a little girl, but I knew he had changed. Oh, it was terrible. He wasn't the same after that. You can't imagine."

Other times, she'd say: "We got beatings for nothing, just for looking at Papa the wrong way. When he came home from collecting the garbage he would be furious sometimes, and if you just looked at him the wrong way you really got it. If Papa told us to go bring in the water from the well and it could be freezing outside—you had to throw a stone down into the well to break the ice so that the bucket could bring up the water—if we didn't move fast enough, that would be enough. We'd get his big hand right across the face and then he would really beat us. I mean really beat us. My sister Toni got it the worst. She always answered back. She could never keep her mouth shut. She'd mutter under her breath and Papa would come after her terrible. Papa would take anything he could find, a stick, a broom, whatever he could lay his hands on and he'd go after her good. Really beat her. We'd want to run and hide. We knew someone was going to get it good. Toni used to hide in the shed where the bread oven was then, behind the oven. She got it worse than anyone. Rocky, too, because he was the boy, but we all got it, believe me. Bad!

"We made sure that everything was on the table just the way he liked when he walked in for dinner at noon. If the salt and pepper shaker wasn't right by his dish on the table he'd throw a fit. *Il Martello* [The Hammer, the anarchist newspaper] had to be waiting for him next to his dish. He'd have a fit. If he didn't like the way something tasted—it didn't have enough salt—he'd take the whole dish and throw the food in the sink.

"Another time my mother bought secondhand dishes to save money and the dish didn't sit on the table right. It wobbled when he went to eat his macaroni—he picked up the dish and threw it on the floor—then he picked up every dish on the table one at a time and broke them all on the floor. That was my father.

"I loved my mother so much and she would get so upset. That day, Mama said she was going to leave him. 'Get my hat,' she said.

"I went to my father and I said, 'Papa, Mama's going to leave. Talk to her, don't let her leave.'

"'Ah, let her go,' he said. That wasn't right at all. She worked so hard for him. Mama loved him so much. He was mean.

"Oh you can't imagine the beatings we'd get. My mother, too. He'd use his hands on her. Bad. She'd fight back, too; they fought like cats and dogs."

Just as angry, we'd hear my grandmother answer him back, "May the rats eat your blood."

"One thing we didn't agree with my father about was him being a communist or an anarchist, whatever he was. He was always holding meetings at our house. This big guy, one of the big shots would come from New York all the time for these meetings. And we had to serve them. They'd all sit around the table and talk for hours. Our house was the meeting place for all of Connecticut. We didn't know what they were talking about. One very big guy, I think his name was Trotta [does she mean Tresca?] used to come all the time. My father hated when the government did something wrong. 'See where they put 'em?' he'd say about an article in the newspaper that buried some important piece of information about the government. 'Goddamn crukadah [crooked] bastards.'

"We didn't think it was right. The way they were running people down. They were talking *against the government*. Communists weren't supposed to be nice people. They were talking against America. We didn't know what to think. Not that we'd dare say a word against him. We'd get our rear ends handed to us if we did.

"Don't get me wrong. Your grandfather loved America. He hated the old ways of Italy, the way the priests cheated the people. The way they didn't do anything for the people."

My Aunt Toni told me this story very recently. "My grandmother, you know Grampa's mother, had been staying with us. She came a lot from New York. I was going to go back with her for a vacation. I was so excited. She was a very religious person. He said to his mother, before she took me, 'Don't you dare take her to church and have her baptized. Do you hear me? Don't you dare!' And then he took me out on the sun porch and pointed down below, 'You see that saw out there?'—it was the table where they cut the logs—'If you let my mother take you to church to be baptized, if you walk into a church even once, I'm going put you there and cut your legs off so you'll never walk anywhere again.' I'll never forget that. It was so cruel of him to say that to me. He had reason to hate the church but . . ."

My mother explained to me, "Papa's family owned land in Tolve: they planted wheat, harvested the wheat and brought it to town and milled it. They had olive groves and made their own oil. But then they had a bad crop of wheat one year and then another year and they got into debt. Then the church called in their debt. There was some nice property in Italy. They couldn't survive so my father came to America with his father and his brother Dan. They didn't want to lose their land. They'd work and mail the money home so the church couldn't take what was left.

"They went to work in Pennsylvania in the coal mines. He was sixteen years old when they came with his father. But then he said, 'Hey, I didn't come to America to be buried under the earth.' After the mines they all set pins in bowling alleys in New York. 'I'm going to let these *fessa* throw balls at me.'

"Mama was back in Tolve waiting for him. He didn't like it here in America. He'd come back as soon as he could pay off the debt. He promised her he'd come back. And finally he did and they got married and had my sister Ag. But the debt was still there so he went back to America. Mama waited and waited for him. She had the baby and she even built a house for them.

"Then he visited some friends in Waterbury and it reminded him of Italy with all its hills and winding streets. He got a job in a factory here in town. When he saw men losing fingers and hands he quit that job, too. Now he didn't want to go back to Italy anymore. But now he liked it here in America. My mother was still waiting for him to come back the way he had promised. But he wrote and said he wasn't going to come back anymore. Finally she had to give in and come to America. She didn't want to. But he wouldn't come back. That's the way he was. He did what he wanted and if you didn't like it, too bad for you.

"While my father was running the government down, he was buying up land around the farm. He built the first slaughterhouse in Connecticut. He made good money on that. When he saw that the Jewish people were butchering their animals in the woods, he went to the department of health in Hartford and petitioned the government to be allowed to build a slaughterhouse. He got money for every animal killed. We had to wash that slaughterhouse down. Whenever he found us playing, we had to go wash the slaughterhouse windows or the floor, or the blood off the walls. Once we had just washed them that morning and he found us playing with a doll. We'd found a doll's head in the garbage and we put a stick in the head and we made clothes for the doll; he was furious. 'Bunch of fools, playing with a doll. I told you to wash the windows of the slaughterhouse. What are you? Stupid? Idiots? *Stunada a vese?* Go get some work done.' 'But Papa, we already washed the windows.' '*Fa'napol'*. Go wash them, I said, or I'll kill you.' And we had to go back and wash them again."

As head of his own state, Grampa made sure to have diplomatic relations with anyone in power. So he was friends with all the town aldermen. He stopped by the mayor's office to talk to him whenever he went down to City Hall. "Everybody knew my father," my mother said. "He was always talking to somebody. He knew how to get around, my father did. He could be so charming when he wanted to be."

"He was always downtown bullshitting," my Uncle Rocco says. "And he'd leave me with all the work."

"That's true," my mother agrees in sympathy. "Then he bought that gas station downtown, too. That was a good investment. He made a lot of money. Later on when he went to Arizona in the cold weather for Mama's arthritis and he and my brother Rocky were fighting all the time, he made friends with Barry Goldwater so that he could bring over his relatives. *Anarchista, mio nonno.*

"Even when we were grown women we feared Papa," my mother told me.

"Aunt Vicki got a beating twice when she was about seventeen, once because she talked to a friend of our family's who she had run into on the road up to the farm. What was she supposed to do, pretend she didn't see him?

"Another time my father came down from the pigs and Vito Capi was there. And Grampa came home and saw that Vicki had been in the kitchen with Vito Capi alone and he started to yell at her, 'You didn't feed the chickens. I know you didn't feed the chickens because one of the chickens followed me down the path!' He beat her all over the cellar.

"By this time my sister Toni was married. She came up to help Mama can the tomatoes and he beat her silly. My father gave her such a black eye. Who knows why? He was always looking for an excuse. Toni was so glad her husband Al didn't go and do anything silly. Like get in a fight with her father. 'Oh, I was so relieved,' Aunt Toni says. 'You couldn't win with my father. Thank God! Who knows what he would have done to my husband?'

"Once he offered some of his subjects, all of his son-in-laws, a reward for following his dictum: He'd give fifty dollars to the first one who gave one of his daughters a black eye. Peter walked out in disgust but a few nights later, he and my father had such a fight about politics. Peter thought the government wasn't as bad as my father was saying. I told Peter, 'You can't get that involved with my father. He's really not right on this subject. Just ignore him.'" With us, his grandchildren, his anarchism was simply never brought up. Never! Our parents, his children, were deeply embarrassed by this affiliation with its subversive un-Americanness.

It wasn't as if my grandfather was some standout bastard. He was just a bastard of his time. It wasn't even slightly contradictory that he could be full of a generous spirit of joy. He and my grandmother both loved the house full of people visiting, the table laden abundantly with the *prosciutto, scarmoz'*, and bread my grandmother had made. He loved everyone gathered around *his* table. A large pan on the stove filled with corn from the garden, trays of '*a pizz*' waiting on the wood stove for anyone to take a slice. There would be cakes and cookies; these Sunday gatherings went on every week, a long ongoing party. He loved a good joke and story. He'd tell the old ones from the old country. He'd make up new ones. Once he bought my grandmother a goat for Mother's Day. "What else could I buy her?" he asked with the pleasure of the absurd. That was typical, too. He loved babies. As each baby became capable of holding it's legs straight, he'd pick up the baby and hold it just by its feet and the baby's legs would stiffen and hold its body erect and my grandfather would laugh and laugh: His grandchild—look, see what it could do. He'd send huge boxes home from Arizona, filled with presents for everyone. Silver jewelry for the women. Mexican jackets for the girls. None of this was even slightly contradictory in our world. That's what the patriarchal men were like back then. That's what a man was: larger than life, a provider, a commander; their masculinity was based on this primitive sense that if they weren't able to rule their families with fury and violence, they were less than men. What would be more horrible than that? All of it went together.

He had become *un' anarchista* in the old country. Certainly those immigrants were too deeply familiar with the misery they had left behind, the powerlessness, the poverty and the debts to the church and the feudal lords. When I was in college, my grandmother was showing me some of the weaving she had done in Tolve and I found a postcard from him in her bureau that had sepia-colored *Anarchista* written in script across the front. There was a message in Italian to a friend on the back and it was signed by him. She let me take it. And I began to ask my mother questions about this part of Grampa's life. "Oh that wasn't really true," my mother said. "Well, he was, well, kind of like a communist, but he dropped all that later on."

His affiliation probably deepened here in America when he was living with other young immigrant men, filled with the power of having left the old world, the old ways, filled with the power of their strong young bodies. But in our family, deeply obsessed with its own mythologizing history, how my grandfather's anarchist beginnings came about was drained of all juice and information by the shame that his anarchist leanings induced in his children. They wanted only not to be 'Merican, that dreaded uncivilized state, even while they embraced completely the idea of being so very American. They'd talk about the beatings they got, but never about his politics.

My grandparents were made of the same stuff: two fierce bright wills, pitted against each other. There were horrible fights, beatings, after my grandmother got in the last terrible word. She was smarter than my grandfather, but her love for him was her undoing. He did love her, but he loved himself more. So when her words cut into him, he retaliated against her love with an assortment of *vendetti*.

My grandmother took to her bed for two years when the dampening of his love for her had chilled her bones. After all the cold mornings spent scrubbing the slaughterhouse, collecting eggs, milking cows in the dark, his love for another woman gave her a crippling arthritis. She never walked right again after that.

"My father used to go downtown to get his paycheck at City Hall for picking up garbage. He'd get all cleaned up and dress nice. And he'd go talking to everybody at City Hall. And he'd leave Rocky with all the work on the farm and heaven forbid he didn't get it all done. My brother hated when he did that. 'He's down there bullshitting again,' my brother would say.

"He was riding around Waterbury, all dolled up, out of his work clothes, riding around in the other woman's American Roadster. The woman was American—well she was Italian, but born here—she smoked cigarettes, drove a car. She'd wait for him when he came out of City Hall when he went to collect his garbage collecting check. How could my mother compete with that?" my Aunt Toni asked when she told me this secret.

When I told my mother what Aunt Toni had told me she said, "My sister shouldn't have told you that." Then she proceeded to add this to the story: "When I was very little, he'd take me with him and leave me in the car while he went up to see her. She came out afterward and gave me an orange. I remember that orange sitting in my lap. I didn't want it. I knew something wasn't right. Sometimes he even brought this woman up to the farm. Like she was a friend. What did we know? My sister Ag spotted him downtown with this woman and she came right home and told Mama. The next time he brought her home my mother said to us, 'When she comes in just ignore her. Don't say hello to her. Don't offer her a cup of coffee. Just go about doing your work like you don't even know she's here.' After a while the woman comes in with Papa and we did just what my mother said. We pretended she wasn't even there. After a while the woman said, 'Well, I can see where I'm not wanted.' We all just ignored her. We were so mad at Papa."

My sister and I were sitting with my aunts and uncle in my mother's apartment at the assisted living home, The Village at East Farms, where she lived the last five years of her life. They were in their late eighties, early nineties. Aunt Toni made cream of broccoli soup. Aunt Bea, Uncle Rocco's wife (he was the only uncle left by then) made fried *sisciel'* (pumpkin flowers). Aunt Vicki made an apple cake. Once we'd dispensed with how their grandchildren were, how quiet their lives had become, they'd always circle right back to their childhood. How hard they worked. How many people came to the farm, to visit, to live, how hard their mother worked. After they paid the usual homilies of respect to their father, how smart he was, how he had a photographic memory, how he read the *New York Times* cover to cover every Sunday and an encyclopedia every night: "It was a big big book. Oh, he knew everything." How he could talk to all the "higher ups." He was never afraid of anyone. After this, they'd get down to business and talk about how bad it had been. As the years have gone by, they have told us more and more.

"You can't believe what it was like back then," Aunt Vicki says.

But I do believe.

"Now, they'd call it abuse," Aunt Toni says.

"Oh, what are you talking about?" Uncle Rocco says. "It was good for us!" This from my grandparent's son and heir.

While my grandparent's only surviving son, Rocco, benefited by being the only male child, he was also the object of my grandfather's anarchic nature. "In some ways, worse than all the others because he was the boy. He missed a lot of school because he had to work so hard. Sometimes he'd fall asleep in class the next day. My father believed in education but . . . well, anyway, Rocky had it good *and* bad," my mother often told me.

"My brother Rocky built himself a canoe, from scratch, from nothing," Aunt Vicki told us that day. A story I had never heard until then. "Remember that, Rock? We were teenagers. We spent a lot of time together because we were the two youngest. First he built the frame— he had to soak the wood and bend it for the inside. That takes a lot of work. Oh, he worked on it for months and months. You know, because we lived on the lake; we couldn't wait until we could take it out on the water. Then he put the canvas on the outside, so careful. Then you have to seal it so that it was waterproof. What did you use, Rock? You have to be real sure there were no leaks. So he kept testing. It was beautiful. He did such a good job. So he had finished it and he was letting it cure, I think they call it. Waiting for it to be ready to be put on the water. Right, Rocky? And you know what my father did? I still can't believe it. One day he got mad, and who knows about what. He was always mad about one thing or another. He went down there with a sledge hammer—I ran after him. 'That's not right, Papa!' Rocky wasn't there. I tried to stop my father, but he just pushed me aside. He smashed the whole thing to smithereens. My brother hadn't even gotten to take it out once on the water. Not even once. That was my father."

I turn to look at my Uncle Rocco, in disbelief. He flings his right hand up in the air. "What the hell. I probably deserved it."

My grandfather, the ungovernable. My grandfather, the anarchist.

Rille

"*Rille, rille,*" my mother says to her mother. The two women sit at the large, chipped enamel table, with the blue and white checked edge which fills the kitchen "up the farm." My grandmother's table is the still point around which we inevitably converge. It's the large flat plane to which we inevitably belly. The rest of us live in a slack, uneven circle on the streets and roads nearby.

"*Rille, rille.*"

Sundays we sweep in, crowding the table as we press and rush to eat and drink and talk and demand each other's attention. We children slip into the crevices between our rocks, the grown ups. *Rille, rille,* tell, tell, we say and the stories from "the other side" are told and retold. The words vibrate and rotate among us so often so they become our stories too. After Sunday dinner, the kids play wild in the woods while the grownups crack nuts, play cards, take long, loose naps, then we all eat and drink again and finally pour off home. Our grandparents are the spin of the planet, the forces that affix us to the earth, then loosen us to the wind.

Rille is our dialect for *dillo,* tell.

Lucia Santorsa, child of cheese makers, is *Lucana,* a woman from the ancient region of Lucania, now called Basilicata. *Su nata in Tolve, provincia di Potenza.* Her daughter, my mother, is asking her to tell us one of the stories about making cheese with her father and uncle. I drift in to my mother's side.

Rille adess, my mother says again. Tell us now.

"*Ma, rille di che?*" But what should I say?

"*Mo' gli dic', u nom' du padre e che facev'.*" Now you tell your father's name and what he did.

My *pader** had cows and he make a lot of cheese. He went to
deliver the cheese every day and he went all over: Naples,
Potenza, all those places. My *pader* sell all that cheese. Eh.
That's the life my father had.

And Papa, he wann' *'a* make me go *a' scuola* and I wann' *'a*
go, but *Mama* no wan' *a* makea me go. I stay home to help my
mader. But Papa was so nice. He talked so nice and he took
me with him to the *masseri'* where they kept the cows. That's
where they make the cheese. I learn how to make 'em. My
pader give me a piece of *'a stuffa* to eat, a lilla piece but I went
in the back to work the s*tuffa*, to make lilla thing, *sola sol'* . . .
And Papa and Zi' Gerardo, the brother of my papa, make little
things for *le* kids: *na cavallozza, na uccellozza, na anellozza*. A
little horse, a little bird and a little ring. The two brothers
always make those things with me. We bring to the kids at
home. When they dry they so hard. Once when I had too
many in my hands, they *cascat' a terr', sono' rott' perchè* it was so
hard, *eran tropp' tost'. E quan' so' cascade, sono rott'*, they fell on
the ground and because they were so hard, they break.

"All right, Lucia," Zi' Gerardo say to me, "I give a little
more. What am I gonna do? We make a little more. We bring
'em home to *tutti le* kids and you give 'em, one each." He was
so patient for *le* kids. *Zi' Gerardo* always thought a bringa
things to the *creature*, for all the kids, not justa me. He brought
cosarella tutti le kids *i vicin'*. How many things my Zi' Gerardo
makea for me! I was always with my father *e* him. He did
everything with me, because I was the only daughter. He likea
so much.

But these *cosarell'*, were so hard nobody can chew him.
One time my uncle Gerardo made *una* special thing just for
me. He *fatta na* doll. From *na stuffa* from the cheese, *Un* doll,
a regular doll. *Cosi* beautiful. I love that doll so much. I'm *a* so
careful. I make sure I never drop that doll. I don't want to
breaka my doll.

Ma one day my doll fall *sulla terr'* and break into little
pieces and my mother she take the pieces and she pick him up
and she put 'em in the *minestra*. I cry. And I cry. I wanta my
thing.

Waiting for Vito

Lucia Santorsa Becce, my grandmother, speaking:

I' mi chiam' Lucia Santorsa. My name is Lucia Santorsa. I was born in Tolve, in the province of Potenza, and I was raised in Tolve. Until I got married, I stayed in Tolve.

And I was in Italy. There were a lot of marriage proposals for me from many young men. My mother was mad at me. She said, "Why do you do this? Why won't you accept any of these proposals. You'll wind up never getting married."

"Ah," my father said, "Leave her alone. We'll keep her with us." But then what happened happened. Vito was taking such a long time to come back from America that my father said, "Lucia, your mother is right. I know you gave your word but are you going to keep your word even if it's for a hundred years?" These words hurt me so much. My father was so nice, no matter what he was talking about. But now he agreed with my mother.

Someone from Tolve had gone to America and he told Vito that there were many young men who wanted to marry me so Vito knew that if he didn't come back to marry me, he was going to lose me.

Well, I used to stand by the door hoping Vito'd come back for me. And I was standing there one day, just standing there waiting. Someone came to our house and said, "Vito is coming."

Vito is coming? No, I couldn't believe it. After all this time he was going to be here in five minutes.

When he arrived at the door, he asked, "Can I come in?" just as my father had always said he would. He shook hands with my father, and he talked to him about America. He told my father about the life he had in America.

Then my mother-in-law came and said to me. "This one isn't going to stay here." And so I got married. And that was the end of that.

While Vito was in Tolve to marry me, he was walking in the town square when someone met him and blurted out, "Your father's dead. Vito, your Papa passed." Vito lost consciousness. His father had died suddenly of pneumonia in New York. That was one of only two times that I saw Vito faint. The other time was later when your little brother Pasquale died. So he went back to America. I waited three years for him in Tolve. I had Archangela (her first daughter).

Tre' Casse

So tell us about when he came to America and then tell us the story about why you finally came to live in America. And tell us about the houses you saw when you came here.

Vito said he didn't like New York, and he wanted to come back, so I built a house in Tolve. My father helped me and I made a home for us. I built a house in Italy. After I had lived in that house for a year—it was such a nice house, built out of stone—so nice. Then he went to Waterbury to visit some people from our town, Tolve. Then he wrote to me and said, "I like Waterbury, it's like Tolve and I'm not going to come back to Italy no more. You have to come to America."

All my people were there. I didn't want to leave them. I had a nice big family (*tenev' una bella famiglia*) and so I didn't want to go to America. I complained for a year. Then my father said, "You want to lose your husband? Your husband will not come back here; you have to leave." And so I was forced to go to America. It seemed so bad. My parents had to force me to get into the cart. I didn't want to leave them.

Pasquale, my cousin, came with me up to Naples. We were going to travel together to America. But when we got to Naples they stopped him from getting on the ship because he had something wrong with his eyes. Pasquale said to me, "Lucia I can't come."

My father had told us that if someone couldn't go ahead, the other one should go on alone. And so I obeyed my father's words. And so I came alone. I didn't want to leave Pasquale. And I came alone, me and the girl (her daughter, Arcangela). It was really bad on the ship. There was a storm, the water was stormy. I couldn't hold anything down. Not even water I could keep in my stomach.

When you got off the boat what happened with your trunks? Tell us, when you got off what happened with the trunks?

I had three wooden trunks with me. They were filled with linens and things to eat. When I arrived in New York they let us pass through customs, but they wanted me to go through without my trunks. And I said I am not leaving here if these trunks don't come with me.

And there were so many people on line. No, they said, I had to pass through without them. "They don't come through with you." But I wouldn't leave the trunks. I wouldn't leave unless they came with me. I only had three trunks with me. So I sat down on them and refused to leave. Then an Italian man came over to me and said, "Don't worry Signora. You won't lose these trunks. They will come with you. Here take these." And he gave me three papers [claim checks]. "But now you take the boat [off Ellis Island into the harbor of New York]."

Then Donato [her brother-in-law] came to me and I said, "What do you want?" I didn't know him at first. Then I looked at him and said to him, "O Donato, Thank God you are here." And all my fear went away. . . .

I told him these are the papers for the trunks and he said, "Don't worry. I have a friend in New York. He'll help us get the trunks." And his friend helped me.

I got here and there was no one here that I knew, no one from Tolve. Just Vito and Donato. I felt so ill. I was sick. I had come to the end of the world for Vito and I was alone. I was so all alone. When the distance from your family is great it's very bad. What are you going to do? You have to make someone happy, either your husband or your family. I cried many times over it. And datsa's the life.

Keeping Company

Rose Becce Clapps: Her Version:

I met him in the park. He kept trailing me around all night. I didn't realize it, but every once in a while this fella would go by me and I would see this figure. What he was doing was walking by me on purpose so I would notice him. I wasn't paying attention like. Later I said what was the figure going by me, like he was so busy going somewhere?

Vicki and I were walking around Lakewood. Then we decided to go home. We were about to leave the park, when we heard these footsteps in back of us. Since we had to walk down Chestnut Hill and it was dark, we were afraid. So I said to Vicki, "We'd better stop and go back into the park." We turned around to walk back in and there's these three fellas right in back of us. I turned to Peter. He was the leader, you know.

He said to me," You're some lump of sugar."

I looked right at him and I said, "Would you mind not following us?" I hated him then.

"Oh, don't get me wrong. Don't get me wrong. All I want to know is your name."

I said, "My name is Abigail and this is Aloysius."

"No, no, I'm really serious. All I want to know is your name. Please."

Then he says, "I see you're going up that way. There's a Mr. Becce up there. He knows my father, Mr. Clapps. You go ask him who the Clappses are."

I knew who the Clappses were, so I thought, isn't that funny. So I said, "I'm Mr. Becce's daughter." That kind of broke the ice.

He said, "We'll walk you home." So they walked us home. Naturally, Peter gets up front and starts walking with me. He had to take over right away and leave the other fellas hanging in the back. But really it was his friend Ernie that first saw us and said, "Hey look at that girl." He didn't give poor Ernie a chance.

On the way up the hill, he asked me, "What do you do? Where do you work?"

I said, "Well, I work at Kay Jewelry Store."

"Oh good," he said, "That's where I'll buy your wedding ring."

Oh wow, I thought, don't lose you.

It was summer. I could come home from Kay's every night. I would go swimming at the lake. Then I would come home. My mother would say, "Somebody called. A fella called you."

"Oh yea, did he give you the name?"

"No."

So finally he called me down Kay's. And he said, "You know I want to go out with you."

"Oh, okay." I was kind of happy about it, because I liked him right away. There were plenty of fellas that wanted to go out with me but I always said no. Isn't that strange? Good looking fellas, too. I can't tell you what made the difference with your father either that made me want to go out with him. It just was there; it was right.

Oh God, the fellas that wanted to go out with me, they would stand on their heads to go out with me. They would send me other people to tell me how good they were because they couldn't tell me themselves. Quite a few fellas would send another fella to tell me how good this fella was and why I should go out with them. It wasn't like they weren't aggressive. I just had this thing in my head.

I would say no to everybody. I was really ready to be an old maid, for some reason. I don't know what changed me. Because when your father came, that was it.

So I made the date. It was on a Sunday. He took me to a movie and we went for ice cream after. We took the bus and walked up the hill. And he didn't make another date with me.

He said, "I'll call you."

I said, "Oh, when?" and he told me later he thought this was awful pushy of me. But I said, "Look, I come home from work, it's hot. I like to go swimming. I'm not going to sit home waiting for the phone. So I'm here now, you want to tell me something, tell me now."

Oh, I couldn't wait to get in the water and I certainly wasn't going to sit home on a hot day and you know how fellas are: sometimes they call you and sometimes they don't. "Listen I have to go swimming. Then I'm going to wait, then you might not call." Oh, I had to go swimming after those hot days in Kay's. We would die if it wasn't for that dip at night. So I straightened that out right away.

You want a date with me, ask me now. Otherwise take your chance of not finding me home. What he would do was call me at Kay's. And then I would go in the vault. We had a vault and we had a phone in the vault and they would say, "Rose, phone." I'd run in the vault so no one could hear me talk. The girls used to tease me. They'd say, "You know your voice changes when you talk to Peter?"

And then he said to me, "You know, I never go up to any girl's house because once you go to a girl's house, that means that's it." I met him downtown. But he would take me home but he'd never come in. If you went into a girl's house, you were going steady, you were serious. So he made this announcement to me.

I said to myself, I'm not too sure about you either. I don't want to drag you to my house either. You know I liked him, but. . . .

Then what happened was that we had a date on a Saturday and he never showed up. And I said, Well, that's it. That was all I needed, anybody who did the least little thing, that was the end.

He calls me the next morning. I said, "What do you want?"

"Well," he said, " I had to go to New York with this bunch of boys." They must have gone to a ball game. "I told my cousin to call you and tell you all about it so you wouldn't wait by the phone."

I said, "I didn't get any phone call and besides I didn't have a date with your cousin, I had it with you."

"I told her to call you," he said. "She didn't call you?"

"No, she didn't. And don't blame your cousin."

"Well," he said, "I'm sorry."

I said, "That's all right you had to go to New York, but even so, don't they have phones in New York?" Oh I was really mad.

He said, "Okay when am I going to see you?"

I said, "Never, you're never going to see me. What you did is not right and I just can't be bothered with anybody that's like that."

"Oh no, oh no, I've got to see you," he said. You know he wanted to make a date and I just wouldn't make a date with him. That was it. He said, "I'll be right up," and hung up the phone. See first he says he's never coming in the house and the next thing he'll be right up. And he came scooting up that house so fast and just walked in, brazen. See then my father knew him and he got to meet my mother and he just sits down, like he was welcome. So now what was I going to do? I had to talk to him. I wasn't that way that I was going to walk away. I was kind of glad he did that, but I was mad as a hornet. I mean if he waited on that phone for me to give him a date, he'd have waited forever. But you know he figured, I'm not listening to her anymore. He was very brash. Otherwise I probably would have broken up with him. If he weren't so aggressive, I just wouldn't take a thing.

Really, my mother used to say to me, "*Da va metre la vetrina*,! That's what we're going to do, put you in a glass case, a shop window, so nothing should touch you, nothing should bother you."

We kept company for four years. We met in 1937 and we were married in 1941. We used to go to the movies, one night a week, or two nights a week maybe once in a while. I'd see him maybe not every night but almost every night after he had a nap after he got home from work. It wouldn't be that early. We'd play cards. Sit in the kitchen and talk, make coffee or go for a walk. In winter, we would just sit. Everyone, my sisters and brothers and their friends, would just sit and talk. That very first summer it was like I wouldn't go out with anyone else and he wouldn't either.

This girl asked him to go to a dance. When I met him I just didn't go out with anyone else. If fellas would call me, I wouldn't make any dates with them. Not that we talked about it. I just wouldn't make any other dates. I figured, well, he would feel bad, although we never talked about going steady. Then one night he called me and he said, "I've got to see you," and he came running up. He said, "I don't know what to do. This girl that I know," I guess that he must have been dating her, "wants me to take her to a dance."

So this was what was going to be like the turning point. Oh good, I said to myself. Now if he goes and takes this girl to the dance, that means if someone calls me, I'll go out with them. We never talked about it but now to me this was going to be it. So I said to him, "That's entirely up to you. You know how you feel. You want to go to the dance, you go." We'd never talked about just going with each other, going steady or anything. "You want to go to the dance, you take her to the dance. Only I would like to know what your decision is going to be."

He said, "All right, come with me." And he had a car. I don't know if it was his father's car or what. "Let's take a ride." So we took a ride and he stops in front of this house. He runs up. Stays a little while and he comes running back. "All right I went to see her and I told her I'm not going." Isn't that strange?

Didn't discuss it with me at all and just went and told her he was sorry he couldn't take her to the dance. We never talked about it. Then I said to myself, then I won't go out with anyone else either. I was just waiting to see what he was going to do. So that was it. He just didn't go with anyone and I didn't. And he just kept coming up every night, never said anything. I think it was the end of August, he told me he loved me. Then that Christmas, he bought me a hope chest. He said to me, "You know I bought you a hope chest."

I said to him, "You've been doing some serious thinking."

"Well," he said, "that's what a fella gives a girl." He must have asked someone, he didn't know. Because to give a girl a hope chest means you are ready to marry her. He probably didn't know it was that serious a gift. I don't know what he was thinking. Or maybe he had made up his mind that he would like to marry me, but we never talked about it. We went along that way.

We were really thinking of getting married but then his brother Frank got sick and we had to wait. They needed his money for the hospital bills. So that was why I went with him for four years. Then later his brother died. We had to wait a year for mourning. It was really heartbreaking. He was so sick, poor man. You mourned for a year. We didn't do anything. We didn't go to a movie or a dance for a whole year. We just didn't. We didn't do it and be upset. You just did it. That's the way we felt. Well, you were just happy being together. We'd sit there playing cards. And my mother sitting waiting for him to go.

He was very brash. I'll never forget he embarrassed my mother and father to death once. I had put this pretty print dress on. It was really pretty. And when he saw me come in the kitchen, "Oh," he said, "That's so beautiful. I've got to see this dress on you really good." So he picks me up and puts me on a chair. "Now, turn around," he said to me. My mother and father were looking at each other. And I was embarrassed to death, but nothing bothered him.

Peter Clapps: His Version:

I met Rose up at Lakewood Park [an amusement park very close to my grandparents' farm]. It was so popular in those days, there was no place else to go. I'd walk up with Charlie and Ernie. On a Sunday night, the whole town would be up there. If you were looking for someone, you'd go up there to find them. Everybody would go up there and scrounge a free night, just stand around and look at everybody else. Maybe you'd have an occasional quarter to go on a ride. I saw her walking there with her sister. I met her up there. She was so pretty, so pretty, you can't believe it—like Hollywood pretty. I knew immediately she was the one.

Flesh and Bone

My father was always man of the flesh: as a young man he was lean, muscular, even sculptural, in his beauty. This was the result of a time and place where fruit was an occasion, where hard physical work *was* daily life, and where using the body to play often and extremely was as natural as using the body to do brutal work 12 hours a day. It came from the daily business of raising iron to build buildings: it came from picking up long, large, heavy pieces of metal; it came from carrying them into place and working to affix them into the planes and corners where they would be essential elements of the buildings he was helping to raise. As he lifted and carried, held and welded, an exchange of sorts took place: you might call it a dialogue between structures, his own and the buildings he worked on. Doing construction built the strength he used to construct more buildings—this conversation built over time.

He walked with ease across I-beams ten stories up to get from one part of a building to another. To make that crossing you have to have muscles that are so sure, so agile, that it's not a possibility that they won't carry you across this very narrow piece of metal with casual grace. A confidence comes from that kind of physical strength and balance that has nothing to do with thought or decision. As the rest of us walk down the street without thinking about it, a special few lift heavy things with self-assurance, move them at will, climb heights, walk easily across dangerous spaces. My father was one of those creatures, moving with the pleasure that a strong body gives, easily, playfully, unselfconsciously, not a cause for arrogance or pride, but a locus of pleasure because your body always does what you want it to as if it is part of your character or nature, seemingly what the fates wrote for you, although it's actually a long slow fabrication of culture, food, attitude, and expectation created in muscle, blood, and bone.

This was the housing our handsome, dark-haired father's large and wild spirit inhabited when my sister and I were children. At the end of a long summer night playing with our cousins up the farm, he'd pick up the two dead weights of his sleeping children out of the back of the car, as if we were two small brown paper bags of groceries, one in each arm, and climb the stairs to our attic rent on the top floor of the Pagano's house. He'd deposit us in our bed, brushing back sweaty bangs from our foreheads, pulling the cotton covers around and then bending down and kissing our soft skin with the pleasure of one who has escaped.

One luminous night of the first snow storm he insists that we all bundle up and go out while the rest of the city is stilled and hidden so that he can pull my mother, my sister, and me on the back of our sled up the center of deserted streets, running and laughing out of the powerful center of his charmed vitality. The snow feathers against our faces as he runs up Grove Street through the enchantment that has been conjured that he has somehow also conjured. His body is a wild horse of an engine, each thigh raising high to the gallop, each stroke of a leg lightly grabbing the snowy ground and pushing it behind him, his thick-soled work shoes churning down in through the thick white blanket to find the crunch of ground below, pulling us up the hill out of reality into this astonishing night. Mid-gallop, mid-flight, lengths from the top of the street, he flings a look over his shoulder throwing back to us the ecstatic light this labor creates in him. A rupture of light escapes, cracking through him from the aboriginal core, flinging phosphorescence out over the quiescent night. Chains on cars on tires clanking slowing through the snow three streets away are not in the same universe with us. He can carry his girls through the snowy night, up steep hills in a world that belongs only to him, only to us. We three, his girls, ride on wooden slats. There at the other end of the rope he pulls his weighted cargo, the clay to his fire, just barely, holding him down to earth.

Within the sturdy frame, big storms blew the wild winds of his big, untamed spirit that had as little control of itself as the flesh had ease and knowledge. Later on my father would thicken, by then he had the solidity of an ancient Greek column, a man who could support weight, burdens. He was a man you could lean into. I can lean into him and feel his profound sturdiness still—that simple comfort that has come to me after my father's death. I can still feel his body's weight and heft. Its volume and stability. This isn't a calculation. It's that the sensation of him, of his presence in the world, lives inside my own body. I know how much weight there is for me to lean into. I can feel how much push it would take to move that body off center. More than I have. This isn't a matter of pounds; it's a simple matter of knowing him.

For all the complications of having come from violence, madness, death and misery, he posited this body to try to hold all of that away from my sister and me. It worked and it failed but his body and his love stay.

Both Are True

I

"Are the girls ready, Rose? Food packed?" My father has taken the stairs two at a time up the three flights. The iron he works with has become too hot to handle in the summer day or the job can wait until the cool dawn to be picked up again. His sleeveless undershirt is hanging out of his back pocket, leaving a red-bronzed outline against the pale skin of his torso, which is usually covered by at least his undershirt. His gray work pants are covered in red paint stains, welding holes, and zigzagged stitching mending old welding burns. My mother washes, mends, and irons five pants and work shirts a week.

The late summer afternoon heat has crept into every corner of our third floor attic rent. Even the chenille bedspread feels warm when I kneel to look for my sandals under the bed.

Supper's packed. The corners of a large, white *mappin'* are tied in the center of a lidded aluminum pot to hold in the heat a pan of macaroni, meatballs and sausage. In the picnic basket there are sandwiches made of baloney, American cheese, iceberg lettuce, tomato and mayonnaise. There's potato salad, fruit, cookies. Forks and spoons are held in place by a ribbon of elastic on the inside lid of the picnic basket. A tablecloth is folded carefully covering the food and matching tin plates and cups. The jars of iced coffee and lemonade are in a separate bag.

Lucia and I are wearing our bathing suits under our starched, ruffled pinafores which my mother has sewn for us trimmed with rickrack and edged in lace. Our white sandals have been polished with chalky white shoe polish that has the same look as Milk of Magnesia. Our mother has packed white cotton underpants, two wool cardigan

sweaters for us to put on later after the sun sets and we are cooling in
our need to sleep.

My father goes into the bedroom to change into his bathing suit.
My mother will pick the work clothes and heavy, very scuffed work
shoes from the floor next to the bed when we get home tonight. When
he's changed we all tumble down the stairs to my father's '49 Pontiac, a
car he ordered after the war and waited for a year to arrive. It's black
and it has a slanted back.

In the summer when the sun shines down on the eaves of the attic
rent at 54 Ward Street the heat accumulates making it unbearably hot
by dinner time, so pretty often we leave to go out for a picnic supper
and a swim as soon as my father gets home from work.

Most family outings are preceded by phone calls to the aunts and
cousins, "We're going swimming now at Hubbard. Should we pick you
up?" Maybe because it's a weeknight, a workday, we go by ourselves.

"You can't swim on a full stomach, you'll get cramps and go under,"
my mother looks up from the blanket where she's reading the newspaper. She has on a halter top and a ruffled yellow skirt that she's sewn for
herself after we're asleep and my father is "down the street," playing
cards with the boys at the North End Social club. But now my father
has his arms crossed under his head as a pillow. He has his fedora set
over his eyes to keep the sun out while he takes a nap.

"Isn't it a half an hour yet? It must be a half an hour, Mommy!"

"I'll wake Daddy up in a little while. Go play."

"Yeah, we're going to drown," we roll our eyes, then "Race ya!" to
see who can get to the sliding pond next to the swings first. Whoever
doesn't get to the bottom of the stairs first makes a show of pulling at
the other one as she starts up the stairs and occasionally even manages
to pull her down the slide stairs, if that one of us hadn't gotten a real
hold on the side rails. But that was considered really mean because it
not only took away the "I win," by undoing it, but it was a humiliation
too—you had lost after already having won. It was so humiliating it
might even backslide into, "I'm telling Mommy," which naturally leads
to, "You're such a *mammone*," and "Baby!! You can't take anything."
That's why it was essential to not just make it to the sliding ponds, but
to actually be a few stairs up so as to make it to the top too. Any kid
who hesitated at the top was "*stunad*." But on a summer night like this
one there were just the two of us so there wasn't that much at stake.
Neither of us was going to have to wait those few crucial seconds at
the bottom of the stairs for "my turn." So the ride down wasn't as
exciting. We would take a few rides in turn, then wander back to the

blanket under the tree to see if Daddy was up yet, or if Mommy would wake him.

After several trips back and forth, my father takes the fedora off his face and places it carefully on one bent knee while he rubs his large rough hands across his face a couple of times. Then he places it on the blanket next to my mother, then turns to us and says, his voice pitched up in mock incredulity, "You want to do *what*? Go swimming?"

My father is never happier than when he can undo, for a little while, the history of his early life, by providing experiences for children that are the opposite of what his had been: the violent beatings from his drunken father, the mother who was institutionalized by the time he was six, the deaths of his two brothers. He appeases these churning miseries by taking all the children in our family to an amusement park, by teaching all of us to swing from a tire out over the swimming hole, taking us for long rides that end in our eating foot-long hot dogs.

He takes us, my sister and me, by the hand to the turquoise swimming pool: this is the central event of these glowing summer nights. Floating: "Let your body rest on the water. It's like a bed if you let yourself go. I've got you, don't worry," supporting our weight on the surface of the water with one large rough hand at the small of our back. Swimming: "Bring your arms all the way around and turn your head to the side to get some air. Good, good, that's the girl." The light glowed warm and red, undulating black and white amoeba shapes shifting over the water.

"It's my turn now, Daddy." One of us is jumping up and down in the water beside him.

Later, after the sun has set and we drive through the summer dusk and the car pulls up along side of the swinging white wood gate at 54 Ward Street, the summer light has faded into a purple night, and Lucia and I will have slipped off to sleep. My father carries us one in each arm up the three flights of stairs. Upstairs, my mother pulls off the chenille spread and folds it three times to rest at the bottom of our double bed so we can be tucked in.

Ward Street was lined with three-family wood frame houses, which had small front yards, canopied by large trees, slightly larger back yards filled with grape arbors, small fruit trees, and tomatoes. There were small front porches on the front of the houses that no one ever used, except for the first floor, where the kids played bride, clapping around in their mothers' old high heels, draping themselves with their mothers' lace trimmed satin slips or what we called "glass" curtains. Our back porches ran the width of the rent where lots of things went on. The kids played, Mom hung the clothes, where the milk, butter, and cream were left in the wood box. It was where the rocking horse sat. It's where the playpen is set up in the summer time for whichever baby cousin is visiting.

A large maple tree in the front yard of 54 Ward Street filled and flooded the small patchy lawn that sat behind the white wood picket fence. Although we knew it was forbidden, the children took turns riding the swinging hinged gate when the grownups weren't around. I'm pretty sure we did a couple of times. Who could resist a lovely piece of perfect apparatus, just the right height to grasp the pickets with our hands, just the right depth to hold our feet on the cross bar? "My turn, my turn."

Mr. and Mrs. Pagano were the landlord and landlady. These *paesans* of my mother's family, smiled at us as we came and went, asking us into their big plain kitchen occasionally, where they offered my parents a small glass of red wine, us a *biscot'*. But landlord and landlady are the first words I learn that mean power. Words that worry me. Will I make the landlord mad? "Don't swing on the gate. The landlord will get mad. You'll break the gate." My parents treat Mr. and Mrs. Pagano, two tiny rumpled people, with great respect and deference. "It's late. We have to be quiet now. You don't want to make the landlord mad at you." Or, "Say hello to the landlady. She owns the house."

The landlord and landlady had four sons, Armand, Tony, Ticaw, Ector, and two daughters, Margaretta and Emilia. Emilia lives under us with her husband but the rest of them still live with their parents.

"I'm going to steal your milk," the boys have settled on as their teasing refrain with Lucia and me, the kind of refrain that workingmen make up with kids to establish an ongoing connection.

I'm always spilling my glass of milk because I leave it sitting there next to my dish. "Finish your milk, then you can have a piece of cake after dinner." I don't like to drink milk, but each time Ector or Tony says, "I'm going to steal your milk," Lucia laughs shyly and runs up the sidewalk that leads around back. She looks up automatically to make sure that Margaret isn't shaking the dust mop out the window. It seems as if Margaret is always shaking the dust mop out of the window when we're passing under it.

I cling to my mother's leg and tears well up in my eyes.

"Oh Joanne, he doesn't mean anything. He's just teasing you. Don't you know that?" They sing this to us on most days and every day I'm upset that they're going to come and take my milk which I hate to drink.

On the second floor Emilia lives with her German husband Art Hornbecker. Marian, their daughter, is five, one of the big girls on the block. She and her friend Patty play dress up with us. Teach us how to play tag, hide and seek, take us out to the front yard and we're even allowed to go out through the front gate to play on the sidewalk with the other kids in the neighborhood if they are with us. They teach us how to pull seeds off grass to make food to go on our tin dish sets. How to make mud by mixing water with the dirt from the garden. They teach us how to play the most intensely absorbing game I have ever played: bride. "I'm the bride today." "No, you were bride yesterday. It's my turn." They tuck my mother's old discarded curtains into our skirts, drape veils on our heads and pin them on with bobby pins so that we can be brides. Teach us how to wobble and scrape along in old high heels. My mother always has a supply of old stuff for us to play with. We're their living dolls. They are five and six, but they are our first experience of the teenagers. They know. We're learning.

This is a relatively carefree time in our lives. My parents are young, beautiful, very much in love. My father's arm goes around my mother's slender body and they sway and dance between the table and the sink after dinner when Nat King Cole's voice changes the air around us when he croons on the radio, "And now the purple dusk of twilight time, steals across the meadows of my heart."

After dinner in the living room where they both read the paper before the dishes are cleaned up, my mother will often get up and go to sit on my father's lap. Or my father lies with his head on her lap on the couch and she runs her hands through his hair. There is an easy, deep physical and romantic love between them.

II

I don't have a consciousness that doesn't include my sister, Lucia. When I think back to living under the hot slanting roof of the attic apartment in that wood frame house, when I think of playing on the large wood porch that runs the width at the back of our rent, I can feel her skin within my reach. She's always there, part of the housing within which I come to consciousness.

She is a round faced, curly headed baby when I'm born—eighteen months old. At that tender time when calculating a child's age is still done by months. When we are asked the age difference between us now, whichever of us is asked will sometimes say a year and a half, but just as often say, "eighteen months"; we're all still deeply conscious of her brief babyhood before another baby replaces her newness in my mother's attention. My mother says now that she made her grow up too soon, "When I was pregnant I told her, 'I'm going to get another baby. Don't forget this baby's for you. She's going to be your baby, too. You're going to be a good little girl and you're going to help Mommy take care of the baby.'" I try to imagine my pregnant mother, after Lucia's asleep, her hair perfectly groomed, the ruffled curtains she's made at night from bleached flour sacks, starched and ironed on the windows behind her. She bends and picks up her fifteen-month-old baby, lifting her to stand face to face on the kitchen table tenderly conferring this adult mantle upon her. What can my sister have understood? But babies take things in. I imagine my sister's round, grave, wide eyed expression, as she is enveloped in garb too large for her. It's an expression I will see on her face often as we go from our joint babyhood into girlhood. I know this from the capacious refuge I will always feel with her despite the vulnerability that never leaves her. A sober covering that never cloaks her worry into stillness.

Back then, in late 1943, my mother assumes it's the right thing to do. This is what Southern Italian women do with their girl children: initiate their baby daughters into training as a woman—which means taking care of little children, even when you are a baby yourself. It's of a piece with the 15th century mores my mother and her sisters grew up with, our generation grew up with and which my family continues to live by today, even as we make our way in the 21st. It's what these women know.

It's more surprising that later on my mother comes to understand that there was something ludicrous about this.

"I made her grow up too soon. You start taking care of a baby, and the baby kind of takes you over. I always gave hugs and kisses to both of you. But I made her stop being a baby. It was wrong. If Lucia had something Joanne wanted she would come crying to me and I would say to Lucia, 'Let her have it,' just to keep her quiet!" My mother, when she tells me this story now, slips back to that time, forgetting that she's telling Joanne this story. "I told Lucia that she was the big sister and that she had to watch out for Joanne. It wasn't right what I did to her.

"Lucia loved the baby right away," my mother continues. "The day I brought the baby home the first thing she did, she went over to the bassinet and she stared down at the baby—she was just a baby herself and she said, 'Look, a pudgy baby.' Staring, staring at that baby. Where did she get that? She always loved babies." My mother looks back at her mistake with her first daughter wistfully. She stares down into her cup of coffee. "But that's what we thought back then."

My mother probably read something about child rearing in a *Good Housekeeping* or *Woman's Day*, the magazines that she clipped recipes from, instinctively studying to be an American. This was in the '50's, even while our family held on to the mores her mother, my grandmother, brought with her from Basilicata, even while our relatives left behind in Italy were gradually abandoning those same mores.

Right and wrong were the roads on which my mother always traveled. She had been trying to teach her first daughter the right way to behave, just as she had been raised in these "*giusta*" ways, and then from America she learns she has been wrong. My mother knew no way to be other than right or wrong. As a result she was always trying to do right, but always certain that she was wrong. This is the code into which my sister is being initiated when I am born. The urgency with which Lucia was being taught to be a good girl, to help with her baby sister, me. Codes of perfection inevitably have failure written into them.

Lucia and I are kneeling next to our bed to say our prayers because our parents are fighting again. Lucia's two chubby inches taller than I am. These inches are the cushion between my baby fat and everything else. If she is vulnerable I am made safe by her being exactly next to me. Even as I feel her panicky worries because of the voices rising outside our room, I feel comforted because her slightly larger body is always in next-to-ness to mine. I can feel about how much she must have weighed. I could lift her now, an aging adult, and feel the weight in the crook of my arm, the baby fat under her soft frightened skin.

I know that she is on the edge of tears as she instructs me, "We have to pray that they'll stop fighting." She kneels down at the side of the double bed that sits in the center of our bedroom that we share at night, I kneel beside her as we lean into the nubs of our pink chenille spread. It's as much of a location for prayer as Sacred Heart Church where we walk to mass on Sunday mornings on our own. "I don't need to go to church," my mother tells us when we ask her why she doesn't go with us, "I'm always good."

We had been playing on the floor of our bedroom when we heard the fight begin to rise and build. "What did you have to buy that for?" My father's anger is swelling now. They're standing just past the pantry door. Is the door open between us? I could press my parents' bones, my father's emptied of flesh in the grave, my mother's shrinking every day, precisely back into position from where their voices carried to us in that room that day.

"What? I bought a bottle of Canadian Club? What's wrong with that?" Her voice pitches into defensive defiance.

"You had to do that? How much did you pay for that?" His voice is on a hydraulic rise. I imagine him staring down at her, fury in his face. "You can never leave well enough alone. You always have to extract every last drop out of every situation. We can't afford that." His large, naturally booming voice is gathering full force. Even when he's just talking ordinarily his voice is one that moves widely into the space around him. Acting coaches could use him as an example of how to project. When it ascends, it builds to a roar. Then his voice is a force. It pounds the walls, a gale whirling through our attic rent.

"Oh, Peter," My mother says looking up at him in disbelief. Her voice is pitched higher. She is not backing down. Her own anger is rising. How dare you has taken over her voice too. "Stop that now! Stop that! Everyone can hear you!" She never backed down. She held her own against the gale, added her own winds and tempest. They were madly in love, passionate for one another: raised with ordinary rage, they knew the exigencies of rage and its absolutes. Never give in.

There has been a family party. There are family parties all the time, at least weekly. When there aren't official occasions, like birthdays and anniversaries, there are picnics, coffee ans', let's get together, having company. We gathered, as tribes gather, constantly. The kids play together, the grownups talk, joke, laugh, brag, cover over their wounds, for human warmth, for the soothing rhythms of voices in concert, for agreement to say we are together, for the sound of dissonance to say I'm a little separate, but even the anger is to tie us together. At our gatherings are always cold cuts for sandwiches, platters of sausage, peppers, onions and potatoes, lots of coffee, home baked cakes and cookies. We gather at each other's kitchen tables as naturally and as often as we shop for groceries, take baths, take the bus downtown. It's part of our weekly cycle. But my mother has upped the ante and bought a bottle of whiskey. "Why do you have to be such a *scialabobo* and squander our money? It's never enough with you! You always have to show off." It was a birthday party. This isn't the norm. Coffee is the grownup drink.

Later, when we're teenagers, my mother will have a lot to say about these fights. "Your father was always loaning people money. Then they wouldn't pay him back. Or sometimes he lost some money gambling; he'd be so mad at himself. Then he would pick a fight with me because I bought a bottle of C&C. He was mad at himself. Not at me. But he couldn't admit it. How many times I wanted to leave him. I'd get so mad. But I was crazy about him too. He was so handsome. You can't believe how handsome he was. I was so in love with him, you can't believe it."

Their voices continue to howl and storm. "How much did you pay for this? I asked you, how much?"

"I only paid ten dollars. What are you so mad about?" Then we hear his voice pitch up to shrill and the "I told you not to do this," the crack of his hand against her face. She really screams now, "Peter, Peter," she's crying, weeping inconsolably, but she's also still furious, "You stop that."

Lucia is crying now. "She shouldn't answer him back. She shouldn't say anything." I'm startled and frightened too, I can feel that Lucia is wobbly with fear. She puts her arms around me and holds me. I'm not as afraid as she is. I'm mystified, but I have what I need, my big sister. She has only her immutable job of being "a good little girl," between her and what's going on outside our bedroom door. "They're the best Mommy and Daddy in the whole world. If only they wouldn't fight."

Later my mother also tells us, "Your father hit me twice. Then I told him that if he ever hit me again I was going to leave him and he stopped. After, when he had calmed down he would feel bad and he used to say to me, 'When I get like that just come over and give me a kiss.' Yeah, I just feel like giving him a kiss then. No, I told him. You better not ever do that again. I'll leave you. I'm telling you. And I meant it!" My mother always triumphs in her stories. No one ever gets the best of her. *She* told *him*. Despite their wild and real love for one another, the screaming fights between them continued for all our years together, waves of the terrible violence they grew up with still flooding through them both—these fights only begin to mellow when my parents reached their seventies, but they don't ever completely stop.

By the time we're settled into our life in the ranch house my father built for us on North Main Street where two of my mother's sisters live, I've joined in the screaming and shouting. It's a part of life. I don't think much about it. Lucia will be stuck with three furious screaming people in her tender, vulnerable world. She will try to get us to stop, but we all rage on. Almost everyone in our family pretty much behaves this way, grandparents, aunt, uncles. In our immediate family, it's so much a part of our days and hours that we don't really notice Lucia's worry. There are so many things that can set these screaming matches off. My disobedience, my mother's spending money, my father "disappearing" down the street to his Social Club, where the boys play cards all night. Lucia doesn't cause the fights.

That late summer afternoon, though, the bottle of Canadian Club is the issue. The party has gone on all afternoon, the sun has slid down behind the other three family houses, just beyond Mr. Pagano's garden. I don't remember how that day ended. I don't remember that party. I don't remember going to sleep that night. The fight is isolated in my early memories. The fight. Is it the first one I remember? I can hear the pitch of each of my parent's voices.

I can feel the nub of the bedspread on our bed. I can feel the scratch of the rickrack that my mother has sewn on Lucia's nightgown against my skin. I can feel my sister's tremulous body next to mine. Her small hand around my shoulder soft with baby fat. I am wide eyed with this new idea, "The best parents in the whole world."

Two

The room rests, a deep afternoon repose. My mother's bedroom: it is their bed, my father's and hers, but it is her room. It is soft with pink and rose, her name. The spread on the bed is a heavy chenille, heavy enough to stay straight on the bed, not so heavy that it weighs on them. It wouldn't weigh anyway. It is always folded down at night, neatly first in half and then again, by her. She is proud of her things and keeps them carefully. He gets into bed after supper for his nap, she comes in to kiss him and to fold down the spread. But now the bed is made without a wrinkle. It's solid with weight. The deeper pink dust ruffle hangs in place below the spread.

All the other furniture was put in place when they first moved here and it hasn't been moved since, except for cleaning. His bureau is near the closet. It's tall with big deep drawers. All his work clothes are in one drawer, the pants on one side and the shirts on the other, full of holes from the welding that he does all day long. The middle drawer has his good shirts and most of his underwear. The top drawer has some brand new underwear and socks for when they go out at night and his watch that he never wears. It's gold; she gave it to him as a wedding present. He wears it when she insists on it because they are going to a dance, but only then. It doesn't really go with his swollen, always blistered hands, that are so crusted with dirt that it never can come out.

Her bureau is lower and wider than his; it's on the other side of the room by the window, with a large mirror held in place by two elongated wooden s's. They are arms that hold the mirror up. There is a statue of the Virgin Mary in pastel porcelains sitting on top of the bureau in the middle of a starched, stiff doily. Her top drawer has boxes of jewelry, rhinestones, flower pins, and strands of costume pearls. In that drawer

112

are her gloves, all piled, each pair placed palms together like the statue's hands, straight and tall, in a state of grace. All her soft things are in the next drawer down. Slips, and stockings, nightgowns, a corner for each category. Folded, piled, waiting to be readily found. In one corner of that drawer are her clean rags. The old ones, that have been softened by hundreds of washings and ironings. She uses those to clean the windows and polish the furniture. They are his old undershorts and shirts, now ripped up into squares, when they became too full of holes to be sent to work again.

In the biggest drawer that opens across the whole bottom of her bureau is her real store, her hats. The big drawer—there are so many of them, and they are fancy and can't be crushed, feathers and flowers and veils and brims. Just now the drawers are all closed.

Things, her hats, his books. The books on the nightstand by the bed are stacked, three of them. The ashtray is empty and clean, the light is out. All these are his. He smokes in bed when he reads and falls asleep with the spread not folded down yet. The book lies on his stomach open, face down. It looks like a little house to me when I find him asleep sometimes, like a little roof. Then the light is on. I wonder how he can go to sleep with a light like that. Some of the time, I find him with his thumb in the page, his arm and the book having fallen to one side, as if he were too tired to put the book like a roof on his stomach.

What makes the room hers, though, aside from the colors and its order, is the table I am standing by now. It is the first thing your eyes rest on when you enter the room, because it is so dressed up. It's a vanity table with a long gathered skirt with a full ruffle at the bottom. On the wall is a big round mirror. The top of the vanity table is blue glass, curving gently to each side of her. In front of her, atop the glass, is an array of bottles, short and knobby and tall and slender, bottles with gold caps and black letters and blue bottles with atomizers, that's her cologne. Then powder boxes, pink and worn, with a pink powder pad inside. It smells, this powder, like the sweetest closest stuff I've ever smelled. The lipstick tubes smell sweet too, waxy sweet, and the cologne has a dry clinging sweetness that hangs in the air, but the powder is the closest thickest smell that tells me that it is a woman's table and hers. There are drawers down under the skirt where she reaches for her hairbrush.

That's what I like best, when she does her hair. I could watch forever. She is standing here now in front of the big round mirror, taking each bobby pin out one by one and putting them in the small white cardboard box, edged with a thin blue stripe. It used to be an aspirin box. The bobby pins make x's all over her head like a decorated cap, they hold her hair tight to her head. I am standing at the side, in front of the double windows. There are white filmy curtains on them that filter the heat out of the late afternoon sun to a slightly cooler gold than it is outside. It filters in bands of light that lie diagonally across her to show the deep reds in the brown of her hair.

As she removes each set of crossed pins a curl springs out; with a gentle bounce, it hangs waiting to be tended to. The aspirin box fills up with the little squiggly black pins, her head becomes thick with curls, popping out in all directions. She runs her hands through for stray bobby pins she's missed. There are always one or two that get lost in the curls. Her fingers loosen the curls as she searches for the pins, and thicken her hair to a luxurious mass of silky brown fleece. With a quick shake of her head, she reaches for her brush lying on the blue glass. The shake loosens one last pin and it drops to the floor with a clink.

"Would you get that, pumpkin?"

I scramble to find it and put it in its box and quickly sit down on her chair, the one that goes with the vanity table, so that I won't miss any of the rite. I lean back so that I can look up comfortably and see just how she does it. I can always sit in her chair when it comes time for her to comb her hair, she never sits when she does that part. Too cramped, I guess, sitting.

The brush goes through the longish dense mass. The strokes whoosh through to the end of the hair. The bristles make a hollow sound against the soft thick hair, a roughish sound for one that makes lush silk. Each stroke gently moves the hair, blending the curls into thick waves. Soft patches of gloss appear curving down her hair. Back away from her face she brushes; as the right hand sweeps the thick flying mass of gossamer around the back of her head, it spills into the left gathering hand. Then the other way, this time her left hand guides instead of gathering. Now the brush goes up under the hair, from the base of her neck, several high sweeping strokes, then she starts over again from the front. She does it over a few times, more than she needs to, more times than it takes to tame the odd angled bounce to lush wave. I'm glad; I love this part the best.

She puts down the brush and begins to coax it with her hands. First, the front waves by her forehead: softly she nudges them so that they make an easy curve across her temple to her ear. She reaches for a bobby pin to hold that in place, holding the hair with her left hand from around the back of her head. She puts the bobby pin in her mouth, opens it with her teeth, quick, and then tucks it into place. Now, fingers held lightly apart, she prods the hair gently upward to match the other side.

Satisfied with the front, she gathers all that remains in the back; with a quick twist of her wrist it is massed on top. Again she holds it with her left hand while she bends forward carefully so as not to disturb the hair settled in place so far and reaches for some bobby pins. It's almost ready now. Some combs in the back, she pulls them up through the hair and then tucks them down tight against her scalp. Some extra bobby pins for security, now on the side, now on the top, each adjustment made with a light touch. She tips her head to one side, reaches for the top of her hair and fluffs it up a bit, then she leans forward again to check, a slight frown on her face. Her middle finger runs over the first curve she put in place, near her forehead, not because it is out of place, just to make sure, to touch how pretty it has become.

The light has deepened outside and in. She turns to look at me to see if I approve.

The house belongs to my mother. My father belongs in the world. My mother goes out into the world to bring back feathers and food and shoes for us all and to pay the bills.

My father comes home from the world to bring us money and himself. There are places in the house that are his and his alone. His side of the bed, his place at the head of the table, the couch down in the cool damp basement where he takes his nap in the summer, listening to the baseball games, but above all his reading chair in the living room.

He is an outside man. He works on the hottest days, out in the sun, as raw as the steel he puts into place. He works in the heat with his shirt off and just his gray work pants belted on. His skin gets red, the color that the steel is painted so that it won't rust, or as red as the rust itself, above the waist. His legs stay as white as soap. He smells good to me when he works out in the sun. It smells like skin and him.

In the winter he smells like the cold he has worked in. He works in the icy cold, out on the steel, high up. No gloves, walking the beams against the wind. His swollen and cracked hands and the folds of his face tell how hard he works, but he tells us, too. He can't understand how some men who work out of the union hall work only by the rules. "Those men don't know what it is to enjoy work, I mean really enjoy it." He puts his cracked hand low on his belly, "I mean from down here. I mean the real satisfaction of doing a day's work, a real day's work."

My father comes home from work every night, starving. He stands in the doorway, awkward, sure, "Is supper ready?"

My mother kisses him, "Go wash up. It will be ready in a minute." Supper never is quite ready, though we start it promptly at four and eat at five-thirty every night. As he washes up, my mother shouts, "Cut the bread. Get Dad's cold coffee. Fix the salad." He sits in his place as it is rushed onto the table.

The aftermath in our kitchen holds the chaos from cooking, rushing, and eating. For twenty minutes or half an hour we sit in the peace of this mess. It is the only time in each day that both the women of the house and a mess are allowed to be still at the same moment. My mother has a cup of coffee. The women's page and the funnies are passed around. You have to say, "I'm next," to get them.

"All right, girls," my mother signals, "time to clean up."

"Five more minutes, please, please, just five more minutes," we plead. We make the same plea every night.

There are half-empty pots on the stove. The table is covered with a disarray of dishes pushed out of the way, glasses with the last sip not drained, strewn forks and spoons, a bowl coated with oily dressing—two or three bits of lettuce and a soggy curl of onion stuck to its glass side, bread crumbs cling to the food left on the plates and are scattered in between. The newspaper is opened on the floor or left on the chairs.

My sister and I are cleaning the kitchen. My father goes to read in his chair in the living room.

His chair. Low, comfortable, plain, by the window. With a standing lamp on one side and the ashtray standing on the other. It is where he reads. Behind his book, as if he were somewhere. His cigarettes are on one arm of the chair, his shoes are kicked off to one side, his legs are stretched out, his eyes are fixed on the pages he holds in front of him.

"If you open a book and start to read and the first sentence gets you into the story right away, then you know that it will be a good book. But if you have to struggle to keep reading, it's not worth it."

Alice in Wonderland has a bad first sentence. We carried it to him one night after we had gotten ready for bed. My sister and I each sat on an arm of his chair. I liked getting to look at his face close up while he read to us.

"That's enough for tonight, girls," he said after a while. "I'll read you some more tomorrow night." He hadn't finished a chapter. The next night we carried it to him again. He only read a little that night before he said, "You don't want to hear anymore of this, do you? I'll read you some of my story." He picked up *The Caine Mutiny* and began to read it out loud to us. I don't remember that story either.

But often he came into the kitchen in the middle of cleanup. "I don't want the girls to finish the dishes tonight." My mother frowned. "No arguments about it now. I want to read them 'The Ancient Mariner.'" "She let us go into the living room with him. It was the only time that ever happened. He read to us that night for hours. "Do you understand what's happening so far?" He read us each note on the side of the page. He wanted us to see what a strange figure the old sailor cut in the fancy wedding hall, the other people there didn't know what to make of him. I looked at the book where it lay on his knees. His cracked hands held the blue book against his gray work pants, he fingered the tips of the white pages a little, while he explained and waited to be sure we understood.

I liked the part about the albatross, he always comes back, and the part about not having to do the dishes. The next night we had to do the dishes, before he read to us. Mom made that clear, but then he finished the rest of the poem. The reading of "The Ancient Mariner" was a one time thing, but *Wuthering Heights* was as seasonal as spring.

He read it over and over. Each time he insisted on just how very good it is, how very well written, as if someone didn't agree, as if anyone would dare to. Again the kitchen, always after supper.

He appears in the doorway between the living room and the kitchen. Standing there in his ripped clothes, in his sleeveless undershirt, shoes off, *Wuthering Heights* in hand. "Rose, I want the girls to stop cleaning the kitchen. I have something I want to read to you. I want you all to listen to this."

My hands still covered with soap suds, I turn around, cross my arms, and lean against the sink. My sister is leaning against the stove with a washrag in her hand, my mother frowning slightly, quizzical, rests in a chair near where he stands. She seems pleased but puzzled after ten years of marriage that this reader of the high steel, this Heathcliff of her own, is her husband. "Now I want you to listen very carefully to this. You have to appreciate the setting, to see what a good writer she is, you have to understand that the guest doesn't know that the room that he is sleeping in is Catherine's bedroom. So he goes to sleep and has these dreams. . . ."

He created those reveries for us, these waking dreams, "Just listen to the way she puts this, just *listen to this*," and teaches us that the words written on the moors of one century can be taken into the middle of a dirty kitchen in the next and make someone say, "listen to this." And we listen and listen. Rapt, mesmerized.

Before and After Tinfoil

It all started with tinfoil.

Or maybe tissues.

Paper napkins?

We lived one way—a time of constraint—before tinfoil and a completely different way after tinfoil—one that rapidly raced toward the future. Definitely using tissues changed the way we lived. When paper towels came along they changed even more. But, really, *really* it was tinfoil. Tinfoil changed everything. Tinfoil, rolled out in a long shiny line defined one way of life before and another way after.

Before tinfoil the way we looked at life went something like this: You said no thank you a lot before you said yes thank you once. You took pride in renunciation, containment, bucking up. You knew how to do things, rewire a lamp, sew a prom dress, pull an old nail out of hard wood and hammer it straight, use again, how to wash and wax Dad's car, which you did before he asked you. If grandma was making brains for lunch (Italian) you tried it and said you liked it even if it tasted weird at first (that organ texture under the tomato and garlic) so that eventually you did get to really like it. The same went for blood pudding. You wanted to be tough, able to take things, a fight in the school yard, swim out to the island in the middle of the lake, to do complicated dives which you learned on your own, to ride your bike up really long, long hills, until it got easy. You had the idea that it was up to you. And your cousins. And of course we'd all die for our religion.

Before tinfoil when there was leftover food you put it in a small bowl and put a dish on top of it and put it in the fridge or the icebox to keep. There was wax paper, but you used that only to wrap sandwiches for lunch or picnics. And sometimes you reused the wax paper. You never balled up anything and threw it away if it had any life left in it. Wrapping paper. String from bakery boxes if your relatives brought Italian pastry from New York. Brown paper grocery bags were not just saved and reused. They were cut up to be used as packing paper.

Before, we all wore hand-me-downs. We passed our clothes down the family line, we remade our mother's discarded dresses into skirts for ourselves, "The fabric is still good." Ironed our sheets and pillow cases, hankies and Dad's work clothes. We lined the garbage pail with newspaper in such a way that you could pick it up and carry it outside as a bundle.

When you traveled away from your family you made a collect call to your home asking for, say, Joanna Has Arrived. The operators asked incredulously, "Your *name is* Joanna Has Arrived?" Baldfaced, you asserted, "Yes, it is." Your mother told you to do that.

If an actual long distance call was made to Grandma and Grandpa in Arizona where they went for the winter, say on Thanksgiving, it was organized long before and the whole family arrived in one of the family kitchens at an exact predetermined hour. Every man, woman, and child in the family got on the phone, all the grandchildren, all the children, each in-law, to say, "Hello, how are you? What's the weather like in Arizona today? That warm?" In the background others said, "Come on. Do you know how much this call is costing? We've been on for ten minutes now." Afterward when the phone bill came the cost was divided by five families. $1.16 per family.

Before tinfoil we had company over for coffee and, after tinfoil people watched TV.

We had been living in an era of good constraint. So at first tinfoil was an amusement—a fascinating new toy. "What will they think of next?" Our mothers all bought it. But its shiny presence seemed more like a Christmas tree decoration, delightful, charming, but not real or practical. It was used very sparingly for special situations. "Mom, can I use the tinfoil on this?" Maybe it was Christmas and we used it for the Christmas cookies.

"All right, but be careful. Use just what you need." But it was confusing. Buying box after box would be ridiculous. Why would any normal person do that? The same with tissues too. And paper towels. All that excess, all that using and discarding. That was opposite of everything about the way we lived.

We had hankies and we washed and ironed them. Everyday ones and fancy lace ones for Sunday and holidays. We had rags to mop up messes.

Being wasteful was as bad as being conceited. Using too much of anything showed a carelessness that meant you weren't thinking right. You were too smart for your own good, you had no respect, you were a *citrull'*. There was plenty in our lives, plenty of food, clothes, toys, dolls, trucks, bikes, sleds, plenty of air, water, snow, sun, stars, trees, grass, plenty of slaps and laughs, but just because there was plenty that didn't mean you should be stupid about it.

But this was a pivot point on which life was turning, a spinning outward and away from a life grounded in making to a life of using up and throwing away.

Later there would be fights between mothers and daughters and mothers-in-law and daughters-in-law, "You should see they way she tears off paper towels and mops up the floor with a wad of them when something spills. What, does she think we're made of money? What a waste."

"Oh, my mother watches me like a hawk. Every time I use a piece of tin foil she's after me. 'Oh Ma,' I say to her, 'Why do you even buy this stuff if you don't want anyone using it?'" But back then at the beginning we were all the same careful and sensible people.

We looked to each other, we had our own opera, our own tornado. We were in our own vortex, not seeking the world or looking outward. Who needed the opera of having too much? We *were* too much. But when tinfoil came it signaled a new way, stretching its long silvery road out toward the world beyond us, beckoning us to throw our money away, to use things up then to throw them away, to throw ourselves upon the winds of change, to go off, out, away into the world, away from our centers, our families, ourselves, off into the land of want, want, want. And we did.

By the time we were using it without thinking about it life had changed—a new kind of desire had been let loose in us, in the world and we were all changed irrevocably forever. *Che pecato*. What a shame.

Stitching Our Voices Together

Italian cousins are a special kind of intense friend siblings. Gilda, Diane, Lucia, Joanna, Clorinda, Beatrice: we were the six older girl cousins in my large Italian family in Waterbury, Connecticut. There were two older boys, then the six of us girls, then six younger boys and finally two younger girls. So symmetry and alternation: boys, girls, boys, girls. The six girls were planets in our own universe, orbiting the sun of our mothers and aunts—playing house, dolls, school, secretary, doing acrobatics, swimming, riding our bikes, hiking, running, running to the store, climbing out of windows, climbing trees, doing housework, lolly-gagging in order not to help our mothers, fighting, skipping, cooking, sewing. We slipped in and our of each other's yards, houses, chairs, beds, swings, and cellars. We used our hands to hold and twist everything within reach to make what was at hand into what we wanted. Working with needles and threads for the women and girls was one of the intense centers of this making. All the grandmothers, all my aunts and all my very first friends in the world, my girl cousins, were involved in this.

We lived in each other's hair then. We live in each other's heads still: these women are my sisters. Our lives and voices were bound together by needle and thread: Jill, Didi, Lulu, Jojo, Linda, Bede, I have spun our voices in one.

I

The needle is held precisely between thumb and forefinger, the thread is licked between the lips and the tongue, the end of the thread is bitten sharply off with the front teeth so that the tip is clean and wet and will slip easily through the tiny eye of the needle.

"You roll the end of thread around your finger, like this, and pull it tight, down to the end to make a knot. Now you try it. No, just one knot is enough."

The needle penetrates the fabric, the long gentle pull through, then the final satisfying tug, to join, to hold, to finish. The soothing repetition of these motions, a kind of breathing, each stitch an inhalation, exhalation, each stitch bringing a deep immersion, disappearance into this other, like reading, meditation, swimming, or prayer.

II

We watched as the fingers of the elders flew and fluttered, fastened, fixed with needles and thread and yarn in the air around us as commonly as brushes and combs, forks and spoons. Needlework was a major idiom, the language of thread of our women. The older the woman the more elaborate her skills. In Italy as girls, they grew up spinning and weaving, making their linens for their future homes, putting them in *le casse*, the chests for keeping their *biancheria*. They learned to make lace to trim those *lenzuola* and their *fazzoletti*. All this came on the boat with them carefully packed in *le casse*.

They sewed, crocheted, knit, embroidered, tatted: made clothes, blankets, spreads, shawls, embroidered pillowcases, all of this flowing out of their dexterous fingers and needles. We'd stand near them watching the art of something from nothing come from threads and yarns and needles using patterns they had learned as children and given to us in turn. Needles and threads were at one with sitting.

They made most of their family's clothes and although our grandmother had her own treadle foot sewing machine in the sun parlor, she might just as often sew a garment by hand.

"A peddler would come around selling bolts of fabric and we'd all look. Then Mama would chose one or two bolts and that would be our fabric to sew for that year. She would cut out the patterns for dresses, shirts, and pants for everyone, for her own dress suits—from memory." Only the patterns they had learned at their elders' knees. Pleating was embedded in the shoulders and under the arms of these clothes to allow for many growth spurts.

"After Mama made all of our clothes we were allowed to have the rest of the fabric to sew with for ourselves. That was a big treat."

III

Sewing provided my mother the first aesthetic control she had over the chaotic life of the farm. She told us with pride, "Once when my mother went to Saratoga for her rheumatoid arthritis I decided to paint the downstairs and sew all new curtains for the dining room and living room."

She made her own clothes as soon as she was able, elaborate outfits: dresses and suits with inset panels and complicated pockets. She tailored each garment to sit close and easy on her lovely young body, to be elegant and stylish, like the women in the movies she and her sisters went to see. Her sewing machine always sat prominently in our kitchen. It was her passion, her joy.

"After I bathed you girls and put you to bed—Dad would be down the street—I'd put on the radio and take out whatever I was working on at the time. I always had something going, something for you girls, maybe matching dresses—remember the plaid taffeta ones? or Easter suits for all of us or a dress for me. If the weather was warm I'd open the windows and lay out the cloth and the pattern, say, and I'd pin the pattern and cut the cloth. That might be all I'd do one night, but it made me so happy. I looked forward to it all day. That I would have that time to myself. Oh how I loved it."

My sister, Lucia, reminds me on the telephone, "Mom always said, even if I only sew one seam, I'm satisfied. Always have to have something going. Promotion dresses stand out! Turquoise taffeta. And all those matching dresses we had. I remember waking late at night to the sound of Mom's machine tearing along. She really worked that thing! It was not a contemplative activity for her!"

If stitching was meditation, sewing on the machine often started as a hum, then a revving up, zip, zip, then into a tearing roar—the machine speeded up into an explosion of stitching. It was less a machine than an animal of stitching, its needle moving up and down so fast it was a small terror of mouth eating up fabric and thread. The sewer fed the creature as fast and straight as possible.

She made our sundresses, our pinafores, our ruffled skirts, our halter tops, first Holy Communion dresses, our confirmation dresses, our first day of school dresses, our promotion day dresses. While we watched, we got fitted and later wore her work proudly. Later than that, the pleasure of these skills was passed to us.

IV

"Button, button, who's got the button?" we sang to each other as we sat lined up on the bed in the kitchen. Each of us had hands folded prayer-like in front of our chests. The one who had the button hidden between her prayer hands went down the row, chanting, "Button, button, who's got the button," while she put her hands between all of ours and dropped the button into a set of waiting hands. The giving over of the button was partly to hide it and partly to confer honor on her cousin. Each girl pretending ostentatiously that none of us had the button while one of us guessed who actually had it. If you guessed right, you got to be the one standing up to become the next button giver. Otherwise, the person who had the button secreted in her hands, got to continue. Oh, the importance of that position! It seemed to me we played that game for uncounted hours. The pleasure of whiling away hours playing Button, Button!

"Grandma Becce taught me to embroider flowers and leaves. We embroidered on dish towels for practice first and then we moved onto pillowcases. We'd cross-stitch—little samplers—but I think Aunt Antoinette showed me that. I have these amorphous memories of being surrounded by women who taught me things, and each picked up where the last one left off. There were so many visitors to our house on the farm that I don't have clear memories about who taught me what. And of course all of you older cousins taught me what you knew as well."

"How do you do that Aunt Dora?" She's sitting in our kitchen by the pantry crocheting. There I watch her nimble fingers fly fast, rhythmically, evenly, the stitches quickly accumulating row upon row.

"Oh you want to learn how to do that?" a big laugh, she lays her work down in her lap. "Okay, I teach you," she picks it up again. "Here. You take this crochet hook. First wrap the yarn around this finger here like this. Hold it tight in your hand. Now hold the hook like this, see, now bring it under the yarn in the other hand, see. . . ." It wasn't so much language as it was all in the way the hands showed and guided. The needle is looped through the yarn, not the quick bird plucks now, but the exaggeratedly slow ones so that we can watch its loop, return, loop back in, pull up, finish. Her large belly sits back in the chair, she holds up the work, then we both bend over it to inspect. "Hmm, you see." Nod, nod.

V

Someone showed us a new thingamajig. I can't remember where the first one came from or who showed us how to do this. We'd beg for the largest empty wooden spools of thread. Then tiny nails were hammered into the top, and voila, we had made small knitting machines. Thin cotton yarn was wound in a very particular way around those nails then using a crochet hook in a series of loopings and hooking you released a tail of knitting, which emerged row by row from the bottom of the empty wooden spool. Each of us would try to outdo the other girl cousins in making the longest one. I remember that eventually we all reached the length of the sun parlor which was about twenty-five feet. That was the goal. At some point we'd tie them off and sew them into circles which we made into trivets for our tables. But that was an afterthought. The point was to do one longer and faster than anyone else.

VI

We'd be strewn around the room—a couple of us lying on couches, two or three of us stretched out on our bellies on the floor, or sitting on the arm of one of the solid old maple chairs the older cousins sat in, standing and sitting, all talking at once—each trying to get their say in, but there was no question that Gilda was the oldest of the girls and special for it. She was also taller, and had already finished first and second and third grades. Gilda had two older brothers and a newspaper route, and knew about everything first, long before we did. So she was our queen, what we all aspired to be like, a dancer, full of what I would later know was called savvy. So Lucia and Diane, the next two cousins in age, her handmaidens, could get her attention easily. Linda, Bede, and I had to push our way into the talk trying to have our say too. But Gilda and her handmaidens would loftily tell us, it wasn't like that for third graders. We'd have to wait until we were older. Then we'd see. Still, it was all girls and talk and connection. "Look at how long mine is. How do you tie on some new yarn?"

It was just us, the girls, wrapped around each other in play, in hierarchy, in competition: Gilda, Diane, Lucia, Linda, me, and Bede. Yes, we'd see.

VII

"Remember the packages to Italy? The boxes would go on the table up the farm. They'd take whatever they were sending, put it in a box, but then they'd wrap it in fabric. Was it heavy muslin? And we'd hand stitch all the seams. After that they'd seal the package with wax, melting it all along the seams with an orange wax. I wonder why we did that. Was it to make sure that no one opened it before it got there?"

We were taught early to darn socks, to sew buttons back on our own clothes.

"Do it in a pattern, either from hole to hole or in an X. But don't do it every which a way. It looks funny that way. Take it out and do it over again."

"All the baby bibs we made. Then we'd embroider them. I made one for Rocky. I was sitting with Aunt Bea up the farm while I was embroidering and shyly saying I know a song that is just right for him. What's that? she says (I can still see her sweet and bemused smile). I sing, 'Baby face, you've got the cutest little baby face, and there is no one who can take your place.' She laughed that lovely gentle way she had. We had so much time. We simply inhabited our days then. I don't know what we do now."

VIII

Every summer Grandma Crawford and Aunt Antoinette came to visit the farm and helped with the mending—some of it having accumulated from their last visits. There would be baskets of clothes with holes and missing buttons and torn sleeves, socks with holes, piled high in the sun parlor. They did this with pleasure and ease. They wanted to help my overworked Aunt Bea. Aunt Bea had five children. She did all the cooking, always had food and drink for all the endless company coming and going on the farm, for all the extra harvest help, did all the canning and cleaning of the vegetables, did all the cheese making, and all the making of sausages, and, with Grandma, all the putting up of the prosciutto.

After they'd sewn back three buttons, a deep draught of the icy lemonade made for and carried to them by my cousin Bede. A deep breath, a careful wipe of the bottom of the glass on their aprons, the glass set back down on the table at their side. They sat for hours looking up from their work over the high grassy fields and the wide blue lake, and back down to their work, slowly reducing those piles into submission.

"I'd thread a bunch of needles at once so that they wouldn't have to stop when they were in the middle of their mending and they could just keep going. They'd tell me how many to do with white thread if that's what they were working on right then. Later my brothers Rocky and Vito would thread the needles for them too. But you know that was usually our work. The girls inside, the boys outside."

IX

All day our fingers moved: quickly, deftly, delicately, twisting, turning, tying, binding, joining; if we pinched, pinned, picked, prodded, poked; our hands lifted, threw, sorted, stirred, smoothed, soothed; these, our most essential tools, fingers and hands—the co-joined extensions ready for our endlessly capacious manual life—cooking, gardening, laundering, ironing, cleaning, painting, bathing, picking, preparing, *but* needlework was also our artisanal satisfaction.

"I was about eleven, I think—my mom was expecting Danny, and I wanted to make something for the baby. Grandma wasn't happy that I was allowed to know my mother was expecting. I don't know how we got past that to the sweater.

"But that was the first time I made something that was actually useful. I can remember learning all the hooks and loops. Grandma taught me a stitch that was called a triple loop. You crocheted three loops before hooking into the next loop. I made a hat to match, a little layette. I felt competent to be able to do that. I wonder what happened to that sweater set. My mother had him wear it. So I guess it must have come out all right. I'll have to ask her.

"As we got older, we made our own Easter outfits. I remember staying up into the middle of the night to finish an outfit to wear that next day."

As hard as the men and women in our world worked, still there was time enough for coffee, coffee and, sitting on the porch talking, platters of watermelon eaten with huge slurps on a hot summer day. We were all of one place, all of this family, all of being together.

X

"In my mother's kitchen there was a small yellow cupboard. One drawer was filled with buttons that had been cut from clothes that had been made into dust rags. Another drawer held jars of hooks and eyes, snaps, black or silver, each jar color sorted for when you needed them. The next drawer was filled with neatly sorted and color coded rickrack, bias tape, binding tape. Another drawer held zippers that had been ripped out of old clothing.

"On shelves at the back of my mother's closet there were shoe boxes filled with more zippers, sorted for color and length. There was one box just for beige, another with just white, then a box of black and finally a multicolored box. You never bought a new zipper unless, strangely, there wasn't one that matched the cloth you were working with."

Our eyes fell naturally into the laps of our grandmothers, out great-aunts, our mothers, our aunts as they sat and worked. It wasn't even always a passing on to us of these skills, this capacity; it was the natural order of things. Needlework was a major idiom, the language of the threads of our women.

Running stitch, basting stitch, backstitch, blanket stitch, buttonhole, hem stitch, slip basting, the whip stitch. Each one carefully demonstrated—the older woman looking over the girl's shoulder, "Make small, even stitches, the smaller the stitches the better the work." The girl bent over the fabric, the needle in her hand, the fabric passed back for another careful and slow demonstration, "Now watch, see how I put the needle just under the fabric here."

The girl's chin is lifted in concentration. Initiate, novice, apprentice—there is only mutual concentration between them, the fabric, the needle, the stitch, and the passing on of this dexterity. "You should almost not be able to see the stitches if you've done them right."

"The buttonhole stitch is the same as the blanket stitch only very tiny and very close together. You cut the slit later. First you do the two rows of each side, leaving enough to cut open the middle." A revelation: big made little creates another skill.

XI

"When I was about twelve or thirteen I bought ten yards of an orange calico for ten cents a yard with my allowance money. I was so thrilled with my bargain and I started to make my first dress. It was going to have a fitted bodice, with a very full gathered skirt and puffed sleeves a zipper in the side. I worked on that dress for probably a week. When the dress was finished it was all there, but. I knew I would never wear it. The sleeves weren't set right. The zipper was set in lumpy. First I took off the puffed sleeves. I was going to make it into a sleeveless dress. Still not right. I decided to take the bodice and the skirt apart and make a blouse and a skirt. It would be easier to do separate zippers. It still didn't work. I decided to just make a full gathered skirt. With a cummerbund waistband. I can't remember why that didn't work. In the end the ten yards was reduced to a not so great orange calico cummerbund, and I was deflated but after that I knew how to sew. I learned everything on those ten yards and the endlessly revised dress and that final cummerbund. I think I may have worn the cum-

merbund twice. I can see it hanging on a hook in my closet, the banner
of my apprenticeship."

XII

All the aunts and mothers used the tiniest stitches for hand finishing,
careful button holes, invisible hems. We were taught to do the same. A
hem should barely show, if the stitches were small enough and even
enough. We had contempt for hems that were doubled over. You could
see the bulk at the bottom of the shirt or leg. Terrible. Bad sewing.
Their mothers didn't teach them right.

"Whenever I wanted my mother to sew something special for me,
she'd say, 'Well then, you have to cook!' There were four kids and I was
the oldest. I'd desperately want something special, a fancy sleeve or a
pocket so I always agreed to cook!

"She'd be sitting at the sewing machine by the window looking out
over the yard and my father's garden. I'd be at the other end of the
kitchen by the stove. From where my Mom would sit, she would give
me my instructions. She'd never look up from the sewing, to see if I was
doing it right or come to the stove to check on things. She'd sew. I'd
make the meatballs—'Now put breadcrumbs in,' she'd say as she bent
over the Singer 'How much?' 'Just shake some in.' Of course, we had
made the breadcrumbs by rolling dried bread between two sheets of
wax paper. Every ingredient gained me a seam or two.

"'Now chop the garlic, and add it to the heated olive oil. When the
garlic's brownish, add the tomatoes.' 'How brown, how much tomato?'
'Brown, not too brown. Golden brown,' as she concentrated on the
sewing. 'You know, one of the jars of tomato we canned this summer.'
As long as I heard the sewing machine humming along, I kept cooking.

"You know, the sewing machine stool was always my seat at the
dinner table. No one ever sat on the sewing machine stool at dinner
except me. Every night, I'd carry it from under the sewing machine and
bring it to the kitchen table. I guess that stool brought the cooking and
sewing together. She did teach me later, but it ended up that I liked to
cook better."

XIII

Auntie Ag would carefully pull out the hemming stitches if something
had to be rehemmed so that she could reuse the thread. She'd wrap the
old thread around an empty spool she had saved just for this purpose to

be used again. If she didn't have an empty spool she'd use a piece of folded paper. The crimped threads from the commercial hems unwrapped as she threaded the next needle. The lick, the point, the aim, and the slipping of the thread in. She'd pull the thread through, then flatten each crimp with the wet tips of her fingers. A head tilt, a leaning toward the window's light. Yes, it looks good.

"Even though I never liked sewing, after I took sewing classes in grammar school my mother would make me take the old sheets when they were worn out in the middle and cut them up into squares and rectangles. Then I had to hem those pieces to make handkerchiefs and *mappines*. Nothing went to waste in my mother's house. Nothing. We reused everything.

"My Grandfather Louis always wore a white dress shirt and when his collars got frayed my mother would take them off and turn them the other way around and sew them back on. My god how hard she worked.

"And she used to make all my dance costumes for the recitals. Then the other mothers asked her to make them for their children too. She made a little extra money on the side that way every year. She'd be sewing until the middle of the night in the room off the kitchen.

"But I was never interested it sewing. I was always at the dance studio working with Barbara Hyland."

XIV

We were all taught early to darn socks, to sew buttons back on our own clothes.

"Do it in a pattern, either from hole to hole or in an X. But don't do it every which a way. It looks funny that way. Take it out and do it over again."

Over stitch, over casting, over basting, interfacing, linings.

"My Grandmother Padula made gigantic bedspreads of fine lace for everyone in her family from thin, thin thread. So delicate, so intricate—she crocheted them. Then she made me a gold crochet dress from brown satin ribbon. So beautiful. I still have it.

"Did you go to the Girls' Club too? I was so excited. I asked my mother to sign me up for art classes, but instead she signed me up for sewing and cooking. 'What good are art classes going to do you?' I was so disappointed. But it was a nice place; it had a lovely feeling to it. The women were so lovely, made it a warm welcoming kind of a place. I loved learning to sew, but I had been so excited that I was going to take art classes."

XV

In seventh and eighth grades we took sewing and cooking classes at school, but by then our mothers had taught us more than the teachers could pass on. We used those classes to make new clothes for ourselves. Half the time we were teaching the other kids how to do it.

"Iron the fabric first. The pattern will sit better on the fabric. Lay it out on a hard surface. Take the time to clear everything out of your way. Use the floor or the table. Pin it slowly. Basting can save you a lot of mistakes. Don't skip that step."

Iron, layout, pin, cut out, pin, baste, sew, press the seam open. Seams, darts, gathers.

"Remember the circle skirts in grammar school sewing classes?"

We didn't use thimbles; the tips of our fingers were filled with tiny perforations, sometimes tiny drops of blood, especially if it was a big project—over the years the hems of our skirts got wider and wider, and then came the years of crinolines.

XVI

We loved going down to Bedford's and Fishman's fabric stores. We'd spend hours there looking through long rows of pattern books, Butterick, McCall's, Vogue, each of us roaming around, feeling fabrics for long contemplative hours.

Silk organza, taffeta, satin, pois de soie, boucle` chiffon, silk crepe de Chine, the luxurious sounds wrap around my tongue, the feel of their lusciousness in my hands; muslin, lawn, tulle, georgette, white eyelet, madras, for summer; the lightness in the hand, the heft and substance of gabardine, corduroy, a good Scots wool plaid, herringbone, and mohair, for winter. We'd run the names over our tongues with the pleasure of touch and competence as we discussed which to use for which garment.

"The first prom dress I made was out of gorgeous white satiny fabric. The top was strapless and it was very fitted and came down just over my hips. Then I made a skirt that sat under the top. I think I used two different patterns for that gown." ·

"We went on to suits and prom dresses, kind of fearless. Well, because everybody did it and nobody acted like it was hard. I remember having to stand on the kitchen table and turn slowly, slowly while someone else 'pinned' you. Mom bought that weird contraption with the movable ruler to measure how high from the table you were to mark the hem. Then we squeeze that rubber bulb with white powder in it and it would puff out of this thing to mark the place. It was all marked for you to pin it up. We thought this was the height of fancy. We did sew like crazy, didn't we all?"

"What do you think of this pattern? Does this color work on me?"

We'd savor the touch and weigh the fabric gently in our hands. We'd consult each other. Enjoy each speculation. Satisfied with our decisions, we'd take our fabric and patterns home on the bus to the North End. There was the sheer joy of entering those tiny jewel-like notions stores with their shelves running to the ceiling, their cabinets full of sewing supplies: pins, needles, chalk, buttons, snaps, zippers, ribbons, tapes, rules, buttons, scissors. I can see the spools of ribbons. Grosgrain and satin ribbon spools, lined up in by color and width so that you could look, touch, unspool them, imagining that someday you might be able to buy as many yards as you liked in every color and width—buy the widest one in blue for a sash on the next dress you're going to make. But for today you had enough to buy a half of a yard of one inch red grosgrain ribbon to tie up our pony tails. Row upon row of what we might need, all calling to us for what we might make. "I'm going to have to take this in. Would you pin it for me?"

"For my junior prom I was still sewing my prom dress, my hair up in curlers when my date arrived, with his corsage. My mother tsk tsked, 'I'll finish it for you. Go get ready.'

"'It's okay Mom. I'm almost finished.' I couldn't have her take that powerful I-made-it-myself feeling away from me at the last minute.

'I'll be ready in a few minutes.'"

As much our world as the world of the women now.

"When I was in high school I worked at Eli Moore's and I told them I'd do all their alterations for customers. How nervy. I'd never do that now. But I did it then.

"Later I worked for Mister Marshall who had an upholstery store. I learned so much from him. I learned how to make draperies; how to put fabric on the walls, how to make piping, cutting the fabric on a bias, how to make slipcovers. He was from Scotland. I helped him make huge fantastic drapes for some theater in Waterville. That was amazing. Whenever a customer was coming in the store he'd say, 'Hide these other bolts of fabric and get her fabric out so she'll think we're only working on her job.'"

XVII

After college, my sister began to spin and weave and she brought her work up the farm to show our grandmother.

"She went quietly off into the dining room and pulled this spindle out and pulled out a beautiful piece of heavy linen, a dish cloth, and she described the whole process to me. How they raised the flax and then they would cut it, then lay it in a brook with stones on top so that the water running over it would break down the fibers, softening it, getting it from a piece of plant life to something you could spin."

"That's a old thing. I use it when I was a little gal in *mia madre*'s house. I bring it in *le cass son venute con me. Tre cass'. Biancheria e roba da mangiare. tutt le bianchiari,* [in my chest, three chests came with me *ala'merica,* my linens and stuff to eat]," Grandma said to Lucia, laughing showing us her old spindle. "Grandma gave me that spindle."

XVIII

By the last part of her life, when she wasn't working, my grandmother's hands, twisted and broken with rheumatoid arthritis, lay mute and stupid, two drugged *bestie,* still in her lap like the merely momentarily abandoned tools that they were. As twisted and as full of pain as they were she'd always pick them back up and set them going again.

We were a world unto ourselves; the Girls Club, the Home Economics classes, these were all just small extensions of the important center—us, our fabric, our family, the girls, all of us on the couch playing Button, Button, on the sun porch making our long, long tails on the thread spools, at our machines making our clothes, measuring and pinning each other's hems. The outside world just wasn't that important. It was just there for us to live in. We were almost too busy with work and play and ourselves to pay it much attention. It was 'Merican and bland. Our world was rich and complicated, full of us and making. One generation to the next, the grandmothers, mothers, aunts, and the girls.

We didn't know whether what we did was highly skilled or astonishing. We were having fun. We made things. From baby bibs to prom dresses. We lived in a land where what isn't—then is. The reach toward the fatal human aspiration—trying to touch the divine—making—the making—ex nihilo—from *not* to *is.*

Coffee And

Coffee and sugar were the narcotics that stimulated the days and nights where I learned about intimacy in that great and terrible school, the Italian American family. We pressed up against one another as if our very breathing depended on our merciless connections.

The adults in my family drank pot after pot of coffee throughout the day, from when they woke early in the morning, until very late at night when they fell into bed exhausted from their caffeine-fueled, furious days.

With the coffee always came the "and." A couple of times a week we baked so that there would always be "and," that little bit of something sweet that inevitably accompanied the many cups of coffee they drank to keep themselves bound to their relentless routines. We used recipes my illiterate grandmother carried in her head from Tolve when she followed her husband to America; *mastachiole, pizza dolce, torta di ricotta, cartadade.* We added to this abundance other recipes our mothers clipped from *Woman's Day* and *Good Housekeeping,* learned on the assembly line at Scovill's Factory, or got from their neighbors: Russian Wedding cookies, jam cookies, brownies. Intimacy and coffee "and" were inextricably connected in my family.

The chemistry of the caffeine, the sugar, the connection with one another (so intense as to make us vibrate) combining as they did with a rage for perfection, made for standards of behavior so exacting, so naturally inevitable, that we threw ourselves at every task, work or play, ferociously, with a blind certainty that this *was* reality. Nothing was relative. Everything was absolute. Must and should was the air we breathed.

Our mothers had been raised in America but with 15th century customs; on the pig farm where they lived as children, they had drawn their own water from the well and baked their weekly bread in the brick oven my grandfather built down by the road. They had risen at dawn to milk the cows and collect the eggs. After school they weeded the garden, cleaned the chicken coops, helped with all the endless chores of farm life. One summer they spent hours in intense heat picking bones out of the pig manure, because my grandfather had heard he could earn money for bags of bones. They grew most of their food. In addition to everyday cooking, they made their own sausage, proccintto, many kinds of cheese, and of course, their own wine. They grew up with screaming and violence as an ordinary response to even minor deviations from these 15th century mores.

This drove them to heights of great accomplishment: Whatever they undertook they did flawlessly. They were accomplished seamstresses, amazing cooks, wonderful hostesses, extraordinary gardeners. They were beautiful, immensely strong, extremely hard working and had no idea that they were allowed to take note of this. That was the family standard.

For most of my generation the violence had diminished, but fury still raced along our currents. "Get over here. Who broke this cup? How did this happen? Come here. Right now! I'm going to kill you." The hand hung in the air, swinging, a cupped threat, the twist of skin tight between your mother's fingers. For some of my cousins, real beatings.

In my time too, the children were expected to work at their parents' side. Our fathers painted and wallpapered the rooms and redid our kitchens after long days of physical work. The kids helped. Our mothers and fathers grew the vegetables and the flowers. The boys were in charge of all yard work, garage work, and basement work. The mothers and daughters did the housecleaning, the laundry, the ironing, the sewing, and the shopping. We canned the tomatoes, the peaches, the pears, pickled the eggplant, made the jam.

When we were little our mothers made our communion dresses, when we were in high school we sewed our own prom dresses. As soon as my generation was able, we sewed most of our clothes, shopping for the best quality fabric, spending hours in Fishman's Fabric Shop on Bank Street, fingering the wool, cotton, satin, considering it, matching it to the Butterick Patterns we spent more hours choosing. But we wouldn't buy it unless the fabric was on sale.

For fun we made our own liqueurs, fresh pasta, baked panetone, pizza, (*'abizz'*) bread, focaccia (*fucazz'* we called it), made ricotta, *scamozza*, and *provolone*.

It wasn't as if we didn't play. We did, ferociously. When we swam we swam to the farthest shores and learned to do the most complicated dives, elaborate ice skating tricks. When we climbed trees we raced each other to the highest limbs. When we gathered for our annual Memorial Day picnic there was first an homage to America, bowls of chips, trays of nuts, dips. Bowls of macaroni salad, potato salad, trays of cold cuts. Our food followed: trays of manicotta, lasagna, meatballs, sausage, roast chicken with potatoes, sausage, onions, and peppers.

Coffee carried in jars wrapped in *mappines* to keep it warm. Gallons of lemonade, orangeade, iced tea, the bottom of each jar coated with a thick syrupy layer of sugar. There were platters of desserts.

If ferocity was our code, oblivion to the code was our commandment. Making any comment on how the family operated was a sin. Calling attention to yourself was another. "Can you imagine she had to go and brag about her sauce. We all make sauce. Who does she think she is? So conceited."

It was the hidden price of silence that was the most exacting. Fueling this illusion of ordinary and easy perfection meant you weren't allowed to get credit for what you naturally worked so hard to accomplish. Instead, there was only blame for trivial failures. Perhaps we thought that if we were silent maybe someday we would be declared *good*. But, to my knowledge, no one ever was.

Often, deep in our night's sleep my sister and I were shaken loose from our dreams by my mother's caffeinated screams, "Peter, Peter, Peter," she'd cry out for my father to protect her. "There's a man, a man, he's coming in the window." That murderous man came to get her so many nights. He was there to tell her she hadn't done enough. She should rise from her sleep and wash the kitchen floor again. Her father had repeatedly condemned all his daughters, in his Tolovese dialect, *"Quest' non mai ess' femin' della cas'* [You'll never make good housewives]." In Italian it would be, *Questa non devono essere femine della casa*, but in any language it's the ethnic father's controlling insult.

My mother cut back her coffee intake a little, when Dr. Lombardi, our family doctor, explained that unlimited amounts of coffee might be contributing to those nightmares. But never enough to stop her real nightmare. She would never be sufficient. No one could. *Basta cosi.*

Weekday afternoons after school the girls helped their mothers start dinner. Then the kids all went outside to play while the mothers had their coffee and. Pretty typically, the only time these women sat still was when they served each other coffee.

"Papa had no business leaving everything to Rocky." They are sitting at one of the Formica tables that dominated our kitchens. It's four o'clock, four-thirty. A *chambotte'* or *pizzaola* is simmering on the stove while we're waiting for our fathers to come home, dirty, sweaty, and hungry from their jobs on construction sites or at the factories.

"We worked on the farm just as hard as Rocky did when we were kids. Didn't we get up at six o'clock in the morning to milk the cows and feed the chickens before we went to school? Those freezing cold mornings. The fire in the stove out." My Aunt Vicky, the youngest daughter starts the conversation. She has combed her hair and put on bright red lipstick, just after my mother called her to say the coffee was on. My mother, too, keeps a comb and lipstick just inside the cupboard by the kitchen door, in case she hears someone coming up the driveway.

"After Mama got her arthritis I had to get up before everyone and light the stove to make Papa's coffee. Some mornings I had to break the ice on the top of the water jug to make the coffee. Oh, it was bad. Papa forgot all that." This is from my mother.

"We *all* worked hard. I was always the one that had to carry up all the wood for the stove the night before. And carry in all the water. God how I used to worry about how I was going to smell going to school after I milked the cows. I'd scrub my hands until they were raw." My Aunt Tony who works in the factory has stopped on the way home to pick up her kids, Nicky and Diane, who'd get off the school bus with us.

"What are you going to do? That's the way it is in Italian families." My Auntie Ag, the oldest, the one who accepts her fate. She raised these sisters and their only brother Rocky.

"I know, Ag." Aunt Vicky says, "The boys are everything. The girls are nothing. But that's not right."

The girls, my mother and her sisters, nursed that conversation, nudged it along the same road for twenty years after my grandfather died. Leaving everything to Rocky, he had declared their work null and void. "Do you know in Italy, I read this somewhere, it's illegal to do that? You can't do that in Italy. How's that?" One would remind the others again.

"And Mama too. She could change it now if she wanted to. It's not right."

"You know Rocky's her favorite. 'Attsa' the way you fadder want it.' That's what she says every time. I told her. Mamma that's not right to leave it like that. You have five children. Not one."

"Here try these cookies. Marie gave me the recipe. Her mother, Donna Paola, used to make them, she said. I don't remember Mama making these. They must be Sicilian."

"I shouldn't. We have to have dinner soon. Just a little piece."

"Wait I'll heat you up." The half-empty cup would be filled.

The coffee, the sweet, and the talk got them through. It never changed anything. It never mitigated the unchangeable ferocity with which every job was engaged, it never released their furies, it never changed the fact that no amount of work would ever be enough to appease the beasts that had been reared within.

Sometimes the fathers arrived home at the end of these "gab sessions." They'd sit and have a cup before they went to take a nap, or went out to their gardens. "You girls have nothing to do, but sit and have coffee." In their greasy and ripped work clothes they'd stand in the doorways, teasing their wives and sisters-in-law.

"*You* should have our 'nothing to do.'" The women would turn their heads away in mock and real fury. "At least your day is finished. We're not even half way through. I don't go to bed sometimes until two, three in the morning."

More often though, before the men started pulling their trucks into the driveways one or another aunt would say, "I have to get home. I haven't even started dinner. Joe hates it if I'm not there when he walks in the door. Men are such babies."

"I know," my mother chimes in. "You know what Peter asked me the other day? Where did I keep the toilet paper. He doesn't know how to find the toilet paper in his own house."

"Men! Such a bunch of babies." All the aunts agree on that.

The rich confines of each other's lives enveloped and imprisoned us *and* held us safe against any worry, sickness, or misery. The whole of it encapsulated us and within it we would live and thrive or whatever roared down our roads. We barely knocked on the door as we ran in and out of each other's kitchens. We knew the damp smell of each other's cellars, where tables of dusty tools rested near shelves full of jarred tomatoes, pickled eggplant, canned peaches. When one of our aunt's or uncle's hands began swinging like a small scythe, threatening one of their kids, we knew enough to make ourselves scarce, slipping off into the yard, whispering to the victim's sibling, "What'd she do? Why's your mom so mad?" Someone was going to get a *palliade*.

We formed the populace of our own claustrophobic nation, gulping each other's air. Sometimes only our depleted exhalations were left in the room.

But on weekends and summer nights, when there was usually another round of coffee and, another kind of air filled our lungs. After the dinner dishes were washed, the stove was cleaned, the floor swept, the ironing done, when the relentless appetites of the beastly gods of duty had been appeased and they dozed briefly, most nights someone would suggest, as if it were a brand new idea, "Let's have company." While our angry gods slept we could crawl away.

Phone calls would be made, "Come over," even though only an hour before my mother might well have said, "You can't believe what your Aunt Tony told me on the phone today." Her full complaint would follow. "She said that she and that other one, your other prized aunt, went to the movies last Thursday. They didn't even call me. After all the rides to New York your father has given those girls." This slight would have been cultivated through the day, nurtured into full insult, given room and time to bloom into noxious anger.

But it was evening now. What were we going to do with this brief respite if not bind ourselves to one another more tightly?

"You can't call Auntie Ag and not call the others. They'll be hurt. I don't want to be like them. Call them too. Tell them the pot's already on. To come over." This time period straddled the pre-TV and the early TV years so evenings were still open ended, waiting to be filled with talk and coffee "and."

Sometimes the men joined us, and we laughed and talked in one kind of way. All the old stories came out and were repeated. All the sweet things the little kids had said were passed around the table again and reminded us of other family stories. But the men got tired earlier than we did. My father went down the street to play cards at the Italian Social Club. By the end of the evening it was always the women and the kids. That was when the deepest intimacies curled up around our ears: in the world of women, kids, coffee "and" and talk. At night. As the dutiful day faded and left us free.

These visits stretched deep into the late hours. Whatever bitterness rocked and roared between these women, when they gathered, they naturally fell to alliances with each other again, murmuring assents and assurances, righting each other's worlds with simple certainties, "Cripes she had no right to say that to you"; nursing each other's miseries, "Peter and I will drive up with you and Gilda to the hospital in Boston. Don't worry. I'll stay with you through the operation"; swelling each other's pride, "He looked so beautiful in his first communion suit. His hair slicked back like that. You should have seen the little smile when he spotted me walking out of church. How I wished I had my camera ready." Or gossiped. My great-grandmother would be quoted, "*A che murmurade?* Who shall we murmur about?"

We invariably sat at each other's kitchen tables. At the end of these attenuated nights, long after the men had left to go home or had gone to bed, with cup after cup poured out for each woman, with plates of cookies and cakes emptied, refilled, reluctantly one of the aunts would say, "It's late. I have to get home." That aunt would rise from the table and begin to carry the cups and saucers to the sink to be washed. That was the signal for everyone to get up and help. Although siblings might fight after dinner—"It's your turn to do the dishes"—when there was "company," even our aunts, each of us wanted to show, almost ostentatiously that she had been brought up "right." We'd push the grownups away from the sink, "I'll do them. Don't worry about that Auntie Ag."

Although coffee and was officially over for that night the real "and" wasn't. The mothers might pick up the conversation, while their girls did the dishes. Then we'd walk each other to the door and pause just inside, not quite ready to let go. There the talk might well continue for another half hour. Whatever the main topic for the evening had been, the talk would go deeper now. "You know what I think it *is* about her?" A piece of information that had been hidden through the whole extended discussion would be revealed now. "You know what she did one time to me?" And the murmured one's horrendous act, having lain dormant under the normal rules of discretion, would now be fully exposed. Everyone would add new cluckings and comments. "I always thought it was just me she did those things to. So, you too?"

"Well you know maybe it's because she never was that pretty. Even when we were girls. She was kind of chunky. Remember?" Then another addendum, "Well her father was so mean to her. I hear he beat her terrible. I remember her even in high school. She always had like this scared look. Once I saw some marks on her back when she was changing her blouse, all bruised, red and blue. It was terrible. Like she had been hit with, I don't know what, who knows . . . ?"

"Well we all were scared of Papa too. Don't you remember the beatings he gave us?"

"Yeah Tony, but her father was even worse than Papa. At least Papa laughed and sang too."

"Yeah. When he wasn't whacking us."

"Yeah, but not like that. That was terrible."

"I gotta get home. Joe must be wondering where I've gotten to."

Then we'd leave our posts around the door frame and walk our company down the driveway to the sidewalk, really a dirt path at the side of the road, and kiss each other good night again. We were at the edge of the visit now, under the clear stars, the cool of darkness. A couple of the younger boys would be playing tag on the lawn, the rest of the kids were hanging onto their mothers, but not saying a word. We didn't want to break the spell. The grownups were *saying* things. One of my aunts would quickly dart a look around at the kids upturned faces, asking herself, Should I say it in front of them? before she turned her gaze back to her sisters. But the night would beckon, restraint was loosened a bit more, "But I feel sorry for her. You know what I heard about her husband. He's stepping out on her."

The pleasure of that moment. Being let into the adult world. The women and kids gathered, the talking, the quick intake of small gulps of air at news of the scandal. Maybe my mother's hand would be stroking my hair—a brief recess from our daily fights. "I gotta go. It's late. I don't know what we're doing standing here." We'd all laugh.

Then, "We'll walk you home. It's dark." We'd walk them home just up the street. Another excuse to extend the visit, the talk. Sometimes the night continued this way for another hour. There would be more talk, "You think that's true what they're saying about Toosie's husband?" Then my aunts and cousins would have to walk us back down the street. Two of my aunts lived side by side. We lived two houses away. "It's dark. We'd better walk you back."

Finally, at maybe one, one-thirty in the morning, just between Mrs. Goodenough's and Miss Simpkin's houses, the houses that lay between us and them, we'd tear ourselves away and say goodnight. "Come on girls we *really* have to get home," my mother's arms around each of us shepherding us home.

Each of those almost goodbye moments allowed discretion and defenses to loosen and fall. Each time we declared the night at an end the conversation was free to go in a little deeper, to allow more to rise up. Out there in the safety of the late dark night, the rules slipped and what my mother and aunts had held in their hearts was allowed to emerge. This caffeinated intimacy, had about it love born of the animal grouping, life lived in clusters, the connection of house to house, body to body, breath to breath, whispered secrets in the dark. Our own nation, tribe, and state.

Coffee was the elixir, the fuel, sugar sweetened the bitter, the talk and being together was the "and." If it never made the furies abate, still we had each other in a way that has spoiled me for the thin and ordinary connections in currency now. I escaped my family in a rage, needing to loosen their claustrophobic bonds, but I miss the "and."

Words and Rags

There is a hierarchy of rags in my house on North Main Street; the very good dust rags, the regular rags, the soaked-with-oils-and-waxes polishing rags, and finally the under-the-sink rags. Our old clothes, old sheets and towels and *mappines* are ripped into squares and each, according to the quality of the cloth, designated to its rag station. Work clothes, towels, anything of a rough, substantial cloth are mopping rags, for washing the linoleum floors, or for turpentining and oiling the wood floors twice a year, or for doing rough jobs like cleaning the paint brushes. The rags descend from high to low station, as they rip and wear further, until they are in their final incarnation as under-the-sink rags. Old sheets, napkins, and *mappines* become regular rags. These all-purpose rags do the hard work of everyday cleaning, but these eventually become under-the-sink rags to clean our filthiest messes. There, dried into dirty gray twists, these under-the-sink rags hang over the pipe beneath the sink, ready for the next dirty job, until they shred from overuse.

Good cotton clothes, once they are too frayed to be worn even as work clothes become the "good" dust rags. These clothes have been washed so often they have become flimsy. Worn-out underwear is perfect for this category. That's when we rip them into squares and, inaugurated as dust rags, they float in flimsy lightness over our furniture. These have the highest place and rank, the queen's standard in our procession. I can fold the regular rags—they go in the back of the *mappin'* drawer—but the "good" rags have to be ironed before they are folded, then carefully placed in neat piles at the back of my mother's top bureau drawer behind her underwear.

The *mappin'* is the flag of our everyday life. Though not of the same high rank and station as the good dust rags, the *mappin'* is ever present, always ready to mop, wipe, dab, every ordinary bit of mess and dirt. Slung over our shoulders, it's a mantle conferring affiliation in our female world. It's our job to keep nature and civilization perfectly balanced: nature with all its incumbent mess outside, us neatly inside. All dirt, grass, leaves, insects are to be swept, dusted, pushed back out through windows and doors. If they can't be pushed out, these bits of fluid nature, always wanting back in, are to be vacuumed, scoured, dumped, made to disappear. All wood must be scrubbed, waxed and polished until it resembles a material as far from the wildness of nature as possible. All stone, clay, glass must gleam, glimmer, and shine—vested of every rough uneven bit of soil, or tree or mountain it may have emerged from. Our rags are our implements—the female equivalent of hammers, chisels, and saws—but the *mappin'* is first among these, the most important tool in our polished female world.

"What a mess!"

"Quick. Where's the *mappin'*?"

"Wipe that up!"

Things are often *sciangiat'*, *strisciliat'*, *strambl'*, *sporc'* in Waterbury. Respectively these mean: broken down, tangled up, a mess, confused, or dirty. There're a lot of dirty, mixed-up messes in Waterbury. What if you are *'broglon'*, someone who makes a big mess? *No' buon'*, or *non* good. What if you're *stunad'*, out of it, stupefied, *citrull'*, a cucumber (that dumb), and brazen about it? This could mean that you're *scustomad'*, *mal educa't*, *senza educazion'*, without custom, badly educated, without education, in short, ill-mannered, ill-mannered, ill-mannered. Bad, bad, bad.

If you know what's good for you, you'd better *stata citt'* and *fate fatti tui'*, shut up and mind your own business. Because if it turns out you're *fracomoda'*, too damn comfortable, so comfortable as to be unable to move, lazy—which definitely makes us the kind of girls who will *mai ess femini' della cas'*, never be good housewives—we're going to get straightened out but good, with such a *palliad'*, such a beating because you're making your mother *schiatt'*, burst.

So it's essential to get these messes cleaned up, straightened up. *Subit' mo'!* Immediately! Now! If we're up the farm with Gramma and we answer back, "I didn't make that mess, Gramma. She did." Then she'll say, "*Citt' na nonna.*" Be quiet, Gramma, meaning, you be quiet, so you might as well just be quick about it and get that *mappin'*. Gramma, like all the old-timers, addressed the children with her own appellation. "Gramma, give Gramma kiss," Gramma says, extending her permanently wrinkled, permanently garlicky cheek toward you.

My mother, my sister, and I have a *mappin'* slung over our shoulders as we go about our work in the kitchen, to sweep past our mouths after we taste some steak *pizzaiol'* from the pan on the stove tasting the combination of steak with peppers, tomatoes, onions, garlic potatoes, all simmering in olive oil. Does it need salt? A little more hot? Or if we grab a bit of salad from someone's plate when we're clearing the table, we hold the *mappin'* just under our chins as we lift the tomato dripping with dressing to our lips. Then we whip the *mappin'*, ready for us to whip down to wipe the olive oil that dribbled on to the floor. A quick shake of the *mappin'* into the sink and it's clean again. Like kissing something up to God, shaking it out makes the *mappin'* immediately clean. Unless it's just come out of the *mappin'* drawer, it's always a little damp and makes the perfect rag to swipe every ordinary spill and mess.

The *mappin'* is as basic to our lives as food. We're out to clean the dirt off our hands and the manure off our peasant feet.

There are only two or three "good" *mappines* to use when company comes. The linen ones, always clean, ironed with perfect creases, are taken out of the linen closet a couple of times a year to dry the gold-trimmed etched glass water goblets that my parents still have left from their wedding presents. When company's coming we take the glasses down from over the fridge and wash them in very hot, hot water. Then we dry them with the linen towels—the good *mappines*—until the glasses squeak. But those are very rare occasions. Maybe it's because the New York relatives are visiting.

The everyday *mappines* have been recently laundered (at least one laundry a day), ironed, and folded in the precise and prescribed way—first lengthwise in three, then folded in half—and laid in piles in the *mappin'* drawer exactly to the left of the equally ripped and ironed and folded cloth napkins. None of these are very far from their rag incarnation.

Aunt Toni, *'ntonett*, stops on her way home from Scovills, the factory where she works, to have coffee and with her sisters—*Vittoriuzz'*, Aunt Vicky, *'Rica'*, Auntie Ag, whose name is *Archangela,* and my mother, *Rosa,* who is also Aunt Rose or Ro except for my father who calls her *Bellezz'*, in both love and anger. When the aunts have finished gabbing, Aunt Toni stands up and pulls a *mappin'* from the drawer to dry the dishes, "Rose, I don't have your money, but at least I have real *mappines*. These are holes with a little rag around them. Is this how you buy those hats of yours? Break down and buy a new *mappin'* for God's sake."

Mappin' is our dialect word for dishtowel, but how *'Merican (*pronounced Mer-i-KAHN) that sounds. But the word dishtowel connotes a neat cloth folded over a towel bar near the stove, clean, intact, more for show than use. It has nothing to do with the *mappin'* as we know it. If the idea is to convert this word back to what might be, what no doubt is, the original Italian word, in the singular it would be *mappina*, plural would be *mappine*.

The daily use of dialect words in the course of the day is one of the ways we knew we were Italian and not Italian-American. Although my generation doesn't speak my mother's family's Tolvese dialect, we are definitely *Tolvese*, and Italian. We are Tolvese on my mother's side; we are *Aviglianese* on my father's. Aunt Vicky's husband is *Riminese*, Aunt Toni's husband's people are from *Fondi, Provincia di Latina,* but his parents weren't greenhorns and they don't speak dialect. Uncle Al speaks some *Siciliano* because his friends are *Siciliani*. We usually pronounce the word *Italian* in English except when we're talking to our relatives from the other side, but we always say *Tolvese, Aviglianese, Siciliana*. But whether we were *Tolvese, Aviglianese,* or Italian we used the English nominative plural, the "s" to make the *mappine*, into *mappine*s. To us dishtowel sounds stilted, pretentious. Dishtowel, dishrag, washrag. These *'Merican* words sound awkward, unnatural. Don't *'Mericans* feel stupid when they use those words? A word like *mappin'* should have a kissing closeness to onomatopoeia.

Colander, too, sounds so Anglo as to be Saxon. *Scola maccarun'* sounds real, it rolls off the tongue like it's supposed to.

"What does *scola maccarun'* actually mean, Mom?" It occurs to me in a burst of linguistic awareness as I'm reaching for it from under the sink. It's a Friday so we're making *aglia olio,* no meat.

The three of us are in the kitchen. Lucia's setting the table. My mother is frying the garlic in oil, I'm washing the parsley when my mother tells me, "Get the *scola maccarun,* Jojo." Until that Friday, it has simply been the word for the object we use to strain the water once the linguini is cooked. (NB: You only use linguini for *aglia olio.*)

She pauses, puzzled and amused by what she finds herself saying, after she stops near the sink with the aluminum pot full of linguini. She's ready to pour, "Well, actually it means 'strain the macaroni.'" We don't consider these words. We say them. They are our words. "Here, put it in the sink," she keeps our preparations going.

"You mean you're saying to us, 'Get the strain the macaroni?'"

"I know, but that's what it's called. What can I tell you?" She throws back her curls, just released from the bobby pins but not yet brushed through, and laughs. Dad isn't home yet and we're hurrying to get dinner on the table. She hasn't had a chance to run a brush through her hair and put her lipstick on, which she'll do when she hears the truck crunch over the gravel in our driveway.

I'm asking about the *scola maccarun'* because Miss Collins, our smartly dressed seventh grade teacher, who's just returned from a trip to Italy over the summer, said something today in an uncharacteristically peremptory manner. Just before we lined up in the pink girl's side of the school basement to go back to our classroom, when we were talking about making '*a bizz*' in cooking class that day. "'*A'bizz*' isn't a real Italian word. The real Italian word is *La Pizza* and it means 'a pie.'" Miss Collins stood there head high, certain in her pronouncement. La Pizza? Not '*a'bizz*'! How could that be? How could she know more about our language than we do? Where did she get this? Who does she think she is?

Miss Collins is one of the young women who went to normal school right after high school for two years to train to be a teacher. When these women accepted their teaching positions, they signed an agreement not to marry. If they married they had to give up their jobs. Not so for men. Occasionally we'd hear a whisper about a female teacher who was secretly married until "they" found out. Then she was fired.

We were shocked that women would give up being married for a job, just as horrified as we were about their being punished, fired, for being married. Even we, Waterbury, Italian, *Tolvese, Aviglianese, Rimenese, Salernese* girls, were shocked.

We know our family speaks dialect, so '*a bizz*'. It's our Italian. Aunt Ag's in-laws from Salerno speak "good" Italian. And Aunt Vicky can understand her *Riminese* in-laws' Italian, but when they use their dialect it's completely incomprehensible. Her *Riminese* mother-in-law says, " *Mit' di zou si scaran' 'a*" to tell her to "Put yourself in the chair." Whichever the dialect or language, it's much more important to speak the right cooking language: Each wife must learn to make her husband's family's special dishes, especially the *ragu'*, and give up making it the way their mother taught them. That's a wife's duty. It shows respect.

Tolvese is our dialect and therefore *buon'*. "*Meh*," Gramma laughs and covers the gaps in her teeth with one cupped hand when I ask her one day when she's making distinctions between people who are *Napolitano, Siciliana,* and *Barese*, "What about the *Tolvese?*"

"*Su bas*," she says. Real low. Even so, being *Tolvese* is what we are and it seems inherently to be a good thing. Even if my generation doesn't speak *Tolvese*, it's still ours. The dialect words lace our everyday cadences as naturally as English. They aren't part of another language for us.

The words we used often had to do with the house, *a cas'*, or food, *i' robb' 'i mangiar'*, and to do with insults, mess, confusion, vulgarities. It's a language of the home and street, at the margins of any lexical canon but at the center of our lives. So for example, "I have such a *vuli'*" means, I have such a yen or desire for a particular food, but "Yen really doesn't capture the same feeling," my father said every time he translated it for someone outside our family. *Bugiard', liar, stravers'*, perverse or pigheaded, determined to do things your own way, and therefore the wrong way, *capa dost'*, thick-headed, *capa dur', hard*-headed, *faccia dost'*, thick-faced, or thick-headed. Do you see a pattern here?

Manaccia diavol', damn the devil, *va'Napl'*, go to hell, or go to Naples, going to Naples being the equivalent of going to hell (I had no idea until I was a teenager that what we were saying had anything to do with Naples: the word meant how annoying), *manag' 'a' merican*, damn the Americans, *malandren'*, bad boy, *mammon'*, mama's boy, but really anyone dumb or annoying, *u pazz'*, crazy, you make me *schiatt'*, you make me burst, said with fury, indignation, *sfachim'*, one literally without face, so like any traditional culture, the very worst person you can be (in some circles so bad it's considered vulgar), *che bellezz'*, what a beauty, really, you're unbelievably annoying, *canta tu*, sing you, or go ahead and talk, tell them everything you, *ma sona ma beech bastid*. These words couldn't be wrong. They were what we used to signify meaning and that meaning was communicated. That's called language.

I don't remember knowing there was another "real" Italian until I was ten or eleven, though my mother always said about Grandpa Clapps's second wife, Nanny Clapps, who was from Lucca, "Oh she speaks such beautiful Italian. Her pronunciation is so beautiful." She took the time to pronounce each vowel fully, even the final ones. Our dialect is hurried; our family had to get out to the *masseri'*, the fields. Is that why so many vowels are elided or clipped?

Visiting Lisbon, the old Portuguese women looked and sounded like my grandmother to me, something about the swing and clip of their words. We all know about the influence of the Arab "u" in the southern Italian dialects, but what about the influence of *the Albanese, Francese, Tedeschi*? What about the influence of all those eastern Mediterranean cultures? Like Comma' Luci's family who were *Grigiott'*, the Greeks, who lived in a certain neighborhood of Tolve. What does it mean that they were "Greek"? Does our dialect include residual Greek words and phrases? Whatever the elements that make it up, our dialect has the sounds of intimacy, the sounds of an enclosed, hermetically sealed world.

The words Miss Collins used that day were the strange ones. If she was correct, she was not right. What did she know? I was annoyed and confused. Only now do I have the words to explain what I knew was wrong but couldn't possibly have explained back then.

She wasn't the one who made the weekly bread supply along with 'a bizz'—to be eaten on Saturdays—in the wood oven Grampa built for his 'a figliol' (young girl), Gramma, down by the road once a week. She didn't help to slaughter a pig and then pour boiling water on the pig's skin to get the hair off, then gut its innards so that we could roast the pig carcass on a spit, or butcher it in order to make salscicia for the ragu, or 'a salscicia that was then dried and preserved in olio di'oliv'. She didn't cure the proscuitt', can the peaches. She hadn't gotten up before dawn to feed the chickens, collect the eggs, milk the cows before she went to school as my mother and her sisters did. She didn't shovel pig shit into barrels to fertilize the garden.

Miss Collins doesn't know the smell of pig shit on a hot summer day that filled the nostrils of my mother and her sisters as they picked bones out of the pig manure to sell, because it was a hard time for her family. She doesn't know the intense salty, cheese and prosciutto smell from the wine cellar where all the drying cheeses, prosciutt', salsiccia hang, the smell from the wine barrels soaked with intense red wine, the damp smell from the damp stone walls, and the smell of the fat crisping from the pig roasting on a spit in summer. She doesn't know the smell of tomatoes that have been picked in the summer heat, blanched in boiling water, peeled, then packed along with basilicol' into large glass jars that have been boiled on long hot summer afternoons in gigantic pots to sterilize them. This project alone took weeks every summer, as the tomatoes were jarred, then carried down the rickety stairs in bushel baskets to line the long sciangiatt', creaky, gray with age, wooden shelves in the side canning cellar, not in the root and wine cellar where the prosciutt' and scamozz' and dry salsicci' and other pre-served foods that Gramma makes hang, not the main cellar where the salscicc' is made. She hasn't laid the rest of the tomatoes out on large sheets in the sun to dry to make 'i conserv', which will thicken and sweeten the ragu all year long.

Still Miss Collins has ripped a tear in the fabric of our mapped world. Our language wasn't "real."

Miss Collins went to grammar school with Rosalind Russell. "Even then she was a devil. She'd try anything. Oh, she was a wild one," Miss Collins said, proud to have had such a friend as a child. "She was always climbing over fences. One day she ripped her underpants and she took them right off and threw them on the ground."

Miss Collins was short and elegant: sharp and a snappy dresser. She traveled in the summer with Miss Burney, who taught second grade, who was quiet, sober, not sharp or a snappy dresser, but she wasn't sad and alone like Miss Martino, whose sadness made her mean. Miss Collins, the snappy dresser, liked us. There was always a light in her eyes that spoke of humor, pleasure at being alive, a lack of resentment at teaching us, the sons and daughters of the flotsam and jetsam that had floated ashore in America.

She had been a very young, beautiful beloved teacher at Webster Grammar School when my mother and her sisters and brother were children. When my cousins and I had her for seventh grade she must have been middle-aged. We girls, who sat on the stairs near the baseball field brushing our long flowing hair, so the boys would notice us, couldn't reconcile our sense of our teachers as women who held great authority over us with the fact that they had agreed not to be married. Miss Collins alluded to romance. Men she met when she traveled in the summer? Did I make that up? Did she say she had met someone that summer? Was she independent and didn't want the strictures my mother and her sisters lived with? That I will live with? The must and should that everyone one in my family lives with? The inadequacy that both the old and new world held out to us?

Now I wonder if she and Miss Burney were more to each other than we could have understood. Was teaching a haven for gay women? Was the convent a sanctuary of professional life and respectability for our nuns who taught us catechism on Monday afternoons in the convent on Hillview Avenue?

In the fifties we felt so sorry for them. The nuns were "married to Jesus," we said with our eyes round and shocked, heads shaking in a studied admiration that barely hid our disbelief, our condescension. Most of us would have signed right up to be nuns if it hadn't been for the prohibition against marriage and having babies. For our teachers it made even less sense. They weren't married to Jesus. "They couldn't get married back then. That's terrible. Then it was probably too late." Whose words are these, stored so carefully in my head? Our mother's, then ours?

Miss Collins, the snappy dresser, the very pretty, the teacher who traveled with Miss Burney, who had had Rosalind Russell for a childhood friend, who had the good sense of humor and real affection for us, said, "I went to Roma, this summer," she said with an unmistakable American pronunciation. "It's called *la pizza* and it means pie. It's not *'a'bizz'*." I guess you could call it mutual condescension made of whole continents of misunderstanding.

Miss Collins didn't know that our dialect preserved the ancient first-person form of *sapere*, which is *saccio*, the word that Dante uses for "I know" in *L'Inferno*. In modern Italian it's been changed to *so*, even though the cognate structure for *fare* still uses *faccio* for "I made." *Fare* and all the "made" constructions are practically copulatives in Italian, used the way the infinitive "to be" is in English. *Fare* is used for so many constructions. At Boston University, years later, I sat through years of Italian taught by our old Pirandelliesque professor who refused to do anything but read each book to us, droning for an hour and a half on Tuesdays and Thursdays, reading the Italian, then translating it, looking up in disgust every half an hour or so to ask, "Are there any questions?" daring us to even consider engaging him.

I learned nothing about Dante, but two things about our dialect. I noticed that Dante used *saccio*, just like we did. *Ma chi sacci', i sacci', no sacci' i.* Who knows, I know, I don't know, were all a part of our everyday parlance in Waterbury. Once in my Dante class, the word *sciagurato* came up in the middle of Canto XX. When I heard from the periphery of my miasmic fog, the professor asks if anyone knew what the word *sciagurato* meant. I swam up out of my stupor and raised my hand for that one and only time and said, "I do. My grandmother used to say, '*Chiest' femmine si chiamano sciaguratu', remaniesc' senz u' marit' e senz' innamurat'.*" These bad women who are called *sciagurat'* wind up without a husband or a lover.

He snorted in bitter recognition, then caught himself and stopped, "Yes, it means something like that, a person of a slovenly nature." That was the only spark of life I ever saw in that class. I learned that my dialect had some deep connection to an older world that I barely glimpsed that day.

Miss Collins and Miss Burney who traveled together in the summers sometimes, didn't know that my grandmother sang to all her *creatur'*, rocking them in their baby carriages, one foot rocking the front axle of the carriage, like the treadle of a sewing machine, the wheels of the carriage creaking in rhythm, her hands free to crocheting in rhythm, while she chants, *Ninna nonna, ninna nonna,* which means sleep grandma, implying sleep for Gramma's sake. (It was common for a mother or grandmother to address her child by her own appellation, a familiar gesture of affection and connection.) Individuation was not on our map, only connection, union, and merging. It's not until I live in New York and I hear Spanish mothers and grandmothers saying this to their little ones, "Mami, don't do that." Meaning "my child, child who belongs to me or even child with whom I am one, don't do that." We're one culture.

The summer my husband and I went to Portugal, we spent days
along the Tagus. The next summer we went to Turkey and spent the
same overheated listless summer afternoons along the Aegean coast.
Each end of this Mediterranean felt the same. At times I would look up
and think, "Italy? No, Turkey, no, wait. . . ."

Then the following year we had no money and we spent our long
summer afternoons bleeding into evenings, bleeding from cerulean blue
into indigo, along the estuary of the Hudson rushing out toward the
western shore of the Atlantic, on the promenade in Battery Park City,
in New York. Here again, the same watery edge on the lip of a large
expanse of sea, or headway rushing into the larger body was the same.
Always the golden glow, always the sense of being held just at the edge
of the larger other that an immense highway of water brings to its
shores. All my connections were here: the eastern antecedents of the
Greek, Semitic, Turkish cultures that flooded over into Sicily and
southern Italy, then the trip our Mediterranean ancestors made in distress via Portugal, Spain, France to the shores of America. These connections, the eastern Mediterranean, the western Med, rushing out into
the Atlantic, which rushes across to American shores, they all hold the
same hope, the same imprisonment, the same possibility.

Gramma said, rubbing our bruises in a gentle circling motion, "*San'
e san', ogg' ruot, e crai e` san'.*" Heal, heal, today broken, tomorrow healed.
Years later, when I was teaching a women's poetry class we began to
discuss the ancient oral tradition of love poetry, or ritual songs and
chants that women were often responsible for, marriage songs, funeral
chants, birth songs. We began to discuss our own female oral traditions
and I asked my students to bring in their mothers' and grandmothers'
chants, blessings, sayings and songs. When I sang my grandmother's
healing chant of *san e san* to show them what I meant, Inez, a Puerto
Rican student of mine, said, "My grandmother sang the same thing all
the time, exactly the same way." Did that healing song travel the
Mediterranean from southern Italy to North Africa to Spain, then to
the New World? Did the Spanish bring it home with them after they
conquered southern Italy? Did they bring it to us when they came and
lived among us? This map of oral language was preserved in invisible
ink in my family and connected me to this woman's family. I felt a wave
of our connection between this Latina woman and the women in my
family. Our grandmothers healed us with the same songy chant.

Miss Collins couldn't know that. She couldn't know that in places
like Waterbury we've preserved these ancient words and songs and sayings long after they gave them up. When my mother and her sisters
went to Tolve in 1986, our people laughed when they spoke the dialect

language they had always used, the one which my grandparents had brought with them when they arrived in the first decade of the 20th century. Our relatives in Tolve had given up the dialect after radio and television took over their language. They didn't say, "*Si volema schi schiama nin se no, non schima scen*," "If we're going to leave, let's go, if we're not, let's not go." (Let's stay.)

What could Miss Collins know about a *mappin*? I'm sure she didn't know that the word *map* comes from the same root word that *mappina* comes from. The Latin root word *mappa* means cloth or towel. In Medieval Latin, *Mappa Mundi* means sheet of the world, because maps were originally drawn on pieces of linen. That the word *mop* comes from the same word root. Miss Collins didn't know that. And we didn't. But deep in the south of Italy, in the hill towns, this word root, this idea of the small piece of precious cloth that holds a world together contained that meaning as surely as those Southern Italian women wiped up one mess after another.

If a dialect is a language without an army behind it, the *mappin'* is our flag, our banner, holding aloft everything that has kept us at the edge. Is it because we've been the backwater to every great Mediterranean that the words that come down to us are words without formality, without hegemony, entirely non-canonical words? Is that why the words of confusion, mess, disorder, the curse words, the words of ruin, crippledness, of dirt are the ones that have passed down to my generation? We had *mappines* on our shoulders, shovels in our hands, dough under our fingernails, bits of sausage caught between our teeth. The church damned us from one side for being the pagans we were, and all the Italians north of us, which means most other Italians, damned us from the other. "Those Arabs down there, those Africans," they still say as they dismiss our people with a laugh and a head tossed in contempt, so afraid that they might be connected to us. They shouldn't worry so much. They're not. We're not. Connected.

Em beh', what are you going to do? If anything we're an ancient Semitic, Phoenician, Greek, Byzantine, Anatolian, maybe even Roman *misconbrulia*, mixed-up mess or confusion, an island of people that came loose from the eastern shores of the Mediterranean, more Near Eastern than Western, but from which in desperation, at the end of the nineteenth century, we floated ourselves across the Mediterranean in bits and pieces, in such tiny pieces we floated one or two people at a time through the Straits of Gibraltar and washed up on the shores of America. We collected in threes and fours along the edges of America. We made communities where the ancient mores of our culture preserve something so old it doesn't have a written record, only a song here and a rag there.

My Aboriginal Women

Anger was our true north, our compass, our map, our weathervane.
Without it we didn't know how to traverse the tight air between
us. A matter of heritage quivered along the currents of our tribe, an element in the climate of our simmering days and hours. Screams, slaps,
spankings, pinches, beatings were so much a part of our every day that
fury seemed unremarkable, even ordinary. Just as we breathed each
other's overheated air as a natural part of our daily weather, we took as
usual, too, the thrill of the defiant glare thrown down, the roiling waves
of disgust, high dudgeon, despair. Tears were usually a momentary
giving in from a hard slap cracked across the face before the one
slapped gathered her fury back inside. Some of us buried it deep inside,
making it a permanent sadness, but most of us positioned it at the ready
so that we could pass it on the next time an opportunity arose. Anger,
our theater, our thrill, drove the tempest and turbulence of our storms
and seasons, our personal climate, a mother country.

We were full of anger, but not angst. My tribe hasn't heard of
ennui. Angry, but not depressed. In a land of clarity, there's too much to
be done for introspection. *Runzeling*, nursing things over, isn't a virtue
to us. That's for the self-indulgent. We *did*. We acted. We stood on the
side of virtue.

Simplicity. And violence. Greek theater of Italian American life.

Ma che fai? Deficiente! Idiote, Che suchess'? What are you doing?
Deficient one. Idiot! What happened? This is was the moral code our
parents had been raised with and raised us with in turn. This was *proprio, giusta*, the way to bring up good children, to teach them, to show
them what they weren't supposed to do. That was what had made them
the decent people they were.

153

Each generation in turn.

My mother has left a note on the kitchen table with a list of chores for my sister and me It says she's down at Aunt Vicky's helping her pin up a hem for the wedding next week. We're going to do the "good laundry" when she comes home. She had asked my father the night before to take the stretcher from the attic. She's set it up out on the back terrace while we were in school. You can adjust the length and width to fit any tablecloth or curtain that needs drying. Along each side there are pinpoint nails upon which we will carefully catch the decorative tips and loops of the hems or lacey edges. A flannel blanket has been left on the living room floor; the large tomato pincushion has been readied, too, with its dangling little fruit hanging and bearing, too, a crown of straight pins. We're starting with our parents' bedroom. We'll starch and stretch Grandma's bedspread today, and the curtains, too, as we do every spring as part of our spring cleaning. The white crocheted bedspread is her warm weather spread. Our cleaning ceremonies mirror the agricultural cycle my mother has grown up with on the farm and that of our ancestors from Southern Italy. Each turn of season makes its particular demands. Inside our house the rooms are turned out completely, floors scrubbed with turpentine before they are rewaxed; every drawer turned out and scrubbed and a host of other tasks. Today, "the good laundry."

While we're waiting for Mom, we're supposed to do our ordinary daily chores before she comes home. Lucia picks up the list and reads what each of us is to do. While she's reading I drift out to the cupboard in the garage and take five cookies from the place where we store what we bake each week.

The everyday ironing of our ordinary laundry is at the top of my list. I'm supposed to dampen my father's dress shirts and roll them up, to get them ready for ironing. I'm to iron our blouses and skirts, the aprons, then my father's work clothes, his undershorts, the napkins, the *mappines,* finally the good rags—the ones we dust with.

In an hour, when my mother comes home, we'll make the starch. The large white enamel pot with the chipped black rim is on the stove. But for now I have wandered off to my bed where I am eating my cookies and reading from one of the stack of library books I get twice a week from the storefront library near our school bus stop.

"Want a cookie?" I ask Lucia. I wander back to the fridge to get some milk.

"No, I'll have mine when I finish my work." She'll do her chores. She'll have a cookie. She'll start her homework. I never do my homework. The work is too easy at the beginning of the year. When I look up from my library books months later, it's suddenly too hard.

I like to read my library books instead. I lose myself in them for hours, sitting in the top of the maple tree in the front yard, or draped over the arms of my father's reading chair or stretched out on my side of our bed.

After half an hour Lucia comes into the bedroom, where I've settled for today. "Joanne, you have to do your work!"

"I have time still." I don't even look up from my book.

She grabs my hand and tries to drag me off the bed. "I'm not going to do it now," I say. "I'm almost finished with this chapter, only two pages." One shoulder off the bed, the other still on. I turn the page. She really grabs hold of me, her hands under my arms, and drags my upper body, which I keep in dead weight, off the bed. But I refuse to give her the satisfaction of even looking up. My legs are up, my feet on the bedspread. I go on reading when she's let my head down on the floor and goes to the door. We're not allowed to sit on the bed once it's been made. The dents will tell on me.

She turns and stalks down the hall. "Mom's going to be really mad at you."

"I don't care."

When I hear my mother's shoes crunching up our gravel driveway I race out to the garage, just off our kitchen, and pull the ironing board out of the cupboard, slamming it open and yanking the iron off its shelf while the ironing board is still rocking into place.

"Don't tell Mom," I whisper loudly over my shoulder to Lucia, who is doing her homework at the Formica kitchen table. She closes her eyes, and rocks her head incredulously. "She's going to know." I haven't captured the swinging end of the cord when my mother walks in.

"Mom, Jo didn't do her work," Lucia shouts from the kitchen. She wants no part of this. She's not going to be tarred by the brush of my disobedience. "She was reading instead of doing her part of the list."

The basket of clothes sits where my mother left it, each wrinkled piece piled in a hill of unironed work. My mother glances at the basket, touches the iron with her finger tips. "It isn't even hot." She dusts me with the back of her hand, a mere reference to a slap.

"What were you doing?"

"Nothing," I say. "I was just reading for a couple of minutes."

"Why didn't you do your work?"

I shrug.

"Lucia, why didn't you make her do her chores? You're the older one." She's moved on into the kitchen. Lucia is standing next to the gleaming white stove now, mute, furious. "She doesn't listen to me. I told her." Lucia glares at me. Lucia wants only one thing: for us to all shut up, for the screaming, giving and taking slaps, the yelling, for it all to stop. She's stuck trying to get us all to behave. We don't even notice.

"Oh, Lucia, you're responsible for your sister. Get the bluing out," she commands, "And the starch."

A reprieve for now. I move into place to be extra helpful. Lucia widens her eyes, warning me.

When the bluing, the box of gritty blue powder, and the yellow and red Argo box have been pulled out from the back corner under the sink, they inevitably have one bottom corner mashed and caked from a drip under the sink. Once the water is hot, we stir the silty, mineral powder into the immense pot of boiling water on the stove. The starch slips against your fingers in an unnatural crunch. Lucia stirs the brew: she pours the bluing in.

The dense, sickeningly sweet smell begins to hang in the air above the stove. Soon it will fill the kitchen. "That will make everything really white," Mom explains, again.

"We know that," we insist. We're allowed to do my grandmother's doilies, our training pieces, but my mother moves us both out of the way with a wiping gesture: it's time to dip Grandma's crocheted bed spread.

Her hands extend in an arc out over the pot. Aware of her duty toward her mother's work, "Now watch me girls," my mother says. "When you have a big piece like this, first you pick the whole thing up, making sure that none of it is going to fall, then slowly you dip in one end—Joanne, get me that wooden spoon over there, quick! Then dip each section until the whole piece is in." She allows each row of lacey circles to descend in homage to all the hours of work my grandmother spent making this bedspread, one for each of her four daughters as they planned their marriages. My mother stirs the steaming blue, witchy concoction with the long wooden spoon.

At night, after long days that began before dawn, Grandma sat on the bed in the kitchen, arthritic hands working the smallest crocheting hook into delicate turns and loops. She's working on them for our generation now.

While my mother stirs the spread, she keeps her gaze fixed on the bluing mixture and talks to us. "When you get married, Grandma will give each of you one as a wedding present.

"Grandma came to America with her *cassa*, a big chest, all the linens she had made as a girl for her kept in there. She had spun the thread, and woven some pieces, some tablecloths. There are a few pieces of those left. I have one. All the young girls did this work: cut work, embroidered pillow cases and the *sopracuschin'* and her sheets. They crocheted lace for the edges of some of the linens too. We only used those linens when we had guests. The material is so strong. I'll show you later. I have a couple of pieces. They're still practically new."

"Where do you keep them?" Lucia asked in her quiet, serious way.

"In my hope chest. Daddy bought my hope chest for me the first year we were keeping company." My mother's face lights up when she talks about falling in love with my father, the days of their courtship. She stirs and dreams of seeing my father at Lakewood Amusement Park that July Fourth weekend, when she and Aunt Vicky had been allowed to go for a walk after dinner when the chores were done.

"Mommy, Mommy, why don't you use it now?" I'm hopping up and down to be part of this.

"The Italian nuns used to come to our house when we were girls and Grandma bought good linens. A gorgeous satin bedspread, pink. Auntie Ag got the first set, then as each of us was about to be married she bought a set for us. We lived such a rough life. We couldn't believe Grandma would buy that for Ag. The work is so fine. I'll show you girls later if you behave."

"I don't know. It's too good to be used." Her mother's fine work has to be rinsed and twisted out of its water now. "You have to save those things. All that hand work. It's too much . . . just to use it like that." Lucia holds the new ritual basin, the large aluminum bowl, the first thing our mother bought at the new store, Caldor's, at the new shopping plaza that has just been built behind our house where "our field" used to be. "So cheap, what a bargain," the aunts cooed to each other. Mom's arms outstretched, she carries the aluminum bowl to the sink to drain and wring out.

My mother's muscular arms make a long twist of the spread.

"Now you girls each take an end and twist all the water out."

We know this job well. We move into place, each turning tight, water wrung out.

Lucia and I move next into position following my mother into the living room to stretch Grandma's spread out, to block it. We take the bottom corners, my mother's arms are pulled across the two top corners and we tug the corners out with practiced hands to stretch it into shape. "More," my mother insists, "Okay, pull the sides long. Tight."

When the spread has been carefully blocked on the blanket in the living room, each square tugged and patted into neat obedience, we begin to pin the edges to the blanket, passing the red tomato back and forth, about five pins held in our mouths to use, until the tomato comes back to us. "I need it. I'm out of pins."

We're a working party, each knows her part and place, Lucia and I, initiates in my mother's temple. "Very good, Lucia. See, Joanne, do it like your sister. Keep it flat. No, not like that. Make sure it's squared off." I'm the youngest virgin at this temple. Not quite trained.

I look at Grandma's tiny stitches, the rosettes and circles of design as we pin each loop to the sides of the flannel, our high priestess of needlework. Grandma's teaching me to crochet shawls. I've learned to do the fan, the double stitch, increasing one more fan per row to make the shawl into a large triangle to hang over our shoulders to keep warm when we go to the door in winter or to use as a scarf over our heads. For my girl cousins and my sister and me, learning how to crochet, like all the needlework we learn from our mothers, aunts, and Grandma, bestows on us a filial rank in the hierarchy: each thread ties us back to all the filaments, of spinning and weaving, each fiber to each thread and yarn, to the lace making and knitting to the cut work, embroidery, all our Mediterranean women ancestors have done since before Penelope. We go to J.C. Penney's, to Woolworth's, to Caldor's to choose the chartreuse, orange, purples, the new chemical dyed yarns coming in from Japan, then to sit with Grandma on the bed at the farm while she periodically takes the work out of our hands and shows us again. "Lika des, non like dat."

Her gnarled, dexterous hands are the true language between us.

When we finish them, all the aunts and Grandma admire our work, "You did that very nice," Grandma smiles over her glasses and laughs, "*Nisa nis'.*" When we finish our own shawls, "I made it myself," we brag in the school yard. The shawls make us feel ostentatious, romantic, to wear these mantles, as if we're reclaiming the rights to ancestral life, where women wore long skirts and boots. We're incapable of imagining the brutal labor our grandmother and her sisters did as an ordinary part of their ordinary days. It's the fifties. We haven't discovered the romance of our own time. No one of us has any idea what the sixties have in store for us.

When the spread is in place, we go back to the large pot to starch, stir, rinse, and squeeze the curtains. Everyone in place, knowing her job. When the curtains are done, we each pick up our corner and walk in silence out to the back terrace. Each of us takes a side of a curtain and carefully catches the edges over the pins on the sides of the stretchers. We're all sucking our fingers by the end to ease the pricks and stings of these pins and to make sure not to stain the curtains with our blood.

At times, being brought into this adult woman's life has us self-consciously well behaved. We say things like, "Yes, Mother," the kind of thing we never say. This makes Mom happy. She wishes we lived in a picture of a *Good Housekeeping* magazine. We're all good girls together for the moment. While we're making our homage, Lucia and I are dreaming of marrying anonymous guys for whom we will starch, iron, cook, and clean. And have babies. I name my husband Bob, which sounds so husbandly to me: secure and cute.

The ordinary laundry is still waiting when we've finished with the curtains and bedspread. We return to the bubbling pot to pick up one garment at a time, holding it by the wooden spoon above the pot to allow the hot liquid to cool long enough so that we can wring out the extra starch and Bluing: our cotton blouses, skirts, cotton slips, trimmed with wide lace. We never have the patience to allow these garments the time to get cool enough. The sting of the hot liquid that burned our fingers is part of our initiation into femaleness. The wet starched clothes will be carried to the terrace and hung on the clothes-lines to dry.

"Lucia, dump the starch down the sink now."

"No, I want to do it today," I insist. I wanted to be the good girl, the doer. I knew that wasn't my job; my job was to never measure up. So I was always elbowing my way for position, for importance. Whatever Lucia was asked to do had status, even if it was a chore.

"No, let Lucia do that," my mother says, but I'm determined and I've already lifted the pot from the stove.

"Be careful," my mother is saying, even as the liquid blue is slosh-ing over the edge of the pot onto the stove and floor.

"Oh, Joanne," my mother says, shaking her head. "Why can't you ever listen to me? You always ruin everything." The picture from *Good Housekeeping* has been spoiled. "Lucia, I told *you* to do it."

Lucia looks at her in disbelief. "She wouldn't let me," but we're not paying attention to her. My mother and I have moved into place for our daily *pas des deux*, admonition and defiance.

The pot is heavier and hotter than I had thought it would be. The liquid is swinging its hot weight from side to side in the pot. I can barely hold it. I'm not sure I can keep it from spilling all over the floor. I only just manage to get it over the sink, then I thud it down there, spraying starch and bluing all over the counter and windows.

"You never listen!" My mother comes over and grabs me by my arm: "Now *you* clean that up! Get i *stracc'*."

I need a rag quick. I reach for one of the under-the-sink rags. My mother presses her fingers into my upper arm, propelling me to bend down to get one of the musty rags.

"What's wrong with you?" She says, walking away from me to sit at the kitchen table. The red is rising into her face. Fury is being born.

My mother, like Lucia, had been a good girl. Lucia, as our mother had, usually manages to stay out of the way of the swinging hands that daily fly in our home. She can't understand why I'm like my Aunt Tony, my mother's sister, the one who mumbled under her breath, who talked back. I make no more sense to Lucia than Aunt Tony had made to my mother. "There's something wrong with you."

"I don't care," I say. I rock back on one foot then forward, first averting my face, then locking into her gaze.

"What did you say?" my mother asks.

My sister slips to my side and whispers, "Don't answer her back. Just be quiet."

I shake Lucia's words off, not looking at her. "I said, I don't care."

My mother rushes across the room and slaps me across the face.

"You be quiet," she says, "you stop that." and she slaps me again. "Now go and hang the clothes on the line."

"No! I won't," I glare at her. "I don't care what you say!" I walk away and sit on a chair with my arms crossed in front of me, the large sopping rag still in one hand dripping down my leg and onto the floor, and look out the window behind the sink at the willow tree.

"Come over here. I said, Come over here!"

She has to spank us when we don't obey her. How would she teach us otherwise?

I watch the willow branches sway with the spring breezes.

"Oh yes, you will." She grabs me by my hair and pulls me toward her to slap me across the face. "What did I tell you? What did I tell you? I told you to stop that."

"I don't care," I grumble under my breath. "I don't care anyway," I throw the dirty wet rag down on the floor. My mother looks at the watery mess it's made on the floor and then back at me.

"What did you say?" my mother can't believe her ears even though these bitter winds escalate every day. She slaps me again across the face, holding my arm, as I try to hop out of her way. "What did I tell you, I said?" my mother screams again at me.

"I said, 'I don't care.' I don't care about anything, I don't care about you or our whole family," I'm screaming now.

"Didn't I tell you to let Lucia carry the starch? And weren't you supposed to finish dampening the clothes *before* I got home?" She's slapping me on my arms, on my shoulders, on my head; each whack hits with a sharp sting then lingers with a burn as the target flashes around. "And to iron Dad's work pants? Didn't I?"

I try to get around the table and I'm climbing over my sister's legs to get into the corner where my mother won't be able to reach me.

"Why do you think I left you a list?" she screams from the other side of the table.

"I've had it with you, *had it*, I'm telling you. I'm calling your father at work." She rushes to the olive green phone hanging on the wall. "I'm going to tell him about this." Her body is close to vibrating.

I stand behind the table squeezing my legs together. I can feel the pee pressing just at the edge of my white cotton underpants. When she brings my father in on it, we're on different ground. "You've gone too far this time," she mutters.

"Why do you answer her back?" Lucia looks at me, the white around her pupils clouding over. "Say you're sorry."

My mother is starting to dial. I don't understand why I'm bad, why I go and lie on my bed to read when I'm supposed to do my work first.

I slam the door on my way out to the terrace where a little while ago I was stretching curtains with my mother and sister.

"Is Peter in the office, Mary?" I hear my mother from the terrace where I pick up one of my white cotton slips that we've just starched in unison. Her voice blows into the phone, breathless with anger. "Has he come in from the job? I have to speak to him."

The performance is almost over.

I look off at the back of the Waterbury Shopping Plaza that had taken over our scraggly fields a few years before. A Spinelli's Bakery truck is unloading its goods. There is only surrender and fury behind my defiance.

Lucia, stranded between us, stands in the doorway between the kitchen and the garage, disgusted, helpless, silent. My mother has positioned herself in the doorway between the kitchen and the living room, one arm raised against the doorframe. Each of us is stunned in position.

I bend down and pick up one of my white cotton slips from the top of the pile. I reach to pull the line to me and begin to hang our clothes, making sure to hang each piece perfectly, exactly as I have been taught. Our blouses and skirts will be hung in faultless swags, the clothespins locking the fabric tightly to the rope. As part of my defiance, my retribution, I want to show her I've learned everything. I just haven't decided to do it all the time yet, my way of not being my mother, of not being my sister. My mother's foot is tapping impatiently against the blue and yellow marbled linoleum. Beat, beat, it called my father home.

I'm struggling through these suns and rains, this weather, toward some idea of America from some idea of Southern Italy. I haven't found my own geography, my own climate. Making the bluing, starching Grandma's crocheted bedspread, ironing rags, all the womanly skills passed to us as girls, these are all part of my understanding of who I am, who I will become. But rage and reverence are especially clear to me.

Uffa: Jojo the Monkey

Part One: Myra and Me

Myra and I came upon each other when we were in our twenties living in the West Village. We spent all hours of the day and night talking, taking long walks as we both began to write and become. Once, reading a piece of fiction she is working on, her young female character is lying on her bed, reading and "living in the wallpaper." That small perfect string of words going straight to the unconscious, piercing precisely how we think without hesitation, said everything to me. A person is living in the wallpaper—in only barely a languaged state, but Myra had found the language for it simply and exactly.

It is because she writes images like that and because she thinks like that that Myra is my very intimate friend. We've been living in each other's wallpaper ever since.

When my mother died, Myra came to Waterbury for the wake and funeral, for the whole shebang. Meeting the entire family, the *paesans*, our friends, at the wake and the funeral at Mairano's, the high mass at Our Lady of Lourdes, the burial at Calvary Cemetery, lunch at the Ponti Club.

After the lunch we reassembled on the farm where my mother had been born and raised, gathering around the well in front of the house to place many of the flowers from the funeral as a way of bringing her back whence she came. We went up the stone stairs to the kitchen where my cousins had started a wood fire in the stove and roasted chestnuts for us and brought out their homemade wine to drink and so that we could talk about my mother one more time.

I wanted Myra to see as much as possible of this primal world I had been describing to her all these years. I walked her around the farm up the pigs, to the slaughterhouse, down to the lake, and then into every room in the house, up the narrow creaking stairs to the bedrooms where my grandmother's bedroom overlooked the lake, into the rooms where my cousin Bede and I waited for the answers to our letters to god, down to the root cellar where all the prosciutto and cheese used to hang, and then back upstairs to the living room where the same over-stuffed furniture has sat as far back as life itself.

"I understand something about you I have never understood before," Myra said.

When we went into the living room she turned to me with real surprise and said laughing, "What's that monkey doing up on the desk?"

Her surprise surprised me. "That's Jojo. You know, that's Jojo our monkey."

Jojo sat there with a little fedora on his head on my grandfather's old upright desk, as he had sat for decades. Next to Jojo was the stuffed squirrel and nearby was the stuffed owl and hanging over the couch a deer head wears a Mexican sombrero, its preserved hooves mounted upside down below to hold my Uncle Rocky's rifles.

When Myra asked me that question about Jojo—what was that monkey doing there?—my old wordlessness about my life in Waterbury flooded in—silence filling the chasm between where Myra grew up where there was no monkey on her grandmother's living room, and the place where Jojo sits so utterly naturally on the top of the desk wearing his fedora.

I'm not sure I have really had an actual conscious thought about Jojo. Jojo just is. Jojo lives on the desk. Jojo is in my head in the languageless place that is my *real* life, but which I have learned to call my aboriginal life. Jojo *is* the wallpaper in Waterbury.

Jojo is so a part of the wallpaper there isn't anything to say.

I turned to my family who were standing with us—helpless. Who could explain Jojo?

The next chance I got I asked Uncle Rocky to tell me the Jojo stories. Here they are. Jojo explains himself.

Part Two: Uncle Rocco's talking

Uffa, Jojo didn't like colored ladies. I don't know why. He just didn't like them. Oh, he was a devil. Papa sent him to me on the train from

Florida. Papa asked me before he left, what do you want from Florida? He just wanted to bring me a present, I guess. Him and Mama were going to Florida for two weeks. It was winter. February. I didn't know what to say. Send me a monkey, I said. A monkey? Sure, a monkey, what else? I was joking, for crying out loud. He did it. I didn't think he was going to do it. He shipped him in a crate. Then we got a call from the train station—they had a crate. That was Jojo, my monkey. I wasn't even married yet. I was seeing your Aunt Bea at the time. She was living down on Waterville Street. I brought him up to see her. He came in a cage. He lived in that cage all that winter. He was a smart son of a gun. Then he started to get out of his cage. He must have watched us because he stuck his hand out and opened the latch. We'd catch him and put him back in, but he'd get out again.

All summer he lived in the woods behind the farm, like a monkey swinging from tree to tree. He was really living after he got away. He traveled wherever he felt like it. Once my sister Vicki went upstairs to Mama's room and there was Jojo—he had chewed up all Mama's jewelry that she left on the bureau. The window was open and he had climbed a tree and into the window. And he was sitting there on the corner of her bed playing with her gold necklace. He'd wait quiet up in a tree until someone was underneath them; then he'd jump down on their shoulders and beat them up and then run back up in the tree and he'd be laughing. I mean it, he'd be laughing. . . . He was so damn fast. He'd wait on the well until the dog came by; then he'd jump on the back of the dog and beat him up and then he'd jump back up on the well. Oh, we had a lot of fun while it lasted.

He'd steal things all the time. He'd run in the house around lunch time and jump on the table and steal a piece of bread, while Mama was getting our meal ready. She'd go after him and he'd use two hands on her, across her face: slap, slap, slap. Then he'd beat it out of the house. Son of a gun.

We couldn't catch him for nothing after that. He'd go down to the lake and run along the railings on the side of the road. He'd torment people all the time. Stealing, beating them up. Especially colored people. He didn't like them. I don't know why. The colored ladies like to fish down by the lake. He'd go down there, he'd slap their legs and steal their bait. He took a colored lady's pocketbook once. He scratched her up good. Then he went up high in a tree. She was mad. She came up to the house, really angry. She said, "I'm going to call the police." Me and Joe climbed the tree to try and get him. He was up there laughing his head off. After a while he dumped all the stuff out of her pocketbook on the ground. But we couldn't catch him. Finally Toni's Al climbed up in the tree, threw him a banana and he dropped her purse to catch the banana. But it was too late. He slapped Mama, he attacked the colored lady. I didn't have any choice. I had to shoot him. I went up and got my gun from the house and I shot him. Then I had him stuffed and put him on Papa's desk in the living room. He's still up there.

Dropping in on Sandy

When we weren't cooking, baking, sewing, scrubbing, planting, watering, mowing, trimming, canning, or swimming, skating, biking, climbing, doing acrobatics, playing cards, singing, dancing, or telling jokes—in short, making or playing—we'd have company. Or go visiting. Or drop in on someone. As soon as we sat around for more than five minutes doing nothing one of us would say, "Who should we call to ask over?" Unless someone happened just then to be coming up our driveway with a cake in their hands or a bunch of arugula that they had just picked from their garden.

If it was a nice evening or a Sunday afternoon we'd take a drive. My father worked all over the state so he knew all the small back roads, all the obscure state parks weighted down with cool ancient trees and lustered water falls. We'd take a ride. We might see one of his jobs along the way and we might swim and picnic in a state park. Possibly. But usually the point of these rides was to take a ride. There was nowhere to be. Nothing that had to be done. We'd wander without going anywhere particularly and we'd usually end with a "Why don't we stop for ice cream?" to give the farthest point a nod and drive slowly home.

The hills in that part of Connecticut have been cultivated since the earliest colonization, creating over time a rustic, bucolic landscape—an essence of America. We were not from America. But we lived next door.

We might go up Route 7 to the northwestern corner of our state, say, to Norfolk: "I did that job last winter. This is called the icebox of Connecticut it gets so much colder than anywhere else. It was horrible; my hand was sticking to the iron." Then down toward Litchfield: "This job was a son of a gun. The risers were off by a quarter inch when they came off the truck. I either had to take the whole job back to the shop and lose all that travel time, all that money too. If the riser is off by a quarter of an inch by the time you get to the top you *don't* have a top stair. I had to work like an animal improvising and making do to get the risers on this stairway to fit. And look, at that small turn at the top of the stairway—that made it so much the harder. It was a ghastly day. I stayed and I got it done but that job caused me so much heartache. God am I glad that one's done."

Washington Depot at a boarding school with a bucolic campus: "The grounds of this school are so beautiful, but can you just picture what keeping a lawn like this involves?"

Another boarding school where he had installed a fire escape. "These old buildings are real fire traps so there's a state code that says they have to have fire escapes installed. So much the better for Waterbury Iron Works, but these old buildings are really frightening. I'd hate to be caught in one of them if there was a fire. Especially filled with all these young boys so full of life. Who knows what they'll get up to? That's the way they're supposed to be."

As we, the immigrant family from the brass city of the world, hummed over these roads, my father talked that day about the pure pleasure of his work, "We finished that job in an afternoon. That never happens. You just can't imagine what a pleasure it is when it all comes together the way it's supposed to. That happens so, so, so rarely. It's the penultimate pleasure when it happens." My father, a ferocious reader, very well read for a high school graduate, had anomalous errors in his speech; one was the word *penultimate*, which he used as intensification. If something was the penultimate that meant it was the best or the worse. He used the word *penultimate* often with great pleasure—with one might even say, the penultimate pleasure.

We wound our way through the old back roads, up and down the perfectly sloping hills that Sunday. From the back seat I heard my father say to my mother, "I was up here last week with Chippy and Uncle Paul. It's right around here. He said we should come and visit him sometime."

That was how we came to drop in on Alexander Calder. Everyone called him Sandy. We called him Mr. Calder.

He had been a well-known artist in Europe and in America. An artist's artist.

In the '50s he began to work on a monumental scale in his sculpture—his mobiles and stabiles. By then his reputation had exploded

into his becoming an international and a deeply commercially success-
ful artist. Before then his work had more or less been on a scale he produced himself but with his new monumental scale, meant for large
public spaces, he needed a foundry. In America Waterbury Iron Works
was that foundry.

Calder was working with Chippy (called that because his name was
Liberator Ieronimo), the shop foreman and head layout man at Waterbury Iron. Chippy became his righthand man in producing these
pieces.

Workman to workman Calder enjoyed going to Waterbury Iron
and visiting with Chippy and Uncle Paul and Marco and having a glass
of wine. He might bring a new maquette—a small scale model of the
next piece—to discuss how the piece would be produced. Or he might
be checking up on how a fabrication was proceeding. There were no
blueprints—just the instructions to use the maquette to build the larger
piece to scale, only much larger. The model was taken apart and each
element of the piece was manufactured. Then the large-scale piece was
reassembled. As he and Chippy worked over time—he worked in a
larger and larger scale. Sometimes he'd bring someone from a high end
gallery or museum with him—"people from New York." But often he
came just to hang around with men who were as comfortable working
with raw materials in the heat and mess of making and who loved as
much as he the forms of the raw and the made. Fabrication to fabrica-
tor they saw eye to eye.

When Calder found out from Uncle Paul that one of his favorite
professors at the Stevens Institute, Professor Salvatore, was our
Aviglianese cousin it sealed the friendship further.

We had seen the maquettes lying around on Chippy's work table at
the shop where they looked like bizarre toys. We had seen the larger
pieces as they had been produced. They looked like wild abstract creatures.

My father had talked about these pieces with the same pleasure
that he always took in talking about constructed work. "Do you see
what he's done? Look at the balance in this piece—he's using weights
and counterweights," he might say about a mobile. Then he'd take a
newspaper and wave it at the smallest piece of the mobile so we could
see how a very small disturbance in the air set the piece into subtle
movement. "Look at the way this heavier piece balances against all
these smaller pieces. This is real genius," he'd say with tremendous
pleasure. "Actually he looks a little dopey, you'd never think he was so
sharp, until you start to talk to him. But he is the pen, pen, pen, penultimate artist."

There had even been an article about Calder in *Life* Magazine. So we knew he was an important artist—a man whose pieces were part of the large public spaces.

But none of this prepared me for what we came upon when we arrived at Calder's black house on Painter Hill Road. An avuncular looking man with tousled hair greeted us with warmth and ushered us inside where a great light poured in on a bewildering topography. The room we came into was so unlike any interior I'd ever seen that at first I could only see my own confusion. There was the unruly chaos exactly opposite to the expected order of the '50s. But he *was* famous, I knew that. Calder's mobiles made of strange shapes and colors were hanging from the slanted open rafter beams. There were objects made of pieces of broken glass, broken ceramic shards, primitive shapes of sticks, rusty pieces of metal, wood, scraps of tattered cloth, old coffee cans. But he *was* an artist, I knew too. The objects assembled from these materials were sitting on furniture surfaces, affixed to walls and hanging from hooks. Fabric and metal edges were unfinished. Some were shaped into implements that looked something like the old kitchen implements about which we'd say, why doesn't Gramma throw those old messed up things away and buy some new ones? And the room was strewn with casual chaos. My mother would kill us if we kept our house like this. I knew that too.

Similar pieces of rusting metal, broken sticks, old springs, and empty coffee cans were on my grandparents' farm, at the back of our gardens, in our basements, and down at Waterbury Iron. But these were our dump heaps where this stuff was being held to be burned or collected for the rag man who came around with his horse and wagon, shouting, "Rag man, rag man, ten cents a pound." In Calder's home these same odd bits and shapes had been made into kitchen implements, tools, toys, and art. He proudly showed off many of these and then insisted that his wife Louisa put on the jewelry he had made for her. Primitive shapes wound into his wife's hair, curling around her neck, ears, and wrists.

Looking at photographs of that room now I see that there were large industrial windows letting in a flooding light to fill the main room The walls were white—the floor was brick laid directly into the earth, the ceiling opened up to the house's roof beams. There was a confusion of things primal spraying this large room. Twisted pieces of wire, camel humps of hammered silver and brass, the raw, rough, and rusted all mixed together. We were in the home of an artist imbued with the undomesticated look of what I would come in the future to know as modernity.

The homes we knew were farms, old Victorian New England houses, '50s ranch style houses built after the war, but none looked like this one. The sole aim in my mother's home was to control and disguise any bit of chaos or nature and its incumbent chaos—she had had more than enough of that on her parents' pig farm to last her all of the lives she fully intended to be reincarnated into. Here instead it had been invited in, played with, worked with, and valued. This new country was everything ours wasn't.

My cousin Paul told me recently, "Then, all of sudden, after years of this, Calder wasn't showing up at the shop anymore. Your grandfather ran him off. He couldn't care less about who he was. Calder's sculptures distracted from the main work of the shop too much as far as he was concerned." My grandfather made it so unpleasant that Calder began to work with Chippy at Segre's Iron, where Chippy worked on the weekends. But as soon as my grandfather retired Calder brought his work back to Waterbury Iron again and by then he was so prodigious that he needed both of those shops and a third to keep up with all the work he was producing. What a *cavon'* my grandfather was.

Sometime after that visit my mother left the brown plastic handle of her favorite spatula too near a burner on her stove. The heat melted the handle it twisting it into a gnarled arthritic shape. She pulled it off the burner and set it on the counter to cool down. A little later I picked it up to throw in the garbage. "Oh no," my mother said, "I made a piece of modern art. Don't you just it love it?" For years every time I helped her clean out her kitchen drawers I tried to convince her to throw it away. "No," she'd say pitching to insistence. "That's my modern art." In Calder's home we glimpsed the shock and confusion of modernity.

Notes of an Unredeemed Catholic

The church we went to as children was an Italian parish called, inevitably, St. Lucy's. It was a small wooden church with a wistful young woman holding her gouged-out eyes in a small shell in her hand. She didn't look disfigured; she looked wan and romantic. She had a flowing gown and a regretful tilt to her head. All of this seemed to us reverent girls a deep and romantic calling to passion. We would do anything for the sake of our beliefs. That I come from a Church that is deeply connected to and embedded in paganism, just as the Irish said about us, had to do with all of our families having barely dusted off the earth of southern Italy.

Being a Catholic for me back then had very little to do with what I was later told by both Catholics and non-Catholics was central to being Catholic, obsessing about guilt and sin. Though guilt and sin may be prominent accompaniments of belief in the Irish American Catholic church, which dominates the Catholic Church in America, they had little to do with my Italian American world. No doubt concern about guilt and sin were taught to us in catechism on Monday afternoon, during released time from Webster Grammar School. I even remember talking about sin with the nuns and priests, but it was not *the* burning question.

The burning question, which was clear to anyone who was a real Catholic, was: Were you prepared to die for your religion? This was the true test of whether you were a believer or not.

This was the question that we loved to ask each other, the question we debated at length among ourselves on the streetcorner waiting for the bus home from school, on the sidewalk outside the convent after catechism, and there was only one answer for anyone worth his salt. No

matter how hot the iron rod placed upon your skin, no matter how tor-
turous the rack you might be placed on, you were never to denounce
your religion or your God. As important to knowing you were Italian
was that you would never disavow the central tenet of the one true
Church. You were prepared to die for it.

We were not like those *Protestants*, the most deeply 'Merican state
one could enter. For that's who the enemy was. Not the Jews (they
simply weren't in our picture), but those lightweights, the Protestants
(they were all one thin bland mass of baked macaroni eaters as far as
we were concerned) to whom we flung down the gauntlet of belief.
They would never die for their religion. We would. They were the
opposite of us, who were the real believers. They were the deserters.
Faced with threats of death they would probably convert or invent yet
another religion.

But how did the church manage to engage us so deeply? How did
modest St. Lucy's engender in us a passion to worship in the deepest
way?

All religions invoke ritual, prayer, and meditation to lead their
believers into the spiritual world they seek to enter. The physical body
in the material world is a means by which clergy engage their congre-
gations. The human body is bent, humbled, and prostrated to conduct
celebrant and believer down this path. Functions as basic as walking
and breathing are ritualized. Think of the way religious services use
sound to pull their worshippers into a sanctified state; the sounds of
language, chanting, and perhaps most of all, music. Sometimes,
though, the absence of sound has the most profound effect, imparting
that holiest of states, silence, to hold off all sound not related to the
presence of god.

Our churches, our temples, our holy grounds are the places that
house this sanctified state. Religious leaders know that they must build
a bridge from the concrete into the spiritual, to say, that from *this* place,
we leave the worldly behind. It is necessary therefore for the concrete
details of that sanctified place to be particular enough to signal the
invocation of that state of grace. An altered state of consciousness can't
be invoked theoretically or abstractly. Each religion must create the
world from which to depart.

St. Lucy's was the place I first experienced this state of grace;
therefore, it is about that church and that parish in that time that I can
speak. And although supplication was crucial, guilt was secondary. Our
religious life was much more about passion than guilt. Not only was
religion a matter of passion for us, I would even say it was training for a
passionate life.

There were many things that contributed to this passionate, even sensual, Catholic life. There was the cycle of the liturgy, life, death, rebirth; there was the music, art, and drama, all a part of our daily involvement with the Church. There was the drama and pageantry of Mass.

And of course there was what we learned at the knees of those mysterious women—our nuns. My girlfriends and I spent hours after catechism lessons at "the convent," in front of the three-story wood frame house just a little bigger than the wood frame houses our families lived in, imagining what their lives were like inside. "Why had Sister Joseph Mary become a nun? She was so young and pretty. How do you think she got her calling? How do you know when it's a true calling?" The mysterious air of the nuns made us wonder if we too should become nuns and be like them, lovely and true to their love for God.

Mary, Bernadette, Linda and I wondered: did they have hair under their habits, and what did they look like at night when they took their habits off if they *didn't* have hair? *Did* they take their habits off at night? What did they do when they had to take a bath, since they were the ones who told us that if you wore a slip that was too silky, it was a sin? What a thrilling sense of sin! Not only does this kind of preaching not turn you away from sex. In fact it has the effect of turning our attention to it in delicious detail. Probably it wasn't the young and pretty ones who told stories like that, but the other nuns, so old and obviously unhappy that they had long since stopped attempting anything other than a crabby remark. (Was being relegated to teaching little Italian kids in Waterbury something like a test of their love of God?) Some of the old and some of the young seemed clearly holy and saintly, an air about them of simplicity and even a state of grace, an otherworldliness.

These women, as close to exotic as existed in our small, but fervent world, were the ones who had renounced all worldly pleasures to enter into a holy state of matrimony with Jesus. They had much to teach us about the ardor of mystical love. St. Lucy, our own saint, they told us enthusiastically, had gouged out her own eyes because of what those eyes had been made to see. Her left hand proffered a sea shell, holding the very eyes she had put out. I knelt often and long in front of her statue, lighting a candle and abandoning myself to my prayers, filled with a zeal to submit to true religious feeling—to be prepared to give everything for my love of God.

Then there was St. Ignatius, who joyfully, Sister Mary Francis told us in a beatific mood, *joyfully* submitted his limbs to the fetters to express his love for God, and who upon entering Rome where he appeared before other zealously faithful Christians, begged these same faithful who sought his release not to hinder his joining the Lord. Possessed of his sacred rage he relinquished himself gladly to the two fierce lions that were let out upon him in a Roman amphitheater.

The stories about our heroes and heroines, men and women of ardent faith, excited in us ideas of martyred ecstasy. We swooned with the idea of surrender to our faith, our God, our own eager desire.

To bolster this passionate surrender to religious life there were the sensations of our life in the church. St. Lucy's, tiny in its dimensions, was filled with the vivid details of the old Catholic churches. The fourteen stations of the cross, each a small piece of folk art positioned for reverence, led us through the narrative of the final passion. There were the statues and paintings depicting those central themes of birth, death, pity, and ecstasy. There was the smell of incense that even today evokes indecipherable murmurs of Latin washing past my ears. There were the haunting strains of the music descending from the choir during mass. There were the exquisite lace cloths and flowers decorating high altars. The priests were dressed in garments of gold brocade embroidered by blind nuns with crimson thread. There were the nuns in their austere but flowing black habits. There was the great liturgical drama when this all came together at high Mass. All of these brought one to a state of attention to beauty and to an involuntary focus on the senses. Is there anyone who has been a practicing Catholic who can forget the sensations visited upon him as a child of being pressed up against his religion in a tangible way?

For first Holy Communion, each girl was encouraged to choose the laciest and most beautiful dress she would wear until she was a bride. What an occasion for fulfillment for a seven-year-old girl, who dreamed of little else than lacy dresses. For confirmation, we spent weeks choosing our new middle names. For each of these occasions there would be processions into the church. What a sense of sanctity the children of St. Lucy's had at those moments.

The moment of highest drama, though, was being part of the living rosary for The Feast of the Most Holy Rosary. Each of us became for that occasion almost as good as the nuns and priests we envied for their holiness. We held our candles devoutly and with a great sense of our own exalted state and processed in front our families, our neighbors, those boys, through the streets of our neighborhood, from St. Lucy's Grammar School to the church, wearing special white flowing robes. All the cars, all the daily rounds, the whole neighborhood stopped for us.

Once we were in the church, we each had a turn to recite our own portion of the rosary out loud. It was my first understanding of the thrill of being on stage. Many murmured their Hail Marys, or Our Fathers, showing their faith through decorum. I didn't have one of the important beads to say, just an ordinary Hail Mary in an ordinary decade, but I waited excitedly for my turn to sing out my Hail Mary, to make sure everyone heard me being holy.

But even this moment was surpassed in Waterbury in passionate religiosity by the arrival of the movie *The Miracle of Fatima*. To see those humble Portuguese peasant children on the silver screen joined for us the two most powerful visionary matrices of our world—the one, the ancient beliefs from the Christian-Mediterranean world and the other, the iconographic machine, the movies. The stories of the nuns and Hollywood united as we languished with sympathy for these poor children. They had seen the Holy Mother, and no one would believe them. How moved we were by their devotion in the face of everyone's dismissal of their announcement. They were faced with the hot iron of disbelief and their resolute piety withstood this onslaught. If only we could be put to such a test.

For months after I saw this movie I was up at five o'clock in the morning to at the very least say a holy rosary, but often also going to the six o'clock mass on cold winter mornings. All this rigorous demand that our religion made on us satisfied our deepest yearnings to be stirred by something of weight and moment.

When the cliché that religion is the opiate of the masses is tossed out so lightly I can only think how little it refers to my experience. This was not a life in training for skepticism or ennui, but rather for digging down into the well of interior life.

When I entered adolescence and began to ask the famous "why?" questions, I was still in the hands of the same priests and nuns, whose responses were catechistically ingrained: "Pray for faith, my dear," or "Come to church and ask for God's help." I can now see that I wanted to be asked what I meant, to be asked why I had these new questions. I wanted, in short, to be invited into the world of the adults. But I lived among adults who had come into *their* maturity with these questions neatly resolved. For them, answers in faith resolved a childhood; for me, questions unanswered sent me to the larger world on my own.

I have two other revealing memories from this period in my life. One is how painful it was not to sleep with Gary, my high school boyfriend, whom I was very much in love with. "God wouldn't want us to sleep together," I answered as earnestly as I've ever answered anything. "What if we died on the way home in a car accident? We'd be in a mortal state of sin." We were both still very much a part of the church. We went and lit candles together sometimes after school. What a sense of sanctity, to walk into a darkened church for the purpose of praying alongside the boy you more than anything wanted to kiss all day long.

This didn't interfere with our necking, for hours on end, in dark cars on out of the way dirt roads. Nor do I remember feeling guilty about it. Necking seemed perfectly okay, as long as I didn't consummate this passion. There was no question in my mind about making love. Of course I wouldn't. I wasn't supposed to. I couldn't. We broke up over that.

Still, my other memory contradicts this one—at least partly. I am walking down the hill after school with my friend Joey Matzkin. Joey and I liked to talk about the big questions. That day, Joey turned to me significantly: "What would you do if you knew the world was going to blow up tomorrow?" The answer came to me with precise clarity. I felt cornered. He knew when he asked me the question that if I were honest with myself there could be only one answer: I would sleep with Gary Ursini.

If it was all to be over anyway, why *not* do what I most wanted to do? Where is God in this memory? Where is hell, where sin? How could these two memories be true? I guess the answer lies in the reality that I wouldn't sleep with him, though the part of me free of these Catholic artifacts desperately wanted to.

My first Sunday at Boston University I got up by myself, the only one in my suite astir, and found my way to the cold, concrete Catholic chapel. The mass was sparsely attended. It had none of the folksy beauty of mass at St. Lucy's. The following Sunday, when it was time to get up for mass again, I simply didn't. I lay there and thought as I had on hundreds of other Sunday mornings: maybe I won't. There was nobody around me to notice or care or comment. I could have levitated at the elation I felt at being on my own. It was as if this last habit of my childhood fell away like a vestigial appendage that had withered throughout my adolescence.

In 1962, the year I entered college, it was more and more fashionable to renounce everything you used to believe in. So, of course, I did. But once I found myself loose in the big world beyond school and its imperatives to rebel, I saw that I was in odd coincidence with the church.

It happened when I began to travel and found myself in museums in Florence and Rome and Siena, in a familiar state of reverence, in front of the great Byzantine and Renaissance paintings. I was at home with these works. They were about figures and subjects I knew intimately. I was yielding my sensibilities to them in a new way, but the penchant for surrender was the same.

I found I was not only interested in the art and architecture in the great *duomos* and cathedrals, but rather that I was "of" those structures when I was in them, in the same way that I had been "of" St. Lucy's. I gave myself up to that place at that moment on my knees in front of a lighted candle, searching for a still point inside myself. This was in felicitous opposition to my usual frantic urban life. I began to realize that the church I had left was in me, even though each of us might be more at ease without the other. Passion in my life was now sexual and intellectual, and while both were intensely spiritual, neither filled the spiritual well, empty since I had left Waterbury.

Understanding more deeply what my Catholic upbringing had given me came finally from the deepest part of my secular intellectual life, work, and my Jewish boyfriend. By then I was living in New York and teaching at a small progressive school on the Upper West Side.

One day I was walking down the street with my boyfriend along one side of Washington Square. I was telling him about reading the myth of Demeter and Persephone to a group of fourth graders. I loved reading to these children: they sat rapt, quiet in the spell of the story. I read about how Persephone is abducted by Hades, about Demeter's mourning for her daughter, and about the six pomegranate seeds that must not be eaten, but are. The myth ended, "And so for six months a year when Demeter is separated from her daughter she wanders the earth in mourning and nothing grows upon the face of the earth and for six months a year when they are reunited she is filled with joy and the earth abounds with its fruits. And that is why there are seasons, a time for growing and a time when the earth lays fallow, a time for summer and a time for winter."

Only the hiss of the radiator filled the room that day when I finished reading. Then an audible sigh came from one rambunctious nine-year-old boy, Adam. His voice, filled with great longing, caught by the reverberations of this ending, "How I wish I could believe in something like that."

"I knew just what he was longing for," I said to my boyfriend.

"You would," he said. "You were once a little Catholic girl in Waterbury." I looked at him quizzically.

"Catholicism," he went on. "It's really another myth system—and our whole Western religion relies on the same agricultural cycles and sacrificial myths. The hero is sacrificed and comes back to life—like the seasons. Jesus is prefigured by Dionysus." I was stunned by this—revelation—for he went on and on with this analogizing. And I could now see clearly that what Adam longed for had been something I once had in my bones.

Rediscovering the church in this light was the beginning of recovering the riches of universality I had left behind.

I could repossess what had run deeply in me. I began to understand why I lit candles in churches of a religion I no longer practiced, why I prayed when I didn't know what I thought or believed. I could remember what moved me so deeply and had given me a world to live in.

I think about this every year at Christmas when I am reminded, at the darkest hour of the year, that light will come again, and I light the advent candles; when I am reminded that the trees will bear fruit again, then we carry a live tree into our living room to hang thick with decorations of fruit and birds; when I am reminded that there will always be more babies born and therein lies continued hope, then my son and I carefully unwrap each of the many crèche figures, placing baby Jesus in the position of honor in our home. These rituals frame my passionate understanding of the cycle of life and death. And I know again that there is hope in the time of dark.

My religious life became what I now call a personal catholicism. Because I was raised in the Catholic Church, its stories, its forms, rituals, music, and liturgy are dear to me. My connection to these forms is the means by which I am filled with a sense of reverence. My "religion" houses the place from which I ask the largest questions, think my quietest thoughts, wonder about a small earth in an immense cosmos. It's from here that I follow that worthy, frustrating path of the search for God I've made my own. I seek and pray and sanctify on my own. I pray when I want to. I go to church when I want to. I think about God a lot. Sometimes my belief is strong, sometimes it's weak. But I would say we are in mutual possession.

The Becce family on the wagon

Four Becce sisters as children in front of the old barn

The old farmhouse porch before the renovation

Grandpa Becce feeding the pigs from the wagon and Uncle Rocky as a small boy

Grandma Becce with the sheep on the farm in Waterbury, Connecticut

Aunt Vicki with the doll house

Uncle Rocky with his horse

Four Becce children and the Delalla boy

Aunt Vicki and Uncle Rocky on Farmwood Road

Grandpa Becce carrying barrel

Sunday afternoon on the farm with friends

Grandpa Becce with his daughters

Breadmaking time in front of the oven on the farm

The Uncles and girl cousins with Jojo the monkey in the living room at the farm

Bede on her tricycle in the kitchen at the farm

Halloween at the farm

Grandma Becce's surprise party

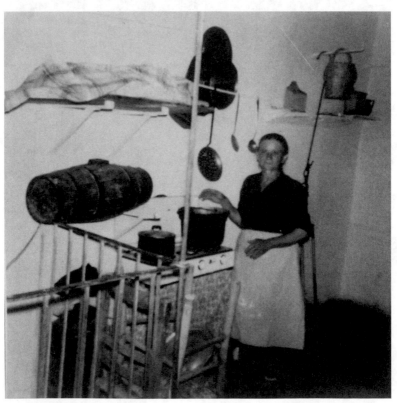

Anna Rosa Santorsa in her kitchen. Grandma Becce's youngest sister.

IV

E' POI? AND THEN?

'U Bizz' di Creanz':
A Piece of Politeness

I

The rules were these: If you are the guest, don't be *'Merican*. Never take any food that you are offered. Not at first, even if you are at your aunt's house. You must refuse any and all food when it is first offered. "Oh, no thank you," you say, "it looks delicious, but I really couldn't. We just finished eating."

Only after the food has been offered over and over, then put on a plate in front of you and the host has insisted repeatedly, "Try some. I just made it this morning," are you even to consider eating a modest portion and saying, "Well, if you insist." Then, "Mmmmm, delicious. That's so good. Thank you so much. I couldn't possibly eat another morsel/spoonful/bite/sip." In fact the food *always is* delicious, scrumptious, delectably sweet, perfectly salted—we like a lot of salt—crisp, fresh. Whatever it should be, it is.

If you are the host you never ask, "Would you like a piece of *'a bizz*?" That would put your guest in the terrible position of overtly having to announce that, yes, they would like something. It would be a profound embarrassment for both guest and host. Showing desire of any kind reveals that you are wanting. As the host your job is to put as much food on the table as you can, to burden the table with food and drink, far beyond the limit of what actually makes sense for you to offer. As a guest you are to limit yourself to a highly appreciated, small amount.

These rules and customs are based on a culture of scarcity of the very old world in southern Italy and Sicily, where it would have been terribly shameful to show any hint of actual scarcity in your household. These rules helped everything keep in balance. The host would offer and save face and the guest would partake of their offerings and reveal nothing.

Lucia was in the home of our dearly beloved Comma Maria and Compa Frank who were our close friends and *paesans* and who lived downstairs from us. Comma offered my sister, a tiny two-year-old, "Lucia, have a piece of cake."

"No thank you," my sister already knew to answer. More than sixty years later she remembers how delicious that piece of cake looked and that she was obliged to say no. "I really wanted that piece of cake. It looked so delicious, but I knew I was supposed to say no."

After Lucia and I left home for "America," when we left Waterbury to go to college, we were very surprised to learn that these rules did not apply in the wider world.

Over a long period of time our new people (friends, then husbands and their families) pointed out that the food offered at our tables, it really *was* too much—more than people could or would want. That it involved too much work and excess and that maybe it wasn't necessary, that it might even be a burden to guest as well as the host. You could just offer something, say, "Would you like to have some?" At first this seemed ridiculous, *ridickle*, as my grandmother used to say, and we laughed as we smuggled ourselves back and forth across this border— with pride and shame and confusion about both, uncertain which country we belonged to. Over time we confided in each other that our own ways were changing under the influence of our new people.

When my mother was staying with my sister long years after the two of us had more or less adjusted to American culture, a world of plenty, Lucia had some friends over. She put out some cheese and olives and bread, she offered wine and poured it for those who said yes. "Then I sat down at the table to talk to them."

"After they left Mom said, 'Uh, you're becoming pretty 'Merican now aren't you? You don't ask, . . . just give it. That's so embarrassing.' Mom was pretty upset with me."

Another time when Lucia and her husband were renting a house in Italy Lucia became friends with an Italian woman living nearby and they were comparing Italian and American customs. Lucia, knowing the Italian customs around hospitality and the ritual offering and refusals that preceded anyone partaking, explained to her friend, Paola, how different these rules are in America.

In America we *offer* food and we ask our guests, "Would you like a piece of cake."

Paola hid her face in her hands and giggling, completely confused, asked, "But how would they know what to do? What would they say?" She was completely nonplused, by even the explanation of this, especially since it was coming from a woman of Italian heritage.

Lucia said, "Oh they might say, 'That looks very good. Yes, I'd love some.'"

Paola thought this was even more hilarious and it sent her into further giggles at the very thought of the baldness of this exchange, so completely naked of ritual grace. Lucia knew what these giggles meant. Even saying this out loud was embarrassing. You have to *offer, insist,* and *never* put the guest into the position of having to expose the fact that indeed you would *like a piece of cake.*

How could you do it that way and not humiliate your guests? The American way can reveal desire, and so expose a position of shame.

II

Of course, my husband Bill, not an Italian, experiences shame too. It's just different in his private universe. Maybe, because he was the golden child joining two distinct families. His father a widower with five children, his mother a widow with three children. Bill was the adored only child of this often disjointed combination. He was the last child of both his parents, the child of his father's later years. And he was the golden baby that briefly bridged the terrible gulf between these two very broken families. Then he lost his father and the gold burned dark and his family was torn apart by mistreatment and mistrust.

So Bill is made of sun and burn, light and dark, which combined into a wicked wit, an artificer, a song and dance man, a bit of the flim flam man, one of wild humor, a beguiler, sending his audience into paroxysms of delight, then disappearing offstage into deep shadows: there he is a man of indifference to all but his darkness. But he will have his way. His are the rules of theater, of the magician more than of society so that if he wants something and he can flick a hand and get it, he does. Then he disappears. These are his own rules, the rules of the golden, then betrayed child.

Stories, humor, charm are his guides. Clannish shame doesn't pertain to him much. They didn't hold him together for long enough so he has rebelled against clan demands.

One long sultry summer afternoon Bill and I were staying at my sister's country farmhouse in a small valley in upstate New York. There was a creek running through the valley and only one way in or out—a wooden bridge over the creek. I wanted to go to town. He was wearing a three day beard, cutoffs and a tank top and had no intention of leaving the hammock on the back porch or the book he was reading. He would read and doze until I got back. When I came to the bridge, five county road workers wearing dark bronzed tans and baseball caps with undulating white sweat rings around the crowns of their John Deere or Agway Agricultural were pulling up the thick boards to do some repairs on the struts. When I leaned out of the window to ask if I could go through, "Road closed," one of the men said, without looking at me.

"When will it be open?" I asked.

"Not until late this afternoon." I drove back to the house the heat of the sun pouring through the windshield—a long hot, desultory afternoon ahead, "Can't go," I said to Bill when I got back, "the men are working on the bridge."

"Do you want to go to town?" Bill said chomping on his small cigar, swinging his legs out of the hammock? "I'll get you out if you want to go."

When we got to the bridge there were no boards left across the struts. Bill got out of the passenger's seat and walked up to one of the men, "Who's in charge here?"

One burly guy flicked his thumb to another and Bill walked up to him, hitched up the waist of his cutoffs, "I'm Doctor William Herman. I'm a brain surgeon and there's a man lying on the table in the operating room waiting for me to do surgery on him in twenty minutes at Fox Memorial Hospital in Oneonta. Put those boards back down. I have to get into town immediately."

The head guy turned away and said, "Put 'em back." Bill and I waited in the car while they did, then I drove across the bridge. As soon as we were just on the other side Bill said, "Now pull over."

"What?" I looked in the rear view mirror. They hadn't pulled up all the boards yet. There were five or six men on this road crew.

"I'm not going to town," he said and got out of the car.

I watched as he walked back across the bridge, nodding to the head man and going up the road. The men kept blank faces as they watched him walk by.

III

Early in our courtship, before I knew his rules were those of his own defiant making and before he knew mine were embedded in the importance of reputation among your people, early in our courtship I brought him to meet my father.

Bill is seventeen years older than I am. When I met him he was a somewhat overweight, middle-aged bachelor college professor who wore long hair, a bushy mustache, blue jeans, and a blue work shirt, full of charm and intellect, more concerned with bedazzling his audience with his brain and wit than worrying about his appearance. My mother, the ruler of rules, had already met him and disapproved. I was an unmarried daughter, but I was *her* unmarried daughter. Still. "A man of his profession, dressing like that," she said crisply.

I had been out in the world for ten years by then, but I was still in the relatively early part of the journey of crossing over to America. Still.

Because my mother had made her complete disapproval clear we decided that the way to deal with this first meeting of my father and Bill was to appease my mother by going to Barney's on 17th Street and 7th Avenue and buying Bill an expensive wardrobe (that he couldn't afford) to wear for a weekend in the country. To go to this very rural dairy valley upstate we bought two suits, one a three-piece Pierre Cardin, three dress shirts, silk ties, and new shoes. I think he may have packed one pair of jeans and a work shirt. We arrived at my sister's house with Bill dressed in his three-piece suit.

"Well, he looks very nice," my mother said as he showed up for breakfast in the new three-piece suit. The rest of us were barely dressed in bathrobes and pajamas. But he was passing the border check. That was the way the weekend went. Bill at his most lovely and kind. My mother ameliorated.

One of Bill's chameleon forms is to agree with everyone, "We don't need another pot of coffee, do we?"

"Oh no," Bill says smiling at everyone.

When another member of the family arrives late to the kitchen, "I'm going to make a fresh pot of coffee. I'll make the large pot so there will be more for everyone."

"That would be great," Bill agrees. "I'd love another cup."

He played with my sister's little son. He helped wash the dishes in his suits and ties with his sleeves rolled up, and wore an apron. He talked politics and current events with Lucia's husband. He talked about literature and scenery with my father. All due respect to everyone. And all went beautifully under this change of costume.

My parents always arrived at our homes with so many grocery bags one couldn't help but protest—where was all this food going to be stored? As my parents took over every crevice of pantries and all the counter tops my father always quoted his Mammanonna, "We should all have this much room in paradise." We were down to millimeters apiece, but the paucity, parsimony, the necessary frugality of our ancestors was appeased by the plenty the Italian family able to provide here in the land of plenty. We all love to cook and everyone cooked more upstate. We had breakfasts of pancakes and bacon, platters of *macaroni* and immense soup pans full of lima bean soup with sausage—my father's specialty. We all ate until we were uncomfortably full and then went for long country walks to undo what we had just eaten. Then we came back and had coffee and dessert.

So I'm not quite sure how this actually happened. It may have been a couple of days after Thanksgiving so that we had been overeating for days and decided to be a bit more modest that night. One night my parents cooked a dinner of chicken cutlets, roasted potatoes, zucchini, and salad. There were at least three desserts waiting on the counter. Bill had passed the clothing test. He had passed the good guy test. His age was non-negotiable. Things were going well. As the meal wound down and we were all happily overeating there wound up on the platter sitting in the middle of the table—one last chicken cutlet. My mother offered it to everyone, but we all knew how this was to go. This rule of the host guest rules is so basic, so important that it has its own name, *'u pizz' di creanze*. The piece of politeness. If the last piece of anything is eaten, all the customs of politeness have been violated. It means that the host hasn't provided enough for all their guests to have as much as they wanted. It means that the guest is demonstrating this fact publicly.

No matter how much the host presses her guests *no one* is to take it. If it is accepted and taken off the platter, emptied space is left where there should always be *more*. You are never to shame your host that way. There is, however, one exception to this rule. After each person has said no in turn several times, there is one person and only one person who has the right to claim it and that is the oldest male in the room. In this case my father—the man whose approval Bill had come to receive.

On what should have been the final round of refusals—my mother once again said, "Bill wouldn't you like to finish this last piece. Don't leave it. It's just sitting there." As an honored guest Bill could have the right to claim it, but Bill was in the petitioner's position.

"Okay, Rose I'd love to have it," he said, smiling all around to everyone at the table.

I sat frozen in my seat as Bill reached his fork out to spear that last piece. My eyes passed across my father's face where I saw suppressed surprise. I quickly looked away. Time slowed and stretched. Should I reach out and stop that fork? As the daughter of the host I couldn't violate giving our guest anything he wanted. As Bill's girl-

friend I was stunned into a realization that this smart, savvy, sophisti-
cated, free spirit didn't know even the basic rules about food and hospitality. He had broken the most important rule—but worse, he didn't
know that he had.

As I looked down and away from the table. The kitchen floor-
boards became intensely interesting I realized I had no recourse.

I couldn't speak on his behalf to my family. I couldn't say anything
to Bill on my family's behalf. I certainly had nothing to say on my own
behalf. So I didn't say anything and waited for the appalling moment
to pass.

I was going to have to take him on a long trip through Italy and
eventually he would get me to settle in America, but I have to say it's
been an awful lot of packing. And I hate packing.

In Absence

An emptying, a leaving, a lack: what was, but now is no more, or should have been but hasn't been. In absence there is what isn't. We lived in an apartment in Upper Manhattan on 215th Street across from a small, abandoned brick convent. Late in the day as the light faded outside, my fat baby James sat in the kitchen sink splashing water onto the cabinets and floor while I began preparing dinner in my tiny galley kitchen. The sink is filled with water and my son. The circle of flame under the pan on my stove heated and transformed the raw into cooked. The window carried air and the turn of day from the outside in.

My attention and my body rocked easily back and forth between the abundance of my son and dinner: a half step to my left to pick up the plastic elephant cup with the trunk handle he had just flung onto the floor; a quick sway and shifting of my weight onto my right hip as I simmered the potatoes and carrots in garlic and oil; now a sway left for a wet smooch on James's exuberant fat little body; back right for a quick stir of dinner on the stove. James's plump hand gripped the elephant trunk handle of his cup tight in concentration; then he'd scoop the water into the cup, raise it up in triumph and dump it, laughing in celebration.

Still, when my gaze fell away from him and drifted to the day draining away outside my window, it fell on the convent's deteriorating brick facade. Large sheets of plywood were nailed over the doors and windows, the weed-like trees crawling up too close along its walls. The abandoned shell of this old convent backed right into a leafy park, rich large old trees, flowerbeds, winding paths all banked into a long sloping hill.

Despite the animal sweetness of that moment—a fat healthy baby and the preparation of good food in a light, sweet balance—loose waves of melancholy often swept over me, always when my eyes dropped on the waste of that abandoned place. Looking at it simply emptied me of hope.

My melancholy over this squander evoked the same repetitive, almost compulsive, questions. Why was this charming old building left to deteriorate? Why let it fall into ruin? Why wasn't it being used for some purpose? Every day I rebuilt and repopulated it. I decided what its best use would be and filled it with people, especially children. It would be reopened as a community center, it would be a glorious children's museum or, if it should be a commercial venture, it could be turned into apartments. Or why not a great restaurant with tables in the back under the trees? I filled it with voices and movement and purpose but most of all pleasure. I favored the community center. That seemed like the perfect use of all the uses the committee of my imagination came up with. That's what I usually decided in the end. I never imagined kids in the afterschool program that I invented there fighting within its rebuilt walls, only kids playing. I made plans for it over and over because its emptiness, its closed-off doors and windows caused too terrible a sadness to sweep through me, a mourning for what wasn't—what had been and wasn't anymore.

I felt I could almost *will* this building back into new life. The compulsion to imagine it renewed and the frustration that it always lay empty eventually, in almost a rubbing away, forced me to accept in great frustration the lack, the emptiness of that place. Still, each day my longing forced me to repeat the same relentless and hopeless task. When we stand on the rim of absence, we can either feel the deep loneliness and fall into that vast chasm or we can try to fill it.

Life and water sat to my left, fire and food to my right and with a turn of my head a beautiful vista of waste and ruin. This was what my world consisted of then. We had recently moved to Inwood, the northern tip of Manhattan, where, down the hill from us, the Hudson and East Rivers curve and meet, where the land is filled with parks and gardens, and ball fields, but which is far from East 9th Street in Greenwich Village.

Greenwich Village: the place where Bill and I had created our beginning. It had been our grounding, where we had courted, made our first home, decided to marry, and where we had planned, conceived, and had James. There had never been any question that it was where our life together as a family would take place. All my friends and all the women I started to raise James next to were there. But we needed more room for James and the second child. The real estate firestorm of 1979 had hit exactly when James was born and we had had to find a larger apartment and move. I was desolate without that world to live in. I wanted the second child that we had planned on and promised. Desperately. Now it wasn't clear that this was going to be either. The two losses definitely account for the longing and loss I felt when I looked at that building each day back then. I wasn't among my downtown friends. I wasn't going to have that second child for whom we had moved to Inwood.

But there was a much deeper longing behind even all of that. I knew exactly how to raise a child. You bring them up with other children, you bring them up with your larger family. Everything I knew about babies and children started with my tribe, with all the babies who came year after year, with all the diapers we changed of the slightly younger children. All the family life I knew about had men, women, girls, boys all jumbled together working and playing, yelling and fooling around together. Now I was without the women from my family. James's cousins weren't here, my sister, my cousins, my aunts, my parents, all of whom knew the ins and the outs of how I was supposed to raise my child, weren't with me. I was as empty of them as the house was empty of life. Here I was with my deepest desire filled—to have a child, but I was without my two tribes, my original one and the one I had created in the Village and lost. Tribeless.

Without My Tribe

James is the dawn on my horizon, the stars in my dark night. He has large dark olive eyes set against golden hair and skin. In the first months of his life when I got up in the middle of the night I felt as if we were the only two creatures awake on a large rusting boat crossing a wide black sea under a starless sky. It was up to me to carry him fearlessly across the night waters. After his mouth had shuddered into quiet, sucking, then whimpering a quick complaint, then sucking again, then whimpering, finally settling into a steady suck, suck. It was just the two of us facing the dark, filled with invented danger, yearning for the sun's rising, for the warmth of daylight. I'd drink a large glass of water, as satisfied as I had ever been.

As that first year continued, he got up two, three, four times a night, nursing quickly, desperately, and descending back into a deep sleep. I usually tossed for an hour or more; then just as I was beginning to be smuggled across the simple crazy waters into sleep, he'd wail into the dark.

When the first year turned into two and went around the corner into the third year of sleeplessness, a terrible misery overtook me. Most days started off achy and irritable with years of too little sleep. On those days I wasn't sure we'd both survive raising James. Motherhood was consuming my brain, my flesh, my spirit.

For years long after he had been weaned, throughout his toddlerhood and well beyond, in addition to still waking several times during the night, however dark or light the season, however blind to light the shades on his window made his room, however calm or frenzied the previous day's activity had been, James woke up twenty minutes before dawn.

Then too a current runs through him, quivering along his wires, whizzing, whirring as his strong legs carry him along. His small sturdy body moves before an idea has finished leaping across the synapses of his brain. The salt shaker sitting next to my glass of wine rains salt into my glass, white crystals falling into the rich translucent red, before my chin has the chance to drop, long before I have the time I need to reach out my hand to stop the salt from raining down.

"I've got him, Hon," Bill said many mornings. But not before I picked James up from beside our bed where he had stood waiting, pulling the soggy weighty bottom, his smell, the tiny musty puffs of breath into my body. Then I'd pass him to Bill and sink back into a headachy stupor. A rage of exhaustion and an aboriginal passion for my son were always at war in me during those years. Some mornings the soft rising glow of light on the horizon wore away at my tired skin like sandpaper. I longed for sleep the way I had once longed for him.

Some mornings, since I was awake anyway, and neither of us had had much sleep, I'd think Bill might as well get some sleep. If it were, say, five in the morning, then at seven when I was completely desperate I might wake him up and say, "Your turn," and fall back to sleep for a couple of hours. What follows is one of the days when I didn't go back to bed.

James appears by our bed, his eyes wide with an eagerness to begin. "Wanna play, Mama?"

"Yes Mama wants to play with you." And I do. The puffiness about his eyes, the simple longing in his request always pushes my sleepiness away. There is only a call to answer his eagerness as I get up from my warm bed. We go to the kitchen and watch as the light comes up behind the buildings outside the window together. James and I mess around in the kitchen. I make the coffee. NPR is on the radio. James climbs up and down from my lap, running matchbox cars over my various limbs. It is only after a couple of hours and at least two cups of coffee that my body starts aching.

"I have a idea," his dark eyes shining, "we could play . . . play . . . do play dough." These words waft up from my two-year-old golden loaf of a boy.

"Okay, let Mama finish her coffee then we'll make it. Okay?"

"Where's the powder machine"—I gulp down my last half cup and wash out the grounds from the coffee maker—"that goes round and round?" James stands on the small stepstool, next to me at the sink. He means the flour sifter that he was playing with the day before. The deep combination of joy and exhaustion of those mornings sits in my body.

"Let me clean out the sink, then. I'll get it for you."

"Where's that powder Mama?" He means the flour. In his haste to look for powder and powder machine, James knocks over the stepstool, which bangs into my ankle.

It is at moments like that in the excruciatingly early morning that his tempo begins to worry me. He is moving faster than I can keep up with.

"Wait honey. Let's get out all the ingredients, the flour, the salt and the big, big bowl. So we'll have everything we need," I say, bending over to rub my ankle. I try to manage our mornings the way I'd always imagined I would when I had been a nursery school teacher, longing to have a child to wake up with. I had pictured making play dough with my longed-for child, but that child had stayed at my side, moving at a pace I generously accommodated.

"Here's a gooder powder bowl Ma." There are several pans on the floor, two pan covers. Proudly, James holds up the bowl he'd gone to find.

"That's a good one, pumpkin." I didn't want to suggest that maybe we'd need a bigger bowl to contain the mess that would soon be rising in our tiny kitchen because he says so proudly, "I, I, I got got got it my own self."

I quickly put away the pans and covers, hurry to get the flour and salt and then measure it myself so that it doesn't wind up on the floor. I put the water into a pitcher so that James can pour the water in himself. I set up the "powder machine" in the bowl so that he can begin to play with the flour. This is the main inspiration for this request to make play dough.

He begins to pick the flour high up above his head. Then he opens his fingers and watches the flour rain down, soft, loose, powdery. Some of it goes into the bowl; some of it lightly covers the sink and the counters. I look at his sturdy male body enveloped by this silky cloud. A floury pleasure rises in the air.

"I like this powder Ma," he says with a big sloppy grin. He coats his arms with it now, carefully patting it on, and carefully watching it fall off.

"I know honey." Not all mothers let their children play with flour like this, I think virtuously, hearing my neighbor Ginny, say, "Flour is for cooking, not for playing with," in her always certain tone. "She's so angry all the time," I think, putting myself in the not-her category. Some of the flour is in the sink, more is on the counters. There is some on the floor in front of the sink. I want to turn away from James for a minute to open a drawer or cupboard looking for the cream of tartar. But I know that can lead somewhere I don't want to go. There is the food coloring in the drawer, but no cream of tartar needed for the play dough. I don't want to go around the corner to the pantry to look for the cream of tartar. Anyway, I don't keep it there. James has by now dumped the water all at one time into the too shallow bowl. The flour goes up into a spray, some floury globs spatter the rug by the sink. I bend down to wipe it up with a sponge. My idealized version of how I was going to be the good mother to a very lively child—I had longed for just exactly the child that James was: a little wild, fiercely intelligent, deeply engaged by what is in front of him—and the reality of being a mother rise into a swirl of anxiety.

"Be careful Honey," I say, hearing the hard edge of Ginny's voice coming into my own. How does that happen? Whenever I congratulate myself on not being like some other mother of whom I disapprove, within seconds I find myself saying exactly the kind of thing that mother would say. It began to seem like a secret rehearsal, concealing from myself that I was about to behave in a way I hate—concealed, until Ginny's high pitch emerges from my mouth. "So what if some of the flour is on the floor? Enjoy your kid," I try to command myself.

By the time I find the cream of tartar in with the vitamins. James's arms are deep into the gooey mess. His gluey fingers are trying to open the food coloring bottle. "Red's good, right Mama?" he turns toward me, his floured gooey hands dropping some more blobs of play dough on the floor. His powdered face looks earnestly up at me for approval. Flour fills the air like chaos, falling covering the counters, the floors. Little bits of wet and dry dough stick to James's face and hair. I sigh, trying to release the distress into the space between us.

"Be careful about where the powder's falling okay?" I hear my voice going up. I look at the clock. It's 7:50. I try to clear my head as I bend down to wipe up the worst of the spills with a wet rag. This is what you waited for all those years—to have a child, this child. Why spend all your time cleaning up now that he is finally here?

James is going at the mixing, kneading the play dough intensely. "Good job James, you're just like the baker, making his bread. Good kneading," I say, trying to stay with my idea of what a good mother would say.

"I'm a gooder baker, right?"

I use all of my self-control not to start putting the ingredients away, when the phone rings. It's a loud demand into our floury disorder, our apartment building management. I've been trying to reach them for weeks to come and inspect the water stains from the leak.

"Ma, I have to clean my hands now." James is tugging on my nightgown with his doughy hands. I try to get him to knead some more so I can deal with the phone call. "Just a minute honey, Mama will be coming back to the bakery."

"Look, you said you'd come and see them last week." I turn to get my appointment book to write this so-called appointment down and the name of the person calling. As I do that I see that James is shaking his hands now trying to get this goo off. The pink dough splatters around the tiny kitchen, on the toaster, on the walls, on the light fixture over the sink.

"I'm not going to be able to match your paint, you understand?" the man on the phone says. But James has climbed down from the stepladder and is racing toward the living room, gooey hands out front. I drop the phone on the floor and race to get James, "Just a minute," I scream to both of them, "We're not going to do that." I march James back to the kitchen, and holding one hand around his middle I place him back on the stepladder. "Look just come and look at the damn stain," I say to the guy on the phone. "We'll talk paint later."

James is squirming away and he is racing toward his father in the bedroom, "Papa, Papa, I'm a bakerman."

By the time I catch up with him in the bedroom Bill's eyes are flaked with dried bits of play dough. "Jesus honey," he says looking up at me, "what's up?"

As filled with turmoil as the dark hours can be, waking into life with a toddler feels more bizarre than a dreamscape. "Oh please," I say, suppressing my sympathy for Bill. I'm afraid to give my sympathy to him or all the sympathy in the house will be used up; there will be none left for me. "I've been up since five-thirty. I've had too much coffee. We've made some play dough. The building management called to harass me. I'm exhausted and your son's ready to rock and roll."

James is watching his mother from his perch beside his father's head, one leg casually over his father's shoulder. His hair is standing up in several doughy peaks. "We going to dance Mama?" He's waving his hands above his head moving his bottom to his own rhythm. I would never know at those moments whether I should hug or strangle him.

"Jeez, is there any coffee left?" Bill asks, shaking his head. The clock claims it is 8:30. The long day stretches out in front of me. I lie back on the bed, "Please tell me tonight's not your graduate course." That course runs very late.

"No not tonight; just a departmental meeting. I'll be home by five. I'll cook tonight, okay?" Bill bends over and kisses me. James pokes his nose into the small spot where our mouths are meeting.

"I'll kiss," he says, "I'll kiss too." I look up and see his dark olive eyes. An intense love for him sweeps up in me, brought by the roundness of his cheeks, the dry play dough in his hair, the confidence that he is wanted in our kiss, emotion floods into the smallest cavities in my body. How could I have yelled at him before? It isn't even 9 o'clock in the morning.

"I'll kiss a Nuggins," I say, lifting him above my head, then I aeroplane him down to my mouth. Bill has wandered off to the kitchen. I'll drink some Coke, I think, vowing that today I won't let myself be exhausted, today. Fuck the house, cooking, everything. And no TV either. At that moment the day stretches out generously in front of me.

"Jo, my queen," Bill yells from the kitchen.

"Mr. Rogers, Mr. Rogers, Mr. Rogers," James begins chanting, bouncing up and on the bed. I hate it when Bill reduces my name to flatness and adds *that* endearment—I picture an old fat woman in a heavy brocaded dress with a weird hairdo. I snap on the TV before I go out to the kitchen. I have to have at least a minute with Bill before he leaves to teach at City College.

"Don't call me that horrible name."

"Look, I just remembered I've also got a poker game tonight, but I'll cancel." Bill is always firmly committed to his winning the best husband of the year award. "I mean it."

"You'll just make sure everyone knows what a devoted husband you are, what a good guy, how I couldn't get through the night without you. Go to the damn game." I am never sure who I hate most at those moments. It is definitely someone in our apartment.

In a furious whirl I pick up the house, make the beds, take a shower, make James two snacks. I feel calmer because the house is picked up—but depressed because what I want seems so minimal and so hard to come by. Triumph for me consists of a bed made and a shower taken. I break all my earlier resolves by noon. James's been watching TV steadily in order for me to manage a few things. I have yelled at him for cleaning the jelly off his hands on the couch and for rejecting the second snack he insisted he wanted and that he had to have that he promised he would eat. The atmosphere crackles with the tension and disappointment I feel.

I get him ready for the park.

We are the first ones at the playground. We have only recently moved to Inwood from our home in Greenwich Village where Bill and I had both made our adult lives. We are new to the neighborhood and I have different rhythms than the other women in the neighborhood: they come out after lunch, James can't wait till then.

"Where's anybody?" James often seems surprised when we arrive at an empty park. He wanders over to the sandbox and starts digging in what seems to me to be a desultory way. I go and sit on the bench and read my *New Yorker*. I am always cold when I am tired and so I sit in the sun to warm up. I start to read Talk of the Town, but my eyes wander back to James; I am inextricably drawn back to watching him—a planet circling the sun.

Often, though we're going to the playground, James insists on wearing his polyester three piece navy blue suit that my mother had given him. He carries a cigar box so that he can be like Bill; the cigar box is his briefcase. He is in the sandbox with his clip-on tie; his briefcase having fallen to one side. He loves holding the sand, feeling it, watching it fall in streams from his hands. Often he lies down in it and rests there, then pushes some of it to one side with one foot, then the other. If he moves, it moves, if he slides it slides. It is one of his mediums. Stuff that moves when he pushes. Water and snow are the others. He brushes the sand back and forth with his fingers, quietly moving it one way, then the other. The sand is completely accommodating, completely accepting.

I should be his sand. That's what a mother should be, I think. I have wanted to be a mother all my life. There has been no other constant for me as old, as utter, as my longing for a child. It had been with me through all my childhood; when I played with my dolls and my tea set during my girlish years; when my cousins and I piled small red berries on maple leaf dishes for our doll babies to eat; it was with me when I climbed the tallest tree and sped on my bike down the steep hills of Waterbury. It was with me as a teenager swimming out to the island in the middle of the lake, daydreaming about what it would be like to lie on a cool bed and make love to Donny—that could lead to making babies. I'd thought about it in those days, with delightful anxiety. It stayed with me when it became a real possibility in my twenties, in the sixties, but then began to look as if it were going to slip away from me—I didn't seem to know how to make a relationship work. I didn't know if I had the ability to make men *I* wanted want to stay with me and have a baby. It finally accompanied me as I fell in love with Bill and he said yes he would carry in his strong arms what I would carry in my body.

Now here I am with my boy and my lungs are filled with tight uncertainty. The sun hits me full on my shoulders now. James is singing some phrase over and over to himself. "I like blue play dough. I like blue play dough." I walk quietly near, hoping he'll keep singing. He is turned away from me and doesn't hear me coming. "Mama don't like blue play dough, Mama says no blue dough." His voice is small, high, sweet. It's filled with a yearning that matches mine for something inexplicably not this.

The emptiness of the swings and slide, the empty benches fill the park with absence. A confusion that is with me all the time, crawls up the muscles of my larynx, fills my sinuses, crawls into the spaces around my eyes; burns in me, in my face, in my neck and shoulders, in every crevice of my understanding, with sadness at what is wrong and unchangeable in my life. I am too often tired, worried, anxious during those—the most longed for—times of my life.

I bend down and pour some sand on James's belly, "Hi Mr. Nuggins."

"Hi Mommy Nuggins," his dark eyes light up, beaming up toward my face and resting there for a minute. Then he jumps up, throws sand in every direction. It goes all over us, in our hair, into the pocket of my jacket, down the neck of my flannel shirt, into my eyes. "Could I do swinging?"

I am determined not to let the sand bother me. I shake off the grains, blink my eyes, rub it off my neck, jump up and down to get it out from under my shirt. "Let me think? Can James go on the swing? I don't know." He stands in the sand looking up at me. The anxious blur between teasing and reality has his face puckered, waiting for the relief of the not teasing. "Mr. Nuggins can go for a swing." The golden inner light in him bursts around him.

"And Mama will push?"

"Yes, yes Mama will push."

"Up high, high Mama."

We walk over to the swings sitting still in the thin fall sun. The diagonal metal poles feel damp in their hardness. Is there any object as still as a swing with its inherent need to move? The metal jangles as I lift James into his seat; he has complete faith that he will get what he wants. I am determined not to let the ache in my muscles, the boredom of the repetition, the necessity of surrendering any wish or need of my own, cut this swinging short.

First I play the I'm-going-to-eat-these-toes-for lunch game from the front. Each time the swing comes toward me I pretend to catch James's sneakers in my hands as if I am going to munch them. Sometimes I say, "Sooo delicious," sometimes I say "Uh oh this food's getting away from me. And I'm hungry!" He flings his head back in abandon, thrilled when the lunch gets away.

"From the back Mommy," he requests.

"Okay Button." I go around the back to push. Each time my boy's back returns to me I'd give it a definite push back into the flying future.

"Higher Mommy." I pace my shove to meet the back of the swing just before the peak of the return comes toward me. I receive it and give it a thrust back for height.

"More Mommy, more," James laughs. The swing is in its rhythm. I push each time with just the right amount of energy. My arms still have their morning ache, but something else is there too, a pulsing to the rhythm of this task.

James is mesmerized by the swinging. He stops shouting for more. "I'm going to give him all the swinging time he wants," I think. This time.

The emptiness of the park has only the sound of the swing moving through the worn fall air. The sound of the brushed air moves inside us. We enter into the trance of the swing and release—return and go away.

A silence descends. A current runs between us. We are deep in the back and forth. The metal swing is received easily into my waiting hands, then swing and hands move backward through the last piece of the sweep; with exact control I push it forward and James flies away, out of my hands into the air.

He is really moving now. I push hard for catch and return, balancing the hard shove for speed against the need for control. I know if my push got even a little off center the swing would easily jerk out of synch twisting in that abrupt violent way, then shiver to a halt—a perversion of swinging.

I begin to feel as if we have arrived on another plane where nothing exists but us and the swing, as if no one else ever came to this park, James is the only child who's ever swung on that swing.

James swinging and me pushing him: the tepid sun falls across our sweaters, on our bones, young and younger, tired and more tired—we enter a world we might not be able to come back from—as if I will have to go on pushing him forever if I don't stop soon. No one will ever come down the hill yelling. Bill will never come home from work. Everyone and everything has disappeared but James and me and the swing in the park.

I decide that I will count to one hundred and then stop, so that the endlessness of this strange moment will have shape. I count silently. When I am up to eighty I reconsider and think that maybe I shouldn't stop. Why would I take us away from this strange synchronicity we are in—this stretching, this elastic silence, this connection, this freedom?

This, then, is mothering, I think—this tearing apart, this ripping and rending and then the return, the coming back together, the inexorable giving in, the yielding—the terrible surrender at either end with flight in the middle.

For that moment, the battle has quieted, the war in me has subsided. There is no me, trying to keep my identity separate from Bill or James, no husband for whom I have too little to give, no son who asks more than I can give. There is only aboriginal love—mother and child.

Inexorably I count down the last twenty swings. As I push James off on the count of one hundred, he speaks for the first time into the quiet—"That's enough Mama. Stop."

I let the swing go, and it moves back and forth, each time a little more slowly, in shorter swings until it wiggles to a stop. I lift James out of the swing and we walk side by side up the long hill home in the thin warmth of the fall air.

The Discourse of *un' Propria Papon'*

"Y̶ou're such a *papon'*."

"What's this new curse you're putting on me?"

"Not a curse. It's a slur on your character."

"What're you calling me now?"

I'm in my Upper West Side kitchen talking to my Jewish husband. I'm protesting, insisting, injecting my ethnicity into the New York Jewish intellectual world I live in. The world I escaped to and by which I am now held hostage.

"Look, a *mammon'* was the worse thing you could call someone when I was a kid, anyone who was a *mammon'* was a putz, a jerk. But really it means mama's boy," I explain a bit pedantically, as I have learned to do in my life in New York. "O-n-e is a suffix for big, so when you add it to the end of a word it changes that word from an ordinary nominative to a noun that is somehow adjectival—the noun, made big, bigged up, remember our son used to say, 'you're going to big them up,' when I borrowed his mittens." Not that my family ever pronounced a vowel at the end of any word. We didn't say *mammone*, we said *mammon'*.

"So if you're a *mammon'*, you're big for your mother—too involved with her."

When Marcello Mastroianni died, the *New York Times* obit referred to him as a sex symbol who was actually a *mammon'*. I was stunned, thrilled, a word from my childhood in the *New York Times*!

"You know how I always say 'I'm a *chacciaron'*,"—*chaccia* means someone who talks a lot, but I'm a *chacciaron'*—a really big talker. "Annie's family calls it *chacciarese, e-s-e*, that's from her dialect." Annie's

213

family is from a different town, they use e-s-e. It makes me sad that I have to explain these words instead of being able to just use them in a community that knows what I mean, the way my husband does with his friends, all those childhood sounds that convey what no other sounds can—*intimacy*. Occasionally, I say to my classes, which are made up largely of minority adults, "*Stata chitt'*." And because I love them I expect them to understand me. My students tolerate my explanation and translation because they are a people who recognize oral affection when they hear it.

When I was a kid, *mammon'* had been the worst insult you could fling at someone. That and *cafon'*, which really meant someone with no class, a lowlife. But for me and my cousins a *mammon'* was worse, anyone who wasn't tough, capable of doing whatever, climbing trees, swimming out to the island, staring down somebody in the school yard.

"But *you*," I say to my husband Bill, "you're a *papon'*." Bill loves this stuff, at least as much as he loves me. My Italianness. It goes with the circles under my eyes, my dark moments, all the garlic browned in olive oil for almost everything I cook.

But where we live on the Upper West Side of Manhattan it is assumed everyone middle-class is Jewish in reality or by association. And in effect I am Jewish by association. It's where I've found a home, where there is enough of the kind of talk I love, lots of it, too much of it, too intensely full of jokes and condemnation. It's where I found people who care more about reading or music or have some similar attachment that burns in them, that has little do with what was valued where I was raised. There people care about food, kids, gardens, fooling around, the loss of which burns in me still. But I had to leave because only my father, who had been an ironworker, had been a serious reader. I am at home here on the Upper West Side of Manhattan. But I hate the fact that it's assumed I will be pleased to have my ethnicity replaced, "You're Jewish—everyone ethnic is Jewish," I've been told many times.

"I'm not Jewish, thank you very much, and I'm very happy being Italian," I've found myself saying priggishly many times. Where I grew up it was a point of honor to declare your ethnicity defiantly. "What're *you*?" we asked the first time we met another kid. Everyone understood the question. We were Italian, Irish, a couple of German kids. Elaine Mann was the only Jewish girl in school. Maybe because I was *Italian* I still feel funny saying "Italian American."

Just as I feel funny saying my family is "working-class" or "blue collar." These are not words my family would use to describe them-selves. They didn't define themselves by their work. That wouldn't occur to them. They worked hard. They were good at what they did. They mostly voted Republican. So those labels, although accurate, sound condescending, or as they say in Waterbury, brass capital of the world, "That sounds stupid." Italian American is a name given to them by people who didn't live in our neighborhood. I feel as if I betray my family every time I use those words.

Another one: "That makes me anxious," instead of, "She makes me nervous," or alternatively, "He gives me *agiata*." My husband's brother would say, "Don't get all noyved up." How about replacing, "She was so inappropriate," with "I'd like to give her a slap?" I can feel the sting in my hand when I say it. Is one more articulate than the other? The one with the sensation attached makes more of an impression on my synapses. But my language has changed. I only occasionally use phrases like, "Gimme the *mappin'*" to mean, "Hand me the dishcloth." But these decontextualized phrases have taken on the ring of pretentiousness, because I use these words deliberately now, I'm doing something, not just talking in a world in which I belong. "Get the *scola macaron'*," I say to my son sometimes, because I don't want him growing up not knowing my language, where the phrase "Get the *scola macaron'*" means literally, "Get the strain the macaroni."

So now I accuse my husband, "You're such a *papon'*."

"You're saying I'm a papa's boy, right?"

"Aren't you?"

"Just because I'm mourning my father after forty years. I was a kid. I was only eight. I never got over it. My father . . ." he looks off dreamily into the kitchen cupboards. "If my father had lived he'd be ninety-eight."

"*Managga diavole!* Bill, if your father were alive, he'd be dead." I can't help it. I'm irritated this morning, sick of the endless talk about the dead father, who's haunted my married life to Bill. We've walked this hallowed walk at least once a week for our twenty years of life together. I'm tired of this man I've never met. Bill looks at me, stunned. Then he flings back his head and roars. He's laughing so hard he's crying. "You, *you* kill me." He comes over and throws his large body onto me, grabs me and holds on while he laughs and laughs.

I never get over this. This is acceptable here, it's expected; you make small deflating remarks and if they hit their target you're a hero. I always feel sheepish for daring to go after "the father."

New York is my home. This is where I grew into my maturity, where Bill and I have lived our lives together. This is where we've raised our son James, a large Slavic-looking boy, who has his father's fine ear, which is why he wins prizes reciting poetry in the Tuscan version of

Italian that my grandparents were unable to speak or understand. This Italian has little to do with the dialect I grew up with and can't speak except for a few scattered defining phrases. "My Russian boy," I call James, when I come upon his large blond presence with surprise again. "My big Slavic boy."

James doesn't seem to be in any way confused by these contradictions. His friends call him half-a-wop. He calls himself a Dago-Yid production. His girl friend is the Freaken-Puerta-Rican. Despite the language police, he and his friends use these terms as forms of affection. For them all this is grist for pleasure.

All his girlfriends have been a pleasure for me. His wife Heather is even more so. She has dark hair, a huge smile. She loves to cook and eat, design and make. When I found out she had dyed James's suit because he got a stain on it I was ecstatic. This is stuff that I understand—second skin to me.

James is a *papon'* too. "What did Dad say when you told him I won the Italian recitation prize? Was he happy?"

Why is there a dialect word for *mammon'* but not for *papon'*? Why is it bad to be a mama's boy or girl, but not mentioned if you are papa's boy or girl? Is it that these things are understood, part of the paradigm?

How about *un propria nu papon'*? Here I've modified in dialect this invented noun to describe the Italian girl obsessed with her Italian father—a real bad *papon'*, that's me.

These are the kinds of questions that I can ask here in New York and the people I'm talking to will pick the question up, look at it, turn it over and add something to what I've just said. Where I came from that kind of talk is considered silly. Anything that made you self-conscious is embarrassing. To be embarrassed is the worst.

"Can you imagine, he called my sister-in-law for *directions*? So embarrassing, a man asking a woman for *directions!*" My father had shaken his head in disgust and deep shame for his Jewish son-in-law when Bill had asked Aunt Tony for directions to the Cape, a place she drove to often. Where do you begin with something like that?

Especially if you are a *un propria nu papon'*—just like my husband and son—I'm one obsessed with her father. Whom I had always adored, who read Emily Brontë to my sister and me, at least once a year, sitting at the kitchen table in his undershirt and grey work pants.

"Listen to this," he had said and I had, though I never learned how to talk comfortably to him. Because girls don't talk to their fathers, they listen. Anyway, after a while I no longer spoke his language fluently.

He said things like, "You know what happened down the street with Cockroach Rhinie?" And this had made me want to ask two questions, "Is Cockroach Rhinie the guy who gets the stolen stuff from the colored kids?" And I wanted to ask, "Is Cockroach Rhinie typical of the environment in the social club setting?" Even thinking the second question was a betrayal of him. Thinking the other was a betrayal to the person I'd become. So sometimes it seemed best to stay in my kitchen among the *paponi* of my own and insult my husband in words I've invented, because he knows what I'm saying.

Lotions, Potions, and Solutions

My mother, Rose, the most obedient person who ever lived, was brought up in a culture that controlled through shame. An Italian daughter learns the rules early. At eighty-nine she still washed out her underwear every night by hand. Most nights of her adult life she sat at the kitchen table with files, papers, and ledgers. She had notes and letters to write to friends and for business. "I don't know what I am going to do," she'd say. "I have so much work to get done." "Poor lost soul," my father would say, and shake his head. "She makes work for herself." No one else has all these papers. She had files with all her sales receipts, records of every financial transaction in her ledgers and a copy of every tax form she'd ever filed.

On the farm where she was born and raised her family spoke only the *Tolevese* dialect. It was only when her oldest sister Arcangela started school that she started to teach her brothers and sisters a few words of English. Firstborn in Tolve, Arcangela was her mother's right hand, my mother, firstborn in America, was her father's. By seven, Rosa was his business secretary.

"At night, after all our farm chores were done, milking the cows, collecting the eggs, gathering kindling, making dinner and cleaning up after, sweeping the kitchen floor, he would sit me down at the kitchen table and dictate letters to me in Italian and I would have to put them into English. But I had only been in school a couple of years when I started to help him with his letters and books . . . in this childish handwriting. Who knows what I wrote? What did I know? Can you imagine what those people must have thought getting those letters?" From then on she kept his books, kept track of his banking, paid his bills, kept receipts, account books, and wrote his business correspondence. So she

218

knew how to keep records. All accounts were in order. Caught between the inchoate, pride-and-shame-driven ancient world of the pig farm and being their official face to America, my mother became lettered in every possible kind of accounting: records, rules, regulations, codes, customs, and judgments. Until she went blind in her nineties she read all the fine print on every bill, letter, or advertisement that came in the mail. She knew what they said, what her obligations, duties, and responsibilities were. What the obligations of others were.

She had a greater investment in keeping the law than Moses. And she made herself responsible for all of them. Herself and us. Especially every breach, break, violation, betrayal, rupture, every transgression. She kept track. Counted all the wrongs.

"Can you imagine? I was going round the neighborhood to collect for the church. And she comes to the door and says, 'Oh, hi, Rose.' And we stand there talking. And she doesn't ask me in. She gave me a dollar, which was very nice of her, but really. She didn't even ask me in and ask me to sit down for a minute. Offer me a glass of water, nothing. What a pill." Our word for almost anything for which we have contempt is 'merican. Because this is what 'mericans were like. They're scustamade, rude, without custom, without manners. They don't know the proper way of doing things. My mother did. She was a clear and definite judge of things.

My mother and I were walking down the street one day in downtown, the center of Waterbury's business and social world. It has the charm of citizens conducting their public lives naturally and with pleasure in their home country. As we were walking, my mother noticed someone she knew coming toward us. "She's looking away, pretending she doesn't know me. Don't ever do that. If you know someone, always say hello. People get odd sometimes, they turn their heads away. I don't know why. But you don't do that. You don't have to stop, just say hello."

"Hello, Marie," she called to the woman passing us on the street. The woman feigned having just noticed my mother, who flashed this woman her dazzling certain smile; the woman's face lit up when she saw my mother's smile and she smiled back just as brightly. The simplicity and rightness of that advice pleased. A deeply rule-bound woman, sometimes she was just right.

Just as when she made up this aphorism when someone chastised her for breaking a dish while she was washing up after dinner at their house. "Hey,' I wanted to say to them," she told me later, "'the one who washes the dishes is the one who breaks them.'" Right again.

My mother wasn't brought up in the Church—her *anarchista Papa* hated the Church for calling in loans against seed money. When crops failed in Basilicata, they'd confiscate the peasant's land. But his loathing was sealed here in America.

My mother told me: "In those days they didn't have the babies baptized right away. You waited a while and maybe they'd take a couple of the children at once. Then when that terrible accident happened and the baby died, when Papa went to make arrangements for the mass, Father Scoglio said that he couldn't bring the baby into the church for mass because he wasn't baptized. My brother was only two years old. That was an awful slap in the face. You have all this pain that you're going through and then Father Scoglio says that to you. After that we were not allowed to go near a church."

But as my mother and her sisters grew up they were embarrassed, ashamed really, not to have been brought up in the Church. After family, it was an important location of right and wrong, sins and blessings, goodness and badness. When my mother fell in love with my father, she snuck off to take catechism classes to be baptized and confirmed. She didn't know my father was "no churchgoer."

Joining the Church was inevitable, since in every way my mother was a religious zealot—every rule-mandating system was for her. Only loosely at first, then more and more over the course of her lifetime, being Catholic became important to my mother. It was always a part of my sister's and my life.

But the Church was no match for her. She drew on all systems of rules, regimes, and beliefs. Her deepest beliefs went far beyond the Church or even religion. Her sense of how things should go was far wider and deeper than a system like the Church or even the absolutes of our Italian culture.

She believed there was a prayer for every occasion. If not a prayer, there was a saying. If not a prayer or a saying, then a remedy. If not a prayer, saying, or remedy, then a vitamin. "If you have a cold you drink a cup of hot water, two teaspoons of apple cider vinegar and honey, every few hours and before bed. Your cold will go away immediately and it makes you lose weight too. Apply vinegar to your varicose veins to shrink them. Warts, rub with castor oil—twenty times or so. Rub with vitamin A too. For asthma apply one tablespoon of corn oil to eyelids at bedtime.

"For high blood pressure paprika and honey at every meal. If you get ridges in your fingernails you should eat more Jello or mix Knox Gelatin every day in a glass of juice. It's good for your nails and hair.

"Vaseline is good for everything. My mother used it for everything that hurt her. I use in on my face at night sometimes. I rotate.

"If you have a water ring on a table from a glass, rub it with mayonnaise and ashes from a cigarette."

If not a prayer, a saying, a vitamin, or a remedy, then *the truth.* "All babies know everything when they're born. They just forget it as they grow up. What a shame. They know everything. Look into their eyes and you can see it. You just keep an eye on them." Then a big sigh, "It's such a shame we have to lose all that.

"All children choose their parents. They decide who they want to be born to. So I want to say thank you for choosing me to be your mother," a solemn, even formal look on her good girl face.

Rosa Rosette, her mother called her when she was annoyed with her. My father called her Sugar Lump the night they met, then Rosy, Rosy Baby, Rambling Rose, Gram Baby, Che Billettz, Billetz, finally Billy. Sometimes I think the world would have been better off with her in charge. Rose by whatever name, my mother knew how things should go.

Kiss the bed, *baci' u letz*, before you leave the house, so you'll be sure you'll come back. When I protested her insistence that I should put paprika in everything I cook: "All right, don't! Get sick! See if I care." Most of her friends saw her as generous, beneficent. She would have made a terrific goddess. They also thought she was modern. I found her ways absolute and exhausting. She could have been a queen, she was so comfortable with an edict: "Take that off. You can't wear that to a wedding. You have to call Mrs. M. and make a time to visit her. Did you write to Mrs. Perugini yet?" Maybe a judge.

By middle age my mother went to church regularly, with us and without us. My mother's involvement with psychics and Edgar Cayce increased, too. Her vitamin regimen and all of her systems of potions and solutions were on the rise. She never went anywhere without her copper bracelet for her arthritis. When she wanted to affect the outcome of the future she went on a complete regimen of fasting and prayers. She might have made a decent wise woman with her potions and solutions.

"I'm not eating any sweets for six months," she'd announce airily at the daily coffeeklatch she had with her sisters every afternoon before their husbands came home from work. "It worked that time I prayed for Gilda and her heart. I didn't eat any chocolate for a year that time. And I said a rosary every night too."

She knew her own power, too. "You know, the other day I really concentrated and I made the clouds go away. I just kept looking at them and really worked at it. And they finally just drifted away."

But her limits, too. More and more, she spent much of her day praying for her children, her nieces, nephews, eventually for grandchildren and her sons-in-law, too.

"Even when he's sleeping, I can't get through to him."

"What do you mean, Mom?" I was on the phone with her. We were discussing a particularly difficult case for my mother. My sister's husband, John.

"Well, you know I pray for all of you at night, when you're asleep. And I think that if you're asleep you hear me better; my prayers can get to you. I've been praying for John Mudd. Even when he's sleeping, I can't get through to him. Maybe because he is Protestant. What are you going to do?"

Once she visited my husband, son, and me while we were living in Paris and she spent most of the time writing postcards to her family and friends. This went on for days and days, buying postcards, going to the post office, getting more stamps. She was driven to fulfill this duty—to each person, she owed a postcard. Finally, one day she said, "All I really want to say is, 'Ha ha, I'm in Paris and you're not.'"

When she died, my sister and I went through all of her files and boxes of papers. An epic archive:

All tax files. Bank books. Nine address books.

All the photograph albums of all the pictures she ever took.

Her grammar school autograph book from 1926–27, where the school yell is recorded as "rah, rah," and with sayings like the following: "When you're in the kitchen drinking tea, burn your lips and think of me." And, "I wish you luck, I wish you joy, I wish you first a baby boy, and when his hair begins to curl I wish you then a baby girl. Yours till the moon shines green." A daring one: "Here's to us, I wish us well and all the rest can go to ____."

My father's pension benefit book going back to 1937 when he was an apprentice ironworker.

A receipt from The Aluminum Cooking Utensil Company dated 9/10/40 for $53.48 for all the pots and pans she bought just before she got married. Also the payment book from Metropolitan Furniture for a houseful of furniture, lamps, and rugs she bought to furnish their first "rent" at 334 Oak Street. In addition, this includes one carpet sweeper and one percolator. The "free" rocking chair she later nursed us in was "thrown in" as a gift from the salesman. The payment book is marked paid off, January 15, 1942.

Many notebooks: On the front page of one of her notebooks in her handwriting is written: "You shall give an account of every word that is spoken."

Tiny travel notebooks which mentioned time of arrival at each hotel, every meal they ate, every sight they saw, every outfit she wore every day of any trip, including which shoes, jewelry, gloves, and pocketbook. The jokes they told on the bus.

A recipe-like file box full of home remedies filed both alphabetically and by organ.

Under *cold sore*: rub with burnt toast. *Infection*: brown soap and sugar. *Mumps*: hemp cut up, egg white, wrap in cloth, apply to affected parts. *Bee or wasp bite*: sliced raw onion, apply.

Under *heart*: carry currants and raisins in pocket and chew slowly while working. Chew tops of rosemary first thing in the morning after breakfast.

A draft of a letter to Wayne Newton complaining because he cancelled a performance on a trip they had booked to Missouri: "You are our favorite performer." The brochure doesn't state in the fine print that this could happen. She signs it, "Two disappointed fans. Anyway we can enjoy your tapes."

She was a dutiful daughter, she was passionately in love with my father, but she was born to be a grandmother—she loved her grandchildren with a joy that made her love pure and complete. She had every single card, drawing, letter she ever got from them. She wrote down every cute thing they ever said. One notebook for each of them. She had their sizes documented through their growing up so that she could buy them the right presents.

She could have worked for the Catholic Review Board: what's acceptable for movies and television. She was watching her soaps one day when she complained to me, "These women, you put them on TV and they all become sluts." She throws up her hands in disgust watching *All My Children*.

"Just leave," she squealed at the TV, "Go! *Chiesta ca,* this one here is taking off all her clothes and drinking tequila and she's trying to seduce him, and he's saying, 'No, no, no,' but he's not leaving the room." She sighs and rests her tired head on her fingertips. She doesn't know what to do. "What's wrong with people?"

As she got older and she started to become legally blind, her handwriting deteriorated, the letters becoming large, rough and crude. Since she couldn't read anymore and it became harder and harder for her to watch television, she began to keep a new notebook, this one of homonyms, "To keep my mind busy." Ate, eight, ail, ale, all, awl, be, bee, buy, bye, berry, bury.

She sent in her weekly contributions to St. Leo's parish until she died at ninety-four, even though by eighty-six she couldn't drive and eventually was afraid to even leave her apartment. She watched Mass on television, prayed for all of us and sent in her money. And made the sign of the cross over every plate of the food she reheated in the microwave. Hers was a clear and moral world. And a dangerous one. If you didn't say the right prayer, if you didn't take your vitamins or bring the right present when your hairdresser's daughter had a baby, if you didn't obey your parents' dictates even when they'd been dead for thirty years, who knew what might happen?

Toward the end of her life things, even taking her vitamins, began to wear her out. "I'm just fixing my vitamins," she sighed deeply. "I'd like to dump them all down the drain. Sometimes you're better off being a normal person." Things were changing a little.

Late in my mother's life, Lucia, a woman with a permanent light in her eyes, longing for a piece of our old world, returned to the church and sang in her choir. This was a couple of years before the pedophile scandals broke in Boston. Lucia and John live in Cambridge. When the scandal broke her spiritual home changed. This was a devastating betrayal of the Catholic world. So it became a part of Lucia and her husband John's life to stand in protest every Sunday outside the Cathedral of the Holy Cross in Boston, with survivors bearing witness instead of going inside to attend Mass. The survivors were men and women who had once been among the most faithful Catholics, who had been raped and molested by priests when they were children and adolescents. One Sunday, when our mother was staying with them, they took her along. She was going to wait in the van for them and say her prayers for her grandchildren.

Lucia and John were getting out of the van, when, as my mother told it, "Then it dawned on me. 'Hey, I'm sitting here. I want to tell the Cardinal *too*. *I* have something to say. Who do they think they are anyway? To children!" Her voice rose each time she told this to a high indignant plane. "These were children! Little children! Their lives are ruined."

So that day my somewhat bent, but clear-minded eighty-nine-year-old, Italian American, Catholic mother descended from my sister's van with her walker: "I call it my chariot," she said and laughed when she told this story, and with John and Lucia at either side, she struggled over the mounds of snow, to stand in protest for the first time in her life. To disobey for the first time in her life.

"We should turn away from the Church and toward the Lord," she said to those she stood with wearing her STTOP button ("Speak Truth to Power"). She toddled along when they moved to the back of the church to man each of the corners of the intersection where Cardinal

Law would have to pass in his sleek black car. "He said it was a sin, but it's a crime," said one protester. "It *is* a sin. And *it is* a crime," answered another. "It is a sin and it is a crime and it is heartbreaking," the chant went further. "It's shameful." Shame is something my mother knew something about.

Transformed into truth teller, lawgiver, my mother lifted her hands from her walker and rubbed one pointer finger along the other, first one, then the other, over and over, pointing toward Cardinal Law, showing her fellow protesters how to make sure someone knows, "that they should be ashamed." She said, "Shame, shame, shame. Shame on you!" In our family there is no greater humiliation you can visit on someone.

Cardinal Law ducked his head as he drove past the protesters. It felt good to be against Law. And he should be filled with dread—especially about arriving at the judgment table in heaven, because my mother will definitely be there, right next to God. She might be elbowing God out of the way. She's always been at ease with a judgment. She knows how things should go and she's kept a record. Law's on her list.

And La La La

"**A**nd wake up, Rosie! People take advantage. What's wrong with me? Why didn't I tell her not to come?" My mother turned to me when she hung up the phone. "I'm still tired from yesterday."

After my father died, Lucia and I went to visit my mother as often as we could. But visiting Waterbury became very different. We weren't just going to visit. We were responsible now for a piece of my mother's life. Since she no longer had my father—the absolute center of her adult life—she ceded to herself new kinds of rights to our attention. We had to replace that center for her. Often, as I drove up from my home, it was as if my adult life in New York disappeared behind me the closer I got to Waterbury. The fact that we lived in other cities in no way lessened our obligations to attend to our mother as she had attended to her own after my grandfather had died. There was no give to the reality of our now living in other cities, other states, other worlds than the one in which we had been raised. We moaned to one another and did our always inadequate best.

On one particular visit the divide of those two worlds became even more intensely apparent and it became clear that two-thirds of me was always in the wrong place. There was no location but in the divide.

On that visit, I had just arrived for a two-day stay, leaving my husband and my son at home in New York City. I knew that they would order in thin, tasteless pizza drowned in rubbery cheese every night until I got back home. It would have none of the fresh tomatoey intensity of my grandmother's '*appizz*'. The pizza boxes would be spread out in every room of our apartment. Unless there was a crisis they'd actually be relieved to have me out of their hair for a few days. "What, Mom? Was that Aunt Vicki?" I asked the fairer, prettier, if now collapsing version of my lookalike self. I am a darker, less glamorous, rougher version of my mother.

"No, no. I just don't listen to her anymore. She's not well at all. We have to bring her some soup tomorrow. No, that was my neighbor Kate. I told her last night how tired I was, but she just sat there. She never takes a hint. I made her a cup of tea, but I didn't want her sitting there all night. What's wrong with people?" Her back collapses further into its curve in frustration at mankind's hopelessness. My mother had a way of faulting the people who stood by her most. For they were imperfectly present.

"But she is good to me, too." My mother straightened herself a little in her chair. "She calls me before she leaves work, to see if I need anything from the store on her way home. What time is it? I can set my watch by her."

"It's five after five. When does she leave work?"

"She leaves around five-thirty, depending. She's got a big job, you know? A lot of responsibility. You should see how hard she works. But she usually stops by to see me." My mother flutters her eyes, and shimmies her body sideways in her chair as if to say, Look at me. See how people care about me? To make fun of this idea, too. "She wants to come down tonight to say hello after dinner."

My mother and I were doing paper work on the laminated surface of a large French Provincial dining room table—the extra leaf permanently in—in the small dinette area of the one-bedroom garden apartment on the other side of town from the neighborhood where she had grown up, fallen in love, and raised her family, and where all of her sisters still lived. Paper work had always been one of the métiers of my mother's life, as much a part of her life as breathing. But she was starting to become legally blind soon after my father died. Kate, my mother's neighbor who called every day and lived upstairs, was much closer to my age than to my mother's.

On those visits I'd be dressed in black jeans and a black sweater. My hair is short and I have two gray streaks above either temple. I wear very expensive, very clunky, scuffed, Mephisto leather sneakers. My mother would never pay that much for shoes. She never wore scuffed shoes of any kind, much less sneakers. And certainly not pants.

At home my mother wore a hostess gown, which flowed to the floor in panels of hot pink and turquoise. This particular one used to be one of the good hostess gowns for when company came. She'd have on beaded slippers. Her bleached hair was curled in a hairdo as well done and formally structured as a Louis XIV wig. She'd have on makeup and lipstick. The powder and lipstick weren't as finely laid on as they once were. If her bright prettiness was crumbling a bit in her mid-eighties, her bright, chic polyester style was still there. She was still more glamorous than my sister or me and still more chic, even in her hostess dress and Caldor's costume jewelry.

"That was very nice of Kate. She calls everyday to check up on me. She's a very sweet girl and all but she's driving me nuts. She's good in a way but there's something wrong with her. Do you know how many times I've had her in to coffee? And do you think she ever invites me into her apartment?

"We'll see about tonight. I'm not sure I want her traipsing down here every night.

"And that other one had to come and ruin me, too. That Jerry." My mother had recentered her irritation now, on Jerry, an old friend of her late husband's, who lived in Florida and who had come by the day before to pay a belated condolence call. Jerry had tried to visit right after my father died, during his annual summer visit to "the old homestead." But my mother hadn't been up for the visit. What had once been her glory, "the hostess with the mostest," decorated on several small flowery serving dishes in her china cupboard in gold lettering, was now her undoing. "I can't do it anymore. It's too much for me.

"I have too much to do. I had all my papers, bills, insurance, everything, all laid out, just so, on the table before Jerry came. You didn't see how organized I had it before he had to come and ruin me. I had to just pile them up and put them in the bedroom. What a mess!" She lifted her hand in disgust, gesturing toward the table full of papers; her crooked pinky pointing back at her, twisted from the time she got it caught in the mixer when she had been making her husband an eggnog at six in the morning before he went to work. Promises of $20 million prizes, envelopes with letters inside begging her to use their credit lines, to take their money, other envelopes pleading the reverse, "Consider poor Sophia and her little sister. Couldn't you give just a little?" Magazines outlining psychic abilities, "Don't hide your hidden powers," catalogs filled with food, furniture, clothes, vitamins and health products—all litter the table.

She'd pick up an envelope and hold it close to the side of one eye. She could see around the edges, but the center was a blurred emptiness. "What's this one?" she'd ask, squinting at the letter. On the floor near my mother's feet sat a large brown paper bag, encased in a smaller, thin plastic grocery bag, which had been pulled out from under the sink where it served as a wastebasket.

"I don't like my name floating around." She ripped her name and address from a piece of junk mail before she threw the remains of the envelope into the grocery bag. Then she carefully tore her name and address from it into tiny scraps and let them float down into the garbage. "That shredder you girls gave me is good, but I don't always have time for it. I heard on TV people go through your garbage. They take old bills and everything. They steal your whole life."

The fact that my mother saw danger wherever she looked was encouraged and enhanced by the nightly news reports. It was up to us to make her world less frightening again. "I live for my children and my grandchildren. You are my life," she'd remind us. There was a large mirror across from the dining table. My eyes would flick away from my mother's squinting face on those visits to that mirror which showed a frowning, exhausted, ungenerous daughter. When I looked away I'd see on the side of the kitchen cabinet a small ceramic tile announcing, "*Il Padrone di casa sono io, ma chi commanda mio e mia moglie.*" (The boss of the house is me, but who commands me is my wife.)

"We have to get back to work here. Here are the ones I want you to tell me what they say. This table is always full, full of paper all the time now. I just do a couple papers and go to bed. It's too much." She'd unwind a rubber band from around a plastic bag whose transparency has been clouded with age. It might hold three small business envelopes which my mother would hand to me. When I'd tell her that each one was for a Catholic missionary school for Native Americans, my mother would say, "I just send them five dollars apiece. I wish they'd just leave me alone. Every month more come."

"Mom, maybe it's time to stop sending them money. I think they might be selling your name."

"What, am I supposed to leave those poor Indian kids, Native whatever, like that? You should read what they say in those letters. I used to be able to read them. I can't any more. It's not much. I do my best.

"Hey, we're put on this world to do good. If you don't do good, why bother?"

"I know, Mom, but . . ."

But at that point my mother would jerk up her head, startled, "What? You don't want me to help those poor kids?"

My only choice was to raise my eyebrows in concession.

"Anyway, that's neither here nor there. What do you think we should do? About Kate tonight? Should I call her back and invite her to supper? She *is* good to me. When you girls can't come I can call her.

And she takes me to CVS or to see Sis, whatever. That's really nice of her." She'd squint, twist her lips to one side, "She might've left already." Kate was kind and attentive to my mother—visiting with her, calling her, bringing her milk. Her sin was that she wasn't my sister or me. Our sin was that we didn't live where Kate lived, upstairs from my mother.

My mother brought her wrist up within inches of her nose and pressed a button on the side of her oversized watch, one of the many devices that she had acquired once she was diagnosed as legally blind. A tinny mechanical voice says, "It's five forty-five." There's a small pause. Then the voice resumes. "PM."

"She probably left already." I knew that this dilemma whether we should share our visit with Kate produced the kind of conflicted emotion that would take over my mother's consciousness. We should include her because she was so helpful to my mother. But my mother didn't want to share her time with me because I wasn't there enough.

"I can try to call her for you, Mom. Or I could ask her when I hear her going up the stairs. But I thought you said it was too much for you."

"We'll see. She tries to be nice. I don't want to be like a *Merican'* keeping my neighbors out of my house. I'll see how I feel."

Each time I looked into the mirror I'd see my skin slipping off bones like hers, the dark circles under my eyes. I'd tighten the muscles under my chin, lift my jaw, and try to put some alertness into my expression. I looked so much older than my mother had looked at this same age. When my mother was in her fifties she was still the belle of the ball. "You're always the prettiest one at the dance," my father had reassured my mother up until the end. And she had been.

When I arrived we'd go to the grocery store, make a visit to the eye doctor, and then attempt to level those mounds of paper. During those visits, my mother always circled her old triumphs. She loved pausing at an old favorite. We were at the point in the story where the suitor didn't speak –"never said a single word to me"—until he suddenly asked Rose to marry him. "Then he asks me to take a walk on my father's farm, out of the blue like, and while we're walking he doesn't talk or anything. Then he says, 'Would you marry me?' He never asks me out. He never takes me to a prom or anything. Now he wants me to marry him. Oh yeah, right, like I'm going to. Can you imagine? Just like that. If your father hadn't come along I don't know what I would have done. I didn't want anything to do with any of them. I was going to die an old maid the way I was behaving. I was so shy."

James was in high school during this era. While he had always been a delightful and rambunctious child, in high school the work finally matched his interest and he was doing beautifully academically and his teachers really liked him. Still, the child who fell in every fountain he had ever walked by certainly hadn't become a saint. Now here was a call coming in from his phone and that wasn't a good sign.

When I picked up the phone, I could feel my shoulders release. A voice from my world. That meant it hadn't disappeared behind me when I'd driven up the Merritt Parkway. It always felt that it had. Then I heard my seventeen-year-old son's low-pitched voice, and realized he was using his calm, I-can-handle-it tone.

I breathed in quickly, "But what . . . ?" I walked over to my mother's picture window and lowered my voice to be out of my mother's earshot. "How did that happen?" I listened again.

"*Ma che bellezz'!*' James. You promised me. I can't believe this. We had a deal—not in our house, not near or in school." I remember struggling to find some footing for this latest problem with my hormone-flooded son. He's smoking weed—just as I had at his age. But whereas for me it had been thrillingly conducted in the strictest secrecy, James had left his recently used redolent bong out in his bedroom, and then apparently had gone to his linear equations class reeking of the acrid leafy stuff. Bill and I were going to have to appear at Stuyvesant High School the next day or he'd be suspended in the middle of the college application process. Not good. *Non buon.*

I could feel my dry skin pulling downward as I looked out the window that day. Outside, an unseasonably soft warm rain joined the early ascending darkness into fog. "I can't believe this, James. . . . Okay. . . . Okay, I'll be there. Yes, eight AM. Blaustein's office. I'll drive from here and meet you and Dad there," I said, as I arrived at the inevitable conclusion. I would have to leave my mother's a full day earlier than I had promised. Wherever I was I should be somewhere else.

I got off the phone not knowing how I would break this news to my mother. I knew how she had looked forward to being with one of her daughters, to poring over her papers with me, to telling Kate she was too busy to see her. How was I going to tell her this? Then *sotto voce,* I reminded James, "Now don't forget to thank Gramma for the twenty she sent you," I walked back to turn the phone over to my mother.

I tried to slip another couple of brochures into the garbage bag while my mother was on the phone with James, but she noticed what I was doing out of the corner of her eye. "What are you doing to me?" She stopped my hand just as the papers were about to fall. "James, just a minute, Honey. Your mother's throwing everything away on me. We're in the middle of a mess here. I'd better go. She's going to *throw me out* if

I don't watch out." My mother giggled, her old girlishness bubbling to the surface.

"I love you," my mother sang into the phone as she said goodbye to her grandson and then pulled the brochure out of my hand. "What's that thing?"

"Remember? We just looked at this. It's a flyer for a dance class at the Arthur Murray Studio."

"What is it? Oh. Okay, okay. Now I remember. Sure, when am I going to go dancing? Your father and I loved to go to dances. We went out every Saturday night, even if it was just to the movies.

"Do you know that men used to follow me down the street to try and meet me? Can you imagine?"

"Hmm." I was trying to figure out how I was going to tell my mother I'd have to leave the following day, at six o'clock in the morning. I knew she had the errands all lined up: the soup drop at Aunt Vicki's, a stop at the Xerox store to copy the family tree her cousin had sent recently from Detroit for all of my mother's grandchildren, a trip to Stop and Shop to return the walnuts that she had bought for $4.99 before Kate told her Bradley's had them on sale for $2.99. That would be if we could find the receipt from Stop and Shop. But my mother always had a bowl full of receipts on top of the china cupboard.

I continued writing checks that afternoon and passed them to her to inspect and sign. I'd make the signature line with a large X. Then I'd hold her fingers a little above the line so my mother's once clear bookkeeper's signature didn't slant too far up above the line. We had purchased a plastic device with spaces where she could fill in her signature when her eyes first started to go. But it had gotten lost. "I swear something's making things disappear on me. You should see how things disappear around here and then show up again. It happens all the time now. The other day I put my wedding ring down on the coffee table for a minute and when I went to put it back on it was gone. I was sick. Why did I ever take it off? I looked high and low for it. The next day there it was like it had never gone anywhere. Now how do you explain that? I think Dad is playing these tricks on me to let me know he's there. The way he does making the lights go on and off.

"Hey, look how dark it is already. What time is it? I need a cup of coffee," she'd announce after a while and stand up to step into the kitchen area. "I'm tired."

There was always a half a circle of cake sitting on the counter. "You want a piece of cake to hold you? It didn't come so good. It's dry. I left it in the oven too long. I can't do anything right anymore."

"Sure, Mom. I'd love some." Cake a little while before dinner is something I still missed in my life in New York.

"Maybe I'll just ask Kate in for a cup of coffee when I hear her on the stairs. Get it over with. Go check and see if her car's in the driveway."

Only my car sat outside in the driveway. The fog had lifted and was drifting just above the houses. Raindrops glistened with clarity on my car. A few at a time they slid down the sides.

In those days it seemed to me as if every time I drove the two hours to see my mother it was always pouring hard, dark rain. I'd drive up the Merritt Parkway feeling all the worry behind me in New York pulling at me and all the worry in front of me in Waterbury dragging me there. About halfway there I'd start to imagine a centrifugal force spinning me out of control and my car careening off the road in the rain into a terrible accident. It seemed as if it was always about to happen. "Kate's car isn't in the driveway yet."

"I brought her nibs a piece of cake last night. I had so much left over from Jerry's visit. Do you think she'd invite me in? She just stood at the door, like blocking the way in.

"That's not the first time. The year Dad died she came down here at Christmas, and she just took over. She decided she was going to decorate my house for me for Christmas. I should have been spending that time with Dad. He was really sick already but we didn't know it yet. But him too, he would say, 'Oh come in, Kate, and have a cup of coffee with my Rosie Baby.' Like I wanted her to do that. Oh, how many nights she came down here for a cup of coffee. Well, she *thought* she was doing good," my mother would say with disgust. "That year she decorated the fireplace, and she put a wreath on our door. She decorated my whole apartment. I mean it was very pretty and all, but who asked her to do that?

"Well, anyway that's neither here nor there.

"When it was all over, poor Dad, he wasn't feeling well even then, we just didn't know yet, he helped me take all of this stuff down. He didn't have much energy. With that, we carried it upstairs. It was a lot. What was I supposed to do with all that stuff? She gets it from her job. And that night, too, she just stood at that door, like blocking Dad's and my way, like we weren't welcome. We stood there talking, 'Here's the stuff. That was very nice of you and la la la.' Then I finally said, 'Well is it all right if we come in?' Then she had to open the door. And we sat there for a few minutes. But do you think she even offered to make us a cup of coffee? That wasn't right for her to be like that. How many nights she sat here. Watch, tonight she'll show up just at dinnertime. 'What are you cooking?' she's going to ask. She wants to know everything."

"Mom!" my voice would pitch up, "I don't think she means anything bad by it. Doesn't she take you for groceries? Don't you go to church together on Sundays?"

My mother would glare at me, then shrug. "Can't I even open my mouth? There's no sense talking to you. I'm not supposed to talk. I'd better learn to keep my mouth shut."

I'd swallow, constricting my esophagus; I'd plaster my face back into neutral. But not before I'd get a glimpse of my stunned, wrinkled face in the mirror.

"I'm not always up for doing that," my mother would pick up her train of thought. "Sometimes I just watch the Mass on television. It's just like being there. I sit on the couch in my nightgown and say my prayers. Then she comes by afterwards to tell me what the priest at St. Lucy's said. She's a very sweet girl. But she's very nosey. She looks at everything in my house. 'What's this?' she asked me the other day. She picked up this glue that I had just bought at CVS. I gave it to her. It glues anything you want. Stick All. She wanted to pay me for it. But I wouldn't let her.

"But she had given me some support hose because she put it on and went to work and it was like too short for a tall person, they hung around her hips all day." She eyes stood up to act out that scene. She put her hands to her hips and pretended to be Kate struggling with the support stockings. Then cheerfully throwing her head back, she laughed, the skin on her face gathered into a younger happier self. " 'So I'm giving them to you,' Kate said to me. She wouldn't take any money for them. I tried to pay her, but she wouldn't take anything. 'I already wore them,' she said to me, 'I know you cut them down.'

"That's what I do, you know? They're better that way. I can't stand them with the panty attached. I can't breathe. I only buy them when I get a bargain at TJ's. Then when they get a run I cut them off at the thigh and use the old elastic tops like big elastic bands. See?" My mother snapped one of those same wide elastic, stocking tops holding a group of manila envelops together, "They're great." Some synthetic material ruffled the edge where the stocking had been cut away.

"So that's why I wanted to give her something. So I gave her the Stick All. I'll have to buy some for you tomorrow when we go to CVS. I glued my window shade the other day.

"I didn't feel like opening the sewing machine, all that trouble taking off the vase and doily, and the pictures," she gestures to the sewing machine where Lucia and I had sewed our first prom dresses, where our mother had sewn all of our dresses when we were younger, trimming them with flounces, ruffles, rickrack all throughout our grade school years. "God, I just loved to sew at night. I couldn't wait to get all my housework done so I could get to it. Dad would go down the club to play cards. I would put you girls to bed and I'd open the sewing machine and I'd put on the radio and listen to nice music. I don't listen to that punk stuff anymore. Now it's on the TV. The right kind of music is healing. I used to put on nice music when Dad was sick. Oh dear God, life is cruel. Now I heard on TV that nice music helps people to heal. You see I'm way ahead of myself.

"But in those days I had my radio right on the shelf, right by the window near the sewing machine. Do you remember in our apartment on Ward Street? I always had something going—dresses for you girls or a skirt for myself. One night I would cut out the pattern. The next night I'd do a little sewing. And little by little. Well, that was my thing."

She stopped and looked around. Whatever was left of her gaze alighted on the glue stick standing in the midst of the piles of papers. "But anyway, you should see how this stuff works so good." She picked up the Stick All and brought it close to her eyes so she could read the letters spelling out the brand name. "I bought myself some more the next day. Vicki and Toni were here when I was fixing the shade. They couldn't get over it. I just put the newspapers down on the table, laid them all out and then I laid out the shade and spread the glue on the pieces." My mother demonstrated her technique, fingers touching, rubbing the glue stick back and forth in the air. "Then I patted it down. You should see how nice it came out. It was perfect, just with Stick All."

She looked up to find me there watching her. "Now when Kate comes in, don't say anything. She means well."

We both listened as a car pulled into the driveway. "Here she comes. God, I hope she doesn't stay all night."

"Mom, why don't I take you and Kate out for dinner tonight," I tried to make my departure in the morning right. To give her a gift of everything I had to give before I had to tell her I'd have to leave in the morning. "We'll go to Diorio's. You can wear your new blouse from TJ's. The blue one. It'll be fun." I thought I could tell her when we got home from dinner that I had to leave in the morning. "I'd like to do something for her, too."

"Don't worry. I do plenty. She's good to me. But I'm good to her, too," she reassured me. She stood up and peered into the mirror on the wall. She put her head inches from the glass, then lifted her chin side to side. After a few seconds of inspection she let her face drop down into its natural folds. "I'm too tired," she said as she turned back to the table.

"Tomorrow we'll go out for dinner, just the two of us," she decided, her glittering eyes filling up with the joke she's about to tell. "We won't mention it to Kate. Don't say a word. We'll go out after we do the errands. Wherever we want." She threw back her head laughing, flung her arms out wide and stiff, and wiggled her fingers at the end, all the easy joy of which she was capable, careening triumphantly back to the center of her life. All her trouble at arm's length.

Psychic Arrangements

My parents came in wonder upon each other on July 5th. They promised as long as they both shall live on July 5th. Death parted them on July 5th.

The first was chance, the second was planned, and the last was a hospital screw-up, but repetition made it seem like destiny.

Both were born in the difficult, chaotic world of the southern Italian immigrants where everything depended on what had come before and was tied to that ancient rocky past. All of my family's blood was mixed and remixed there. If there was new blood it was brought by the newcomers like the Normans, the Angevins, Argonese. It wasn't a place from which anyone moved or changed.

Characterized by the abrupt mountains rising upward, these people brought with them their intense sense of the circumscribed, the insular, the isolated; they were rooted in the craggy mountainous towns where almost nothing has changed or is changeable. Therefore, everything is destiny.

My parents had the good fortune of falling in love at first sight with a romantic sweep on a summer night in 1935. From that wild early love they made a good life, a solid devoted marriage, always the only person for each other. This good marriage included dancing in the kitchen after dinner when the radio was on, dirty dishes still on the table; necking on the couch in the evening while they read the newspaper, and furious battles, over money; over all the ordinary things: "You're driving me crazy! Do you always have to take everything to the extreme?" Doors slamming, fury over ordinary things. But fighting and anger was an ordinary part of our lives; not quite what it means today.

It was just the way we were. Not special, not a real indication of wrong-ness. It was part of the way we lived.

Both romantics by nature and inclination, their love story—meet-ing each other—falling in love, "keeping company," was the passionate heart of their otherwise decent, hardworking prosaic lives—it was the story that sustained them, the one that gave their adult lives an enhanc-ing largeness, a mythic framing that put them in the movie of life, giving their lives glamour and meaning. It embedded them with a sense that the fates had bestowed blessings, when they had been raised to expect yelling and beatings.

They also had the luck of coming from very similar Italian immi-grant families; though they didn't know it when they met, their fathers had known each other for a long time. Both families had real tragedies at the center of their lives. Those tragedies and their fathers' despotic ways had led them as children to assume misery was what their futures held. Instead, the fates turned and delivered these two, young, gorgeous people wild love *and* their families' good wishes. They stayed in love all of the sixty years they had together and beyond that. Since for each of them the most important thing that ever happened in their lives was meeting and falling in love, an endless ritualistic recounting of "Don't worry about falling in love," they both said on many occasions to Lucia and me as we came into adolescence. "When you're young you think love is not anything that will happen to you. It's just stuff that happens in the movies. Then one day you meet that other person and you're in love and that's it. There's no more discussion about it." They'd look at each other across the kitchen table, with a shrug of their shoulders, one hand lifted upward, the same way they might say, "We'll have to drive down to Jersey for the funeral." It just was.

Along with the terrible miseries and *miseria* of their family's lives, the fates gave my parents certain gifts. They lived in the circumscribed world of white ethnic working people where they knew everyone and everyone knew them. They carried themselves with the ease of belong-ing; both were talented at the small everyday interaction. Their glam-orous looks also gave them a confident vitality and they were stars in their own world. Long after their generation had aged a man came up to my mother and told her that when they all had been young, he would wait for them to come out of the Palace Theater, "You two were the best looking people in town. I'd wait to see you."

"Rose, Rosie Baby," my father would exclaim with pleasure, looking up from the newspaper, still surprised at his good luck all throughout their years.

"You were the prettiest girl at the dance, Rose, tonight," he repeated proudly, over and over. "Did you see that everyone wanted to dance with you? You know Johnny's always been in love with you. He never got over you."

"Oh, Peter," she'd say, embarrassed and delighted, and she'd shake her head laughing.

"That's true, you know, girls. He's still in love with your mother. Well everyone loves your mother. I mean you girls are pretty, but your mother, she was something so special. You can't believe how beautiful she was when I met her." He included us in his pride in her. How lucky he was to have found her.

When my parents were first married they lived in what was called a third floor rent. The top floor was always the cheapest rent in a wood frame house. Our rent had slanted ceilings, large airy rooms, nooks, and a large walk-in pantry, as well as a front and back porch.

My mother had been trained all of her life for the job of making a home. But her parents' farm had been rude and rough, and she, who her mother said should have spent her life in a shop window, had been longing to make everything pretty—that was her true art. Now she had her own canvas. She made curtains out of bleached flour sacks, sewing ruffles on the bottom, rickrack on the ruffles. She turned a small barrel upside down and fitted a cushion in the top and made a skirt (with ruffle at the bottom) for the barrel and there was an extra seat in the house. She fussed and sewed and bleached and stitched with the joy of it being her own. There was a shelf in the kitchen with blue plaid oil-cloth tacked carefully to the bottom with a set of blue plaid dishes on the shelf.

"Your mother loves to play house," my father said. "She's always playing." It was exactly this lovely ability to make a real and cozy cottage in the sky that finally made him feel he had found a harbor in the storm.

Which is why it was a perfect place for my father to bring his friends over to shoot craps. "Well," my mother would explain with the same certainty with which she told me not to pass by people I recognized on the street, "Your father never had a real home where he could bring his friends. I mean Grampa Clapps was always there with his cronies drinking and carrying on. Even though Mamanonna was there, it was more like the home of a bachelor. No place for a young man to bring his friends home. So, now this was his first home and I wanted him to have a place where his buddies could always come. You know all those years when he was young he and his friends they shot craps on the streets, even when it got dark they shot craps under the street lamp, so when he had a home of his own I wanted him to make use of it."

My mother made sure there was a platter of cold cuts, lots of soda and coffee, and a cake; then she'd leave so that they could have the house to themselves and she'd go to meet her sisters downtown to go to the movies. Sometimes they went shopping and always they went out for coffee and afterward.

Through all the years, probably preceding us and certainly all the years of our growing up, after dinner my parents always read the *Waterbury Republican* first at the kitchen table, sometimes on the front porch, and sometimes on the couch in the living room. If they were on the couch this often led to one of them laying their head on the other one's lap or to their necking.

Swirled into their destiny and the romantic quotidian were my mother's views of the supernatural. From her mother she inherited typical Southern Italian beliefs: dreams foretold the future, it is essential never to tempt the gods by talking about good fortune, and it was better to be rich in blood than money. *Meglio ricco di sangue e no di ore.*

My mother swept her mother's beliefs into the belief system of Hollywood—the best-looking people are the virtuous ones, hard work always pays off—mixed those with Catholicism, psychic beliefs both ancient and modern, and combined them with her personal system of prayer, vitamins, aphorisms, soap opera wisdom, and certainty. She consulted many psychics, read many of Edgar Cayce's books, watched many television shows about psychics, clairvoyants, read stories in *Reader's Digest* about people with extrasensory perception. She found every word to be true: hers and theirs. At the core of her religious life was the god of her good fortune—that she and my father found each other, fell madly in love, married, and lived normally every after. My father found this ridiculous, hilarious, and charming. "Isn't she wonderful?" he'd ask the room at large and laugh his fool head off, "Isn't she priceless?" whenever my mother declared her psychic beliefs.

"Put it in the air," she'd say. "If you want something, just put it in the air." There was never any question that if you put it in the air properly you would get what you wanted. She had.

If my father didn't agree with her about this, it never interfered with his love for her. "Rose, come and do tucky-tuck," he'd say after he retired, "I have to go and inspect the ceiling." That meant it was time for a nap. "Tell me I'm no bum," he'd say day after day, thrilled that he had her to play out each of these rituals with.

"You *are* a bum," she'd say, and they would both be delighted with these daily games.

When he got sick and was told he had six months to live—in fact, he had ten weeks—he didn't want to be away from her even for a few minutes. Once, when I insisted on going into a test with him because I was sure my mother wouldn't understand what the doctors were talking about and our decisions depended on what they said, he said over and over, "Go and get your mother. I'd like her to be here." Stupidly, I stuck with the practical and insisted that I stay that time with him.

As those last weeks passed, he'd say, "I'm just worried about your mother. How will she handle this?" That was the closest acknowledgment I ever heard from him about his diagnosis. For the rest, we weren't allowed to talk about it. Silence was so essential that I didn't dare say, "We'll take care of her." The rules were that he'd talk if he was allowed to put his thoughts into the air and we didn't address what he had put there.

July 5th made one more fateful appearance in their life together. He had esophageal cancer. His esophagus was so crowded with cancer that no food could pass through. So they put in a feeding tube in order to start treatment. My mother was sitting by my father's bed, shaving him, the morning after the feeding tube was implanted. Then his nurse came in and said in contempt, "He can shave himself." Shamed by this nurse, my father took the razor from my mother's hand and sang as he shaved himself, "They tried to tell us we're too young, too young to truly be in love." He sang through his last shave as he had sung through every shave of his adult life. He was in such pain that day he asked my sister if she could get him some heroin. "I mean it. I can't take this." He was septic from the feeding tube they had put in the day before. He was toxic in the post-op because his esophageal cancer had spread much farther than anyone had figured out. He was strong from all the heavy work he had done as an iron worker, from all the biking he had done since he had retired. He was hours from dying.

But his nurse knew better. "You can shave yourself," she repeated her admonition for emphasis. It was July 5th.

As soon as my father died, it was very clear to my mother that he was keeping in close touch with her. One regular and frequent sign of my father's presence was that he turned lights on and off or set them blinking.

After my mother died, my sister and I found a notebook where she wrote about my father's contact with her from beyond. The first page states: I'm going to write about all the ways my Beloved Peter has kept in touch with us.

Death is the continuation of life—my mother wrote on page two of the notebook.

A typical note goes: *When we were at the wake, Peter I'm sure, put out the lights in the funeral parlor, the rest of the building was lit. Everyone felt that Peter was saying goodbye.*

Another note: *When we came home from Cambridge without our Beloved Peter the lights in the hallway were out. We were still together.*

These occurrences were added to the daily liturgical recitation. *Peter puts the light in the bathroom on and off. I thought I had to change the bulb but it went on fine. I was reading Talking to Heaven by Van Praugh, a book John bought me. Van Praugh says if you want to see a sign from a beloved ask for what you want. So when I said my prayers I asked Peter would he put the lights out in the bathroom when I got up during the night and sure enough they went on and off. I ran to where the light was and kissed the air and thanked Peter.*

I was talking to Vicki on the phone when the bulb in the chandelier went off and I said "I guess I have to change the bulb that just went out." Just as I was saying that it started to go off and on. I told her what happened to the light in the bathroom and it went on and off.

She said, "No Rose, that's Peter trying to get in touch with you. Don't change the bulb." I was so glad she said that. Again, thank you Peter.

Darn it, the next day didn't Terry (her cleaning woman, companion and friend) came along and tightened the bulb in its socket. I said, "Don't do that Terry. That's Peter talking to me." She went ahead anyway. Who asked her? Who does she think she is? What if he's trying to be in touch with me?

One psychic book advised her: "Give yourself suggestions that you will have contact in the right time."

A few months after my father died, she consulted a new psychic who told her she had many relationships with my father in past lives.

This psychic could see that they had been soul mates for many centuries previously. They had lived many different lives together. My mother told me, "I was his husband in Persia, you know.

"I was his Navaho brother.

"I was one of seven women in his harem in Egypt. (I don't like that one so much).

"We had some hassles, but once we found each other, we were soul mates for eternity. Peter came along to restore my faith in love. I hadn't been appreciated before."

She mourned my father with the same intensity that she loved him in life. She looked for all the signs that he was still with her. That he still loved her.

But as time went on, she began to be afraid that she was holding him back from a higher plane where he belonged. Again in her note book: *I don't want to stop your growth. I don't want to stop your growth but I would like to have contact with you. That is going to help my healing process,* she wrote in the book.

She slept with one of his undershirts close to her face as she said her prayers for all of us each night. She told me that she said this prayer: *May I have contact in the right way at the right time with my beloved Peter.* All of these rituals helped her keep my father near her for ten years until her memory began to fade with dementia.

At the end of her life, my sister and I spent long hours with her in her apartment at an assisted living facility. She had become afraid to walk down the hall to the dining room or even to leave her apartment at all. She'd open her door and say, "What's out there? Those streets out there (the hallway outside her door) scare me. You never know who's going to come along. I don't want to go out there." She took the route that dementia takes—"Do you know where my bedroom is? Are you sure? Can you help me find it when the time is right? I'll just stay here on the bench (her couch)." Our hours were as they are at this stage of life, filled with repetitions and a need to fill the air with connection and talk. If she lay down on her couch for a while and closed her eyes, she quickly became aware of the silence around her and would sit up abruptly. "Where is everyone? Where did everyone go?" She had grown up in a noisy, chaotic, but always peopled world. Quiet wasn't a normal environment to her.

When she met my father she found a man she loved, who loved her and the possibility of making the world more like the one she had longed for when she was a frightened Italian girl trying to please her parents and wishing she lived "in a shop window," as her mother said about her.

One day, hoping to revive a favorite piece of her life for her, I asked, "What was the most important thing that you remember happening in your life?"

"Well, falling in love with whoever it was I fell in love with. When I fell in love.

"You know, I was young, and a lot of young men wanted to marry me. But I didn't feel anything for them at all. And I thought I'm never going to find anyone. But then this handsome young man came along; he was the only thing I cared about.

"And I was so glad to be in love with him. I wonder, did I ever turn out to marry him?

"I felt as if I had been waiting my whole life for this person to come along and that now that I had found him it changed my life forever. I finally fell in love."

"What do you remember about meeting him?" I asked her, waiting for the Lakewood Park, July Fourth weekend recitation.

"I remember . . ." she started to say, but the story she had told over and over all her life as if to reassure herself that it had actually happened to her—that she had been that pretty young woman the handsome stranger followed out of the park, that she had been that fortunate, that she had won the love of that handsome stranger who turned out to be a *paesan'*, that their love had sustained them both for all those years, even beyond his death—had disappeared now.

"It must have been my husband, I guess," she said. "I suppose it must have been my husband."

"It was Dad, Mom. It was Peter Clapps."

"Peter Clapps. Who is that? Well, that's a strange name. I don't remember anyone like that."

"Peter Clapps was your husband. The man you were married to."

"Well, then I guess he was the one. The most important thing that ever happened to me was whoever it was that I fell in love with."

Peter Clapps at the shop as a young man.

Mom and Dad at the lake

My mother and father just after they met. Rose Becce and Peter Clapps

Mom and Dad just as they have fallen in love.